ESCAPING PLATO'S CAVE

ESCAPING PLATO'S CAVE

How America's Blindness
to the Rest of the World
Threatens Our Survival

MORT ROSENBLUM

ST. MARTIN'S PRESS

NEW YORK

www.stmartins.com

Library of Congress Cataloging-in-Publication Data
Rosenblum, Mort.
    Escaping Plato's cave : how America's blindness to the rest of the
world threatens our survival / Mort Rosenbum.—1st ed.
        p. cm.
    ISBN-13: 978-0-312-36440-3
    ISBN-10: 0-312-36440-7
    1. United States—Foreign relations—21st century.   2. United
States—Relations—Foreign countries—21st century.   3. United
States—Foreign relations—21st century—Public opinion.
4. United States—Foreign public opinion.   5. Nationalism—
United States.   6. National characteristics, American.
7. Anti-Americanism.   8. World politics—21st century.
I. Title.

E895.R66 2007
327.7309'05—dc22   2007022140

First Edition: October 2007

10   9   8   7   6   5   4   3   2   1

To friends who died trying,
figuratively and literally

CONTENTS

AUTHOR'S NOTE

I've been at this book, one way or another, ever since I persuaded my teacher at Peter Howell Elementary in Tucson that our class should publish a newspaper. We did a pretty awful job, in fact, but journalism is fun when you're six. It only gets complicated when you move beyond the corner of Cooper and Irving into a real world.

A lifetime later, the approach we used then still stands. Someone goes somewhere and learns something. He or she reports that to people who then react, for better or worse. It makes zero difference whether the medium is mimeograph, hot type, voice over airwaves, or gigabits and pixels at warp speed. Journalism is the message.

This book, in the end, is not about journalism but rather about the message we are missing to our extreme peril.

Phil Revzin at St. Martin's Press is a co-conspirator. We worked together in Paris, where he was the *Wall Street Journal* correspondent. When I saw Nicolae Ceausescu about to fall in Romania in 1989, I chartered a plane and offered Phil a ride. After a night of sniper fire, he breathed life into a dead phone line and transmitted poetry via a Tandy 100 proto-computer.

Romania was the last to break free in Eastern Europe, and his simple lead paragraph said it all: "This domino fell in a pool of blood."

For a real journalist, such word mastery is only pastry icing. As a reporter, then as editor of the *Journal*'s European edition, Phil saw a harrowing sort of world taking shape. When I suggested this book, he weighed in with conviction.

I have tried to be objective in the only way that word can make sense: Conclusions are drawn from facts as I have best been able to gather them up close from real sources. During four decades, The Associated Press trusted me to seek observable reality in, more or less, two hundred countries. New executives reshaped AP, shifting crucial judgments from reporters to editors, and I left in 2004. But, whoever is serving time in managerial jobs, AP's historic mission is defined by its journalists—friends and colleagues—out where the news is. All of us across a world in peril depend heavily on them.

A lot of people helped me with this book; an acknowledgments note follows at the end. But particular thanks go to Gina Bentley, an inspired researcher who believes in this book; to Peace Sullivan, whose guidance and various kitchen tables did much to help me finish it; to Mary and Alain Provost, for replanting me in the desert; and, of course, to Jeannette Hermann Rosenblum, for more reasons than I can get on paper.

For having lived long, I have experienced many circumstances of being obliged, by better information or fuller consideration, to change opinions, even on important subjects, which I once thought right but found to be otherwise.

—BENJAMIN FRANKLIN

ESCAPING PLATO'S CAVE

ONE

THE CAVE WALL

*To see clearly is poetry, prophecy,
and religion all in one.*
—JOHN RUSKIN

There is none so blind as they that won't see.
—JONATHAN SWIFT

Plato, who was never much of a populist, believed most of his fellow humans were blind to reality. He imagined prisoners in a cave who could see events outside only as firelight flickering on a wall. These shadows, cropped by the cave's opening, were distorted in size, their details blurred. They loomed suddenly and then vanished. Twenty-three centuries later, these images appear on backlit screens with words like SONY or DELL stamped beneath them. Otherwise, Plato's simile still seems squarely on the mark.

Back then, musing over philosopher kings and a utopian Republic was an affordable luxury in a Mediterranean universe at one corner of the little-known world. Now, blindness to reality is killing us.

Today, a widening abyss between the rich and the desperate erupts regularly into violence. Our planet is dying around us. Lies carry the weight of truth, just as George Orwell and Aldous Huxley foresaw. In practice, we are neither as free nor as democratic as we proclaim. And the world no longer trusts the only superpower it has.

This book is a *cri de coeur* from an American foreign correspondent who spent forty years in the wilderness watching soluble situations in remote backwaters escalate into world-class calamity. Unlike captives in a parable, we are not chained with our backs to reality. To save our world, we need only turn around, take notice, and do what matters.

In the 1960s, as a cub reporter wading into the blood-spattered intrigue of Mobutu's Congo, I was sure my intrepid colleagues and I could right what was wrong. We would report reality; my ennobled countrymen would inspire a "world community" to do the rest. Not exactly. You can almost bank on it: When a crisis looms, Americans somehow manage, with the best intentions, to make things worse. Challenges we face demand sustained deliberation. Yet we approach them with the attention of hummingbirds in heat.

Foreign correspondents who could help us do better are endangered as a species. For all the words and images we call "media," precious few trained eyes see distant reality up close, and these grow fewer by the year. When reporters do warn us of a crisis, we pay scant attention. We react to effect and ignore the causes. And then, overwhelmed, we cite that old saw as a path of least resistance: *You can't worry about what you can't change.* We must turn this around: *You can't change what you don't worry about.*

Not long after Plato, Christian prophets sized up their mysterious world. The Book of Luke assures: "And when you hear of wars and revolts, do not be alarmed by it; such things must happen, but the end is not soon. . . . Nation will rise against nation, and kingdom against kingdom; there will be great earthquakes in this region or that, and plagues and famines; and sights of terror and great portents from heaven."

But back then the extent of plunder was limited to the speed that any particular horde could gallop. Plagues spread no faster than the patter of rat feet or the swarming of locusts. These days, a match lit in any corner of the world can set fires just about anywhere. Electronic-savvy zealots whip up deadly riots over no more than, say, a cartoonist's caricatures. Ignorance, whether in Arabia or America, is a weapon of mass destruction.

We are past blaming anyone for America's collective blindness to a world we cohabit with 6,700,000,000 others. We can no longer assume we automatically come first. Of course, we love our nation. Other people love theirs, too. At a recent conclave of thinkers, Eric Schmidt of Google noted a simple truth we often forget: Nothing in the human genome says that Americans have a lock on brains. Charity or sympathy do not help "underdevelopment." People in trouble need help in confronting the causes of poverty.

Journalism frequently fails us. Yet it also offers clarity and wisdom we ignore. Now the stakes are too high for this hit-and-miss approach. It is up to us—citizens, not journalists—to take notice, and to take action.

A nation of 300 million individuals with the right to vote, and with the freedom to direct their eyes and spend their paychecks however they choose, has ample means to do better. Big government and corporations we let shape our lives depend totally upon our collective free choices.

We can fit comfortably into a wider, safer world of allies who respect us and enemies who have fewer grounds to resent us. The crises we face are essentially man-made; we can undo much of the damage. First, however, we have to understand what is out there.

"You've got to scare people," a veteran editor I admire said recently when we talked about public apathy. "Most people pay no attention until they see it is ten minutes to midnight. Then they panic and do something."

It is now ten minutes to midnight.

Soon after terrorists leveled New York's World Trade Center, I hurried to Quetta, on the Pakistan frontier, to find a way into Afghanistan. As the days dragged on, I tried to understand that devastating message a frustrated underclass had delivered into the heart of America.

One morning, I drove out to a huge lake that drought had dried to cratered moonscape. Long after 9/11 was a historical footnote, I believed, the story of our time would be ecological collapse and famine. During 2000 and most of 2001, I had traveled the world seeing evidence of this. If the news eluded any simple sort of headline, it was dead obvious: We have picked a fight to the death with nature.

Against this stark backdrop, I found three young Pakistani women who had come to visit their village. Each worked for the United Nations, part of that well-educated, multilingual caste of international civil servants that underpins the real world. They knew America and Europe from close friendships, as well as firsthand experience.

The women joked and laughed, but each was deadly serious. I expected to hear the usual opinion that emerges in such encounters: We have this or that quarrel with the United States government, but we know the people are different, and we like America. Not this time.

"If bin Laden were to come here now, I would invite him to my house," one said.

"I would marry him," another added. "I love him."

Each deplored the deaths. But they knew that in most of the world sudden tragedy at the hand of God or man routinely blots out life in stunning numbers, and America barely notices. Osama bin Laden was a symbol. He had arrested the attention of a self-obsessed nation.

United States foreign policy, one woman said, was callous and far more inward-looking than statecraft requires. All three knew how Americans' vaunted generosity translates into reality: Miserly on a per capita basis, U.S. aid is geared toward renting allies. They saw Washington walk away after its proxy ragtag Islamist militia drove the Soviets from Afghanistan. Pakistan, strapped for funds, left much of its primary education to radical mullahs.

The women colorfully excoriated George W. Bush. But they knew that Clinton and his Democrats also did little for Pakistan. If they did not hate anyone merely for carrying a U.S. passport, they were firm on the main point. When a rich, self-absorbed nation declares, "You're with us or against us," they knew where they stood.

That was 2001, before Iraq, Guantánamo, and the rest. Late in 2006, I talked to James Talbot, an Irish-born friend from London, sophisticated and smart, whose fondness for America had grown steadily since the 1970s when he was based in San Francisco to help the State Department attract European tourists. He loves what we are supposed to be, but he no longer comes near our borders. He was stunned that we reelected George W. Bush and his deluded little power cell by an even larger margin than in 2000. "America has become the Evil Empire," James said, with a sad shake of his head. "I just don't understand it."

It is time to start listening to voices like these. It does no good if, via our interactive media, we argue with them. If I have learned anything watching firsthand as people trash what could be a perfectly good world, it is this: Their reality is the issue, not ours. And we cannot begin to address it sensibly unless we first understand it.

You can look almost anywhere. Resentments smolder among peoples in a separate "Third World" to which we give little help. We champion human rights while we find excuses for our own torture and indiscriminate murder. We outsource to contractors accountable to no one the most basic human dealings that should be guaranteed by our flag. We sneak into other peoples' bank records and demand from allies confidential data on their citizens.

When we catch leaders violating our own constitution, we shrug and click on the next item in the computer queue. We seem immune to shock and contemptuous of principle. In time, sensible judges and lawmakers may veer us back toward our basic principles. But far too much is lost in the process. However we explain this to ourselves at home, we pay a staggering price abroad. Our allies no longer assume that we will do the right thing. Our ability to lead by example has eroded badly and risks damage that is beyond repair.

This failure of a lone superpower to see how other societies react to its actions provokes frightening variations on the much-debated "clash of civilizations." When Samuel Huntington coined the term at Harvard in 1993, he used a question mark. These days, it needs an exclamation point.

In this clash, there is no single enemy. It is surely not Islam, a complex belief system of 1.3 billion adherents, which equals Christianity in number. Al Qaeda and other fringe offshoots typify Muslims no more than the cross-burning Ku Klux Klan represents Christians. Terrorism is a reaction, an expression of impotence or despair, not a structure against which we can wage war. Still, we charge blindly on, helping terrorist leaders swell their ranks.

America's muscular pursuit of national interest strays deep into what Webster defines as imperialism. When we swagger, we sow fresh resentment among peoples whose memories burn on for generations. When we over-react to terror, we show pathetic vulnerability. This deadly blend of hubris and fear is what starts world wars. In the meantime, we enslave ourselves with fresh limits on our own freedoms. We need to understand this.

And yet sociopolitical conflict is not the half of it.

We Americans squander oil and pollute as if we cared nothing for tomorrow. We charge off in wrong directions, led by big business, which profits from our confusion. Are biofuels the answer? The world now eats more food than it produces, and we clear-cut Amazon rainforest for farmland. Where do we grow extra corn or sugar for yet more outsized gas tanks? Conscience-troubled rich people drive to the airport in hybrid cars and then burn fuel by the ton in private jets.

The Kyoto treaty was flawed. But rather than find better wording to achieve its essential purpose, a Congress beholden to business shunned it. Our underlying message to the world recalled that 1975 *Daily News* headline reporting Washington's refusal to help New York head off bankruptcy: "Ford to City: Drop Dead." On a global scale, "drop dead" is no mirthful exaggeration.

Soon our society, a 4 percent fringe of humanity, will no longer call the shots. When our kids grow up, China and India will total 3 billion—not "developing" people in a special category but real ones like us who want SUVs and backyard barbecues. Totalitarian leaders in Beijing and freely elected ones in New Delhi both understand the future. We choose bluster over diplomacy in the Irans and Venezuelas and Indonesias. They quietly make deals and build up, just in case, their armed forces.

We need to understand this.

It may well be too late by the time enough of us realize the extent of our environmental catastrophe. What difference does it make if man alone is not at fault, or if damage falls short of worst-case scenarios? Even the best case, over time, is curtains for billions of human beings.

Food production cannot keep pace with world hunger. Each year, China and India eat more but grow less. By 2001, the precarious balance had tipped into deficit. With free markets, cash crops earn more than food. And Earth is a small planet. In a few decades, we will need 40 percent more to eat. Yet aquifers are tapping out. Rivers run dry, and endemic drought is drying up fields. When scarce grain fill gas tanks while bellies go empty, more than our consciences will trouble us.

In New Orleans, a foretaste of new reality spiked our fairy-tale delusion that a Dutch kid could save a nation. When nature strikes back, a finger in the dike won't do it. Hurricane Katrina, close to home, caught our attention. In a global setting, it was barely a major event.

As ice melts and seas rise, with harsh storms and seismic turmoil, a new category joins the 20 million "people of concern" the U.N. refugee agency already succors: climate refugees. If an aftermath can go so wrong in a rich democracy, with victims committing suicide and billions squandered, picture what happens elsewhere.

Big disasters make splashy headlines. Yet few people, even among those who pay attention, fathom the impact of silent scourges.

We often use a single word to symbolize the extent to which man can be indifferent to man: holocaust. War casualties aside, Hitler put to death 10 million people. When it was over, we vowed Never Again.

But if we tally the casualties of lingering wars, episodic famines, and endemic plagues—all as preventable at the outset as stopping a mad Austrian-German dictator—we snuff out 30 million lives a year. That is a fresh holocaust every hundred days.

HIV/AIDS has been killing us softly in the background for twenty-five years. We certainly talk enough about it. But what has been the result? Michel Lavollay, a French specialist who has tracked the pandemic since 1985, knows the numbers as well as anyone. When I asked him, in 2006, how many had died of AIDS, he replied, "Twenty-five to thirty million." The margin of error alone amounts to half of a holocaust. He expects the death toll to surpass 100 million within a generation. That is ten holocausts, more than the combined populations of Canada and Britain.

In developing countries, AIDS hits educated classes the hardest. As a result, entire societies face collapse. Many of us know about Botswana from those lovely little books about a lady detective with a deep respect for her traditional-minded people. But how many of us know that nearly half of Botswana's sexually active population is HIV positive?

If—and many experts say when—our worldwide food supply crashes, those fatality figures could be small by comparison. Rich nations may be among the last to suffer. But although dwindling stocks may go to those who can pay the most, at some point hungry people will storm the nearest Bastille. These crises affect us all, even if we are too fat and complacent to feel our ox being gored.

Count slowly to sixty. When you are done, a jumbo jet's worth of infants will have arrived on our planet, each needing a lifetime of resources and a peaceful place to live, if not a flat-panel TV and a cigarette boat. Desparate populations grow faster than rich ones. Even in the face of famine and AIDS, Ethiopians before long will outnumber Japanese.

We have yet more to worry about. Major corporations and criminal organizations are remaking the world into their own image. It is sometimes difficult to tell which are which. When a company's annual bar bill can approach a small country's gross national product, persuasion is tough to resist. "Legal," these days, is a flexible term. Some states, quite simply, belong to organized crime. As Muammar Qaddafi once put it, it is hard to be straight in a crooked world. We need to understand this.

The hard numbers we throw around so casually are rooted in reality. These days, when a million dollars amounts to chump change, we think in billions. One billion minutes ago, Jesus Christ was still alive. One billion dollars is the annual cost of maintaining only three thousand soldiers, not counting the weapons or bottled water they need while at war.

As a collective, we Americans have what Christopher Dickey of *Newsweek* calls a fleetingly brief "half-life of forgetting." History we so quickly forget, as old wisdom says, condemns us to ever more costly repetition. Why were we surprised by what we brought on in Iraq? Just as in Vietnam, we misunderstood the nature of power. By the time we realized how much wrath we provoked in a place we did not comprehend, we were trapped.

Our Bill of Rights and Constitution were meant to get us through such times of peril. Faced with a changing world we do not understand, however, we allow the very underpinnings of our representative democracy to work loose.

Midterm elections in 2006 comforted many of us; in time, America's inherent wisdom corrects our course. But think of the cost. Iraqi casualties,

according to a carefully done Johns Hopkins survey, surpass 600,000, infants and grandmothers as well as combatants in a formless free-for-all. By
population ratios, that is as if some foreign power caused the deaths of 6
million Americans. A holocaust.

Our squandered treasure in Iraq is heading toward $2 trillion. Remem-
ber those numbers? If you spent one dollar every second, it would take 634
centuries before you reached 2 trillion. But we have lost far more than
money that could have been better used elsewhere.

A friend recently sent chills down my spine. "I want to write letters to
the editor about what's going wrong," she said, "but who knows what list
I'd end up on? I might get denied boarding on a plane." That is the sort of
thing I heard in Moscow during the Evil Empire days. And the scariest part
is that her fear is based on a new reality.

We learned only in 2006 that federal agents had used, for four years, a
secret list of Americans and others who cross borders to rate their potential
as terrorists or criminals. Computers secretly profile driving records, meal
preferences, and God knows what else. No one can see, let alone challenge,
these arbitrary rankings. Civil servants we pay intended to keep this list for
forty years.

There is some good news here. When enough of us notice and make
noise, our representative democracy can correct its course. But this is not
nearly often enough.

Editors who shape world coverage should not need their attention
drawn to what is going wrong. It is their job to tell us. Far too many of
them do not. And the problem is worse than that. When some of them do
warn us, in no uncertain terms, nothing much happens. For our very survival, we need to understand this.

Cave blindness is hardly limited to any one nationality. Yet Americans
have suffered from it acutely since John F. Kennedy's well-intended
folly in Vietnam. For better or worse, America is the dominant player. As
Tony Blair put it, speaking as Britain's prime minister, any solution to a
global problem that does not involve the United States cannot be a solution.

In this crucial role, we see reality via the "media," a collective noun that
is hardly more specific than, say, "stuff." This is a disturbing thought.

Since Revolutionary journalists defied the British, our society has depended on a functional if imperfect system of newsgathering. Publishers and
editors took "conservative" or "liberal" positions on their editorial pages.

Some distorted truth. But among the respected papers, news columns were sacrosanct. Professional reporters had a mission to find reality. Readers formed differing viewpoints around shared basic perceptions.

It works differently now. Never has so much data been so instantly available to so many people. Newspapers, in English or Urdu, are a few keystrokes away. Live pictures show events as they happen. If you miss them, you can find them on your laptop. Google Earth can take us anywhere. We have podcasts, RSS feeds, and streaming radio. Yet never have we been so out of touch with reality.

Taken as a whole, "the media" is a deeply flawed lens that distorts much of what it chances upon. It reduces complexity to tight little paragraphs or a headline crawl. Much of it misleads, willfully or unintentionally. There is still plenty of expert firsthand reporting and insight. But now you have to know how to find it and recognize it.

Knowledgeable voices are drowned out by pundits who guess with the rest of us. As satellites obliterate distance, commentators can form immediate opinions about places they could not find on a map. Actual reporting is no longer a prerequisite. Any real estate mogul can become an expert by buying "media" properties.

With a cheap computer at his mother's kitchen table, anyone can be "media" by relaying headlines from Yahoo! and adding uninformed commentary to fuel a particular prejudice. "Citizen journalists" can call attention to unreported stories, but few have the expertise or the wherewithal to check facts and fit them into context. With so much at stake, a "reporter" must be a skilled worker, with education, on-the-job training, and a professional code. We have no citizen orthopedic surgeons.

What clearer, more costly, example do we need than Iraq? In early 2003, those few seasoned Middle East correspondents who saw the story up close tried to warn that George W. Bush's mission was impossible. An invasion under anyone's single flag could only unite Iraqis against the invader. But editors back home, mostly, blunted their message, if not rejecting it outright then diluting it with long-range guesswork. Unchallenged, official wishful thinking shaped a collective view. Four years too late, with no honorable solution in sight, we must somehow mitigate one of the greatest blunders in world history.

Neither pictures nor words necessarily add up to understanding. Without context and cut loose from the historical continuum, "news" is only confusing noise. What matters is how many practiced and fair-minded reporters are deployed to where reality takes shape. Because of cost cuts and a belief that complacent cave dwellers are happy with shallow fluff, these are diminishing fast. Too often, those who remain are filtered by fearful, unworldly, and inexpert editors.

During the first crucial moments of some distant disaster, Google flashes bulletins on a news site that boasts of 4,500 different sources. As often as not, that means 4,498 sources that are all rearranging the meager facts provided by a couple of local stringers at the scene.

By the time a badly gutted foreign correspondent corps arrives, it competes with "analysts" back home who cannot pronounce the names of the people and places they comment upon. Ranks of editors massage dispatches from the scene into news stories that are too often designed for a low common denominator.

Collective news judgment can venture deeply into the ludicrous. A while ago in Paris, the few remaining correspondents were obsessed for days because Hermès would not open after hours for Oprah Winfrey. Parisians could not figure out why an American tourist, unknown in France, was depicted as the victim of racial discrimination because of a simple "CLOSED" sign. That is an amusing sidelight. The bigger picture is disturbing beyond description. Too many reporters are not only told what to look for but also advised of what they really saw.

News, by definition, is something no one knows about yet. That is, it cannot yet be found on the Web or heard at lunch in Washington. To find real news of this sort, reporters must have a long enough leash to move on their own, according to intuition and solid sources. Now our remaining watchdogs struggle against choke collars.

It is simplistic to dismiss the media out of hand. There remains much to admire, in the mainstream and at the edges. Skillful reporters venture into unpleasant places, and some wise editors back home help them do better. But the good ones are no longer enough. Many will tell you that pressures from their own companies gall them more than obstacles faced on the road.

As the spurs to competition dull, we are left in the hands of only a few influential editors. The *New York Times* is often a grand newspaper, yet it chose to wait fourteen months to report that George W. Bush was spying on us illegally—and broke the news then only because its reporter was about to scoop his editors with a book. When the *Times* finally ran the story, we did nothing about it.

During 2005 and 2006, large U.S. papers cut more than 2,500 editorial jobs. Editors brought home correspondents. This meant a greater reliance on news agencies, which, in turn, were stripping themselves of seasoned eyes and ears. What should be on-the-spot reporting is now often distant guesswork based on secondhand sources.

The effect is more apathy, and not only in America. Andrew Marr, one of Britain's grand journalists, wrote in his amusing but tough-minded book, *My Trade*: "Because of its problems, one would simply try to opt out of the news culture. I know people who barely read a paper and who think most broadcast news is mindless nonsense. I think, however, they are wrong. They might go through their weekly round, taking kids to school, shopping, praying, doing some voluntary work, phoning elderly relatives, and do more good than harm as they go. But they have disconnected themselves from the world; rather like secular monks, they have cloistered themselves in the local. And this is not good enough. We are either players in open, democratic societies, all playing a part in their ultimate direction, or we are deserters."

But this takes some work. No one can absorb reliable news without evaluating sources. We must know whom to trust—and why we trust them. For each "fact," the obvious question arises: Who says? We don't license journalists in America, happily enough, but we should evaluate them on our own. Would you ask some unknown amateur with a sharp scalpel to rebuild your ankle?

Above all, we must add our own human and historical context. At its heart, news is not about faceless nations or simple numbers; it is about people. What matters is to understand how different cultures see things, and react to them, in their own way.

That hoary truism is correct: Two broad oceans isolate the United States from a wider world. Into the twenty-first century, as travelers poked into every corner of the planet, one American in ten held a passport. With scant knowledge of other peoples, we assume people of every culture will respond to outside stimuli just as we would.

Take, for instance, the invasion of Iraq. Saddam Hussein, by anyone's definition, was a perfect Hollywood barroom bully. George W. Bush, righteous and resolute, was just the man to face him down. In American lore, when the good guy punches out the bad guy in a bar fight, the story ends happily. In the real world, the bad guy's buddies wait in the parking lot with tire irons.

After the smoke cleared, 56 percent of Americans who went to remake Iraq from within their isolated "Green Zone" fortress had to get their first passport ever. What mattered more was a *de facto* loyalty oath binding them to the administration's narrow political philosophy.

There is a term for all of this: temper-centric. It means judging things within the context of your own place and time. But different peoples do what they do and think what they think. Reality bites whether or not we approve.

Temper-centric thinkers believe they can shape a world according to their needs. For a resourceful nation, there is a solution to every problem. Perhaps, but at what cost? If our grandkids will need *Dune* suits to trap water, and ray guns whenever they venture beyond their walled borders, we had better know about it now.

In America today, truth belongs to those who can turn a phrase; actual facts come second. Many people cannot even recognize a journalist when they see one. In 2005, the Pew Institute asked Americans whom they considered a reporter. Forty percent chose Bill O'Reilly, Fox News's abusive, ill-informed opinionator. He skunked Bob Woodward, who exposed Richard Nixon's Watergate secrets and now does his journalism in intricately sketched books.

An earlier survey was equally harrowing. The Carnegie Corporation of New York hired Frank N. Magid Associates in 2004 to break down how Americans aged eighteen to thirty-four get their news. Beyond the fast-expanding Internet, local TV scored well above network newscasts and daily papers. Many seemed curious about the world only if it was about to kick in their door. Close to half of those aged eighteen to twenty-four tuned out news as contradictory and irrelevant to their lives. They would rather shop and hang with their friends.

A bigger shock came in a Harris survey in July 2006. Fully 50 percent of respondents—up from 36 percent the year before—believed Saddam Hussein had weapons of mass destruction when American forces invaded. In fact, after a sixteen-month investigation that cost more than $900 million, U.S. weapons hunters of the Iraq Survey Group confirmed earlier U.N. inspectors' findings: Saddam scrapped his banned arms in 1991 under U.N. supervision. Yet White House spin, aided by talk radio, blogs, and misleading headlines about a meaningless find, made its impact.

Four years into the Iraq fiasco, other polls show a plurality of Americans still believe Saddam leveled the World Trade Center. And few see how our own national blindness is swelling terrorist ranks.

Beyond American frontiers, parts of the world flower with new promise. Much of it is eroding into moonscape or simmering at the edge of spontaneous combustion. With applied wisdom, we can make differences that matter. But we simply do not get it.

Plato's image struck a chord, a lifetime ago, as I sat through humanities at the University of Arizona. I wanted to go see things for myself. My journalism teacher, a crusty ex–*New York Times* editor named Sherman Miller, taught me that good reporting takes more than just being there.

After working for the *Daily Journal* in Venezuela, and then the *Arizona Daily Star* in Tucson, I got a phone call to make any twenty-one-year-old reporter's heart race. The Associated Press offered me a job.

In August 1967, I caught a midnight flight to mayhem in the Congo. Back then, I was convinced that hard reporting would set things straight. Today, no one can even calculate the forty-year toll. It is at least one holocaust, possibly two. Most Congolese victims, like trees in Borneo, fall in their forests unseen and unheard.

After the Congo, in a forgotten enclave called Biafra, which seceded from Nigeria, I tried to find words to depict a million children dying of hunger. Eventually, Larry Burrows's photo of a stick-limbed baby sitting in a puddle of diarrhea appeared on the cover of *Life* magazine. The world awoke. Then it went back to sleep. Tens of millions more have died since for lack of a few handfuls of protein.

I went to Vietnam in 1970, as American leaders were realizing they could not chew what they had bitten off. By making enemies of whole cultures, they squandered goodwill built up after two world wars. Americans who assumed natural superiority over off-white foreigners saw their folly. And we paid heavily for a lesson we soon forgot: Any attempt to shape "foreign affairs" that is not rooted in up-close reality will make a bad situation worse.

We tend to romanticize Vietnam coverage. It was hardly perfect. Commentators at home preached about a dangerous, distant place they chose not to visit. Military briefings seldom illuminated. Officials lied like hell.

Editors were conflicted. The *New York Times* sometimes put on the front page side-by-side stories, with diametrically opposed content, from Washington and Saigon. Reasonable observers were tarred as hawks or doves. Honest reporters who managed to see the war from Hanoi were reviled as traitors.

But any reporter who took the trouble could see the story firsthand. We hitched rides at will; pilots and field officers took us anywhere we were dumb enough to go. Editors cleaned up our copy but seldom changed our facts. TV film, when it finally showed up in New York, went on the air untrammeled. Anyone who read the papers and magazines, or the wires, knew early on what America was up against.

If some officers despised us for exposing their weaknesses, others liked us for reflecting their strengths. Either way, we had an immutable place among the war's cast of characters, somewhere between enemy and commander in chief. The military was not responsible for carrying us around. Nor was it their right to deny us access.

The principle is clear. When a free nation goes to war, reporters are no inconvenience to be dealt with as the military sees fit. They are as vital as medics, and they must be just as close to the action. Access is no favor granted by indulgent authorities. It is as fundamental as the administration itself. If a war cannot stand up to scrutiny, why is it being fought?

In Vietnam, we insisted on answers. When a soldier observed, deadpan, "We had to destroy the village to save it, sir," he passed into history. We photographed body bags and napalm victims. Eventually, people back home forced an end to a war that their leaders should not have started and could not have finished.

Over the years, I went to a lot of places for AP, maybe two hundred countries if you count the ones no longer with us. Between main events, I focused on stories that crossed borders and eluded headlines: refugees, recurring famine and drought, the amassing of small arms and big bombs.

I went to Argentina in 1973 as a comfortable beef bourgeoisie was starting to bolt its doors at night against mysterious kidnappers. Soon the threat was plain. Urban guerrillas had discovered the power of terrorism. They bombed businesses and police stations. To fund "people's war," they ransomed industrialists for millions.

At lunch one day, an American embassy attaché spoiled my dessert. He told me how the Argentine military flew suspected terrorists over the Atlantic and pushed them out. Still alive, they gulped water and sank. Police had tortured and murdered young leftists in large numbers, as well as a few personal enemies. He knew because several officers wanted to give him an infant they had just made into an orphan. Washington had his report but kept it quiet. That troubled him, so he told me.

This was a reporter's nightmare. I had a story I confirmed elsewhere, with no source I could even obliquely identify. But my editors trusted their reporter. AP carried my vaguely worded story, anonymously sourced, on how the Argentine government was "disappearing" many of its people. After getting comment from Amnesty International in London, I wrote a harder second dispatch. Soon, others joined in, and the "dirty war" was exposed.

Once, this was standard practice in the news business. Reporters found stories, and editors pushed aside the obstacles. Executives who paid the bills stayed above the mix. Later, they accepted the kudos, or the brickbats. Things can still work out that way—but not often enough.

In the 1980s, U.S. foreign policy, and the press that was supposed to keep an eye on it, turned down a dark alley. President Ronald Reagan bestowed freedom-fighter status on right-wing Central American warlords, the Contras, who fought dirty, tortured liberally, and financed themselves by running drugs. I traced cocaine shipments from a secret Costa Rican airstrip to Homestead Air Force Base in Florida as the CIA helpfully looked elsewhere. My story never reached the AP wire. And I was hardly alone.

Whenever reporters approached the mysterious Contra-drugs story, it seemed, they ended up coated in slime. Their own colleagues in Washington, and their editors, sought to debunk the details. If their stories reached print, competitors knocked them down. For some, the facts seemed inconceivable. Nancy Reagan had told the nation to just say no to drugs. How could Americans be involved? For others, the stories were too hard to match. By then, of course, the White House had learned the value of access. No one wanted to be on an official shit list.

For a time, we foreign-based reporters had to duke it out with our Washington bureaus in covering American adventures abroad. We learned yet another language, in which clear words such as "lie" could be replaced with the warmer and fuzzier "spin." Seeing something for ourselves carried hardly more weight than some spokesman's denial.

Then, in 1989, the Berlin Wall fell, and we all scrambled to keep up with nonstop big news. On Wenceslas Square, my spine tingled as a million Czechs rattled keys in the air, their symbol for freedom. I danced on Red Square the night Communism died. After the first Iraq war, I covered the Balkans, from the first skirmishes in Croatia to the 1999 bombing of Kosovo.

After the millennium changed, Al Qaeda attacked America. And then, for assorted concurrent reasons, foreign correspondents and "the media" in general found themselves in a much different world.

In a nation suddenly terrified by what might be out there, editors saw a new role for themselves. Before, they mostly watched over the gates, assessing what approached and deciding what got through. But with new technology, editors could create their own reality. They buzzed our back pockets anytime some breathless CNN stringer added a dubious detail to the mix. And as the management style of news organizations changed, editors were of a different breed.

By tradition, editors handled world news after prior careers as reporters, seeing events take shape in far-flung settings. This gave them an intimate sense of complexities and a clear idea of how correspondents did their work. Now many of them shape their worldview in Washington. In some cases, editors are seasoned veterans who remember a world that has since changed. Either way, micromanaging by remote control usually distorts reality. This embitters reporters who must ignore their own better judgment.

Horst Faas, a German photographer with a reporter's eye, won the first of his two Pulitzers during eight years in Vietnam. Someone asked him recently what would have been different if editors had satellite cell phones to second-guess staff movements from New York. He replied, Horst-like, "Ve'd all be dead." These days, from a souped-up wheelchair, he blasts around the world inspiring young photographers to use new tools in old ways, depicting what they see, bad or good, not what they are sent to find.

Beyond changing newsroom mentalities, a more tangible factor is at play: money. During 2006, Barry Bingham Jr. died, symbolically marking an end to a style of management he championed. He believed that beyond profits, newspapers had a sacred trust. They were more than simple businesses. He fought with his father and family members whose bottom-line thinking ate away at a *Louisville Courier-News* that so many people had respected.

Media ownership is concentrating into fewer hands. Vast empires belong to investors who watch daily stock prices and are run by managers for whom "public trust" is a cliché reserved for speeches. Network television is simply opting out. ABC, now owned by a litigious Hollywood mouse, marked the fifth anniversary of 9/11 with a fictional "docudrama," as if reality were not significant enough. As grand old newspaper groups are broken up, their less lucrative pieces are hived off and left to wither.

All of this means staff cuts and reduced travel that impact heavily on coverage. Correspondents who deal in reality must learn specific skills and earn their editors' trust over time. But tested veterans cost more and talk back, serious drawbacks for a new breed of managers.

As professional journalism competes with an opaque fog of do-it-yourself chronicling, these factors are doubly important. News consumers must know whom to trust. Some names we can take on faith. Otherwise, we must rely on a familiar logo or masthead. As things now stand, that is not a comforting thought.

News organizations of record—such as AP, the *New York Times,* or CNN—each face a vital responsibility. What they do not report, by choice or by simply missing the story, can be far more important than what they do. These days, far too much is missed.

In cycles since World War II, foreign coverage has gone up and down, depending largely on how executives perceived reader attitude. That is over. Editors know readers want more, but resources are stripped to the bone. The *New York Times*'s national circulation grows because the paper delivers quality journalism and lively voices. But it, too, is stretched thin. When Israel went to war in 2006, the paper's Baghdad bureau was raided for reinforcement. Those are only two stories in a big world.

The *Los Angeles Times* and the *Washington Post* have solid, smart reporters at work. But the *L.A. Times* was savaged by new owners of a once noble *Chicago Tribune*. Two executive editors in a row dug in their heels against cutbacks. Both had to go. Late in 2006, the paper went on the block. After all of its past glory, the *Times* must start all over. The *Post* is reinventing itself, with a free stripped-down street version. The newsroom made famous in *All the President's Men* now has a TV studio and an online control room. A foreign staff of more than twenty has been cut to seventeen while editors focus on what they call "hyperlocal" community news.

In a nation such as ours, a sampling of bits of the world in chain-owned dailies does not amount to "coverage." When you probe the details, the picture gets worse. As everyone downsizes, for instance, old files are tossed to save space—irreplaceable reporters' gleanings from earlier in the historical continuum—and we lose vital collective memory. Short staffs mean reporters work by telephone and press handouts. Official or company propaganda, once shunned, helps to fill in the gaps.

Many circulations are dropping precipitously. Middle-range newspapers that once provided sensitive dispatches from abroad have been eviscerated. Stockholders demanding more auctioned off the venerable Knight-Ridder chain. The McClatchy group in California, which had earned respect as a family-controlled chain with solid values, bought up pieces and ditched the rest. The *Philadelphia Inquirer,* once a groundbreaker, was sold to a public relations mogul.

Even at its best, television rarely offers the depth of newspapers. And TV is hardly at its best. Commercial broadcasting, as Bill Moyers put it well, "is too firmly fixed within the rules of the economic game to rise more than occasionally above the lowest common denominator." It has, he notes, made peace with "the little lies and fantasies that are the by-products of the merchandising process."[1] Public broadcasting, meantime, is fighting against broad indifference and outright assault.

Foreign correspondents found one cause for optimism after September 11. If the attacks exacted a grievous price, Americans saw up close that they shared a big world they had best understand. But a reverse effect set in. Many people shut out the outside, reducing complexity to a simple matter of us–versus–them.

Marketers decided that distressing reality reduced audiences. Responsibility is one thing; profit is another. True enough, news of Angelina Jolie's baby born in Africa might outsell the uncounted millions who die of neglect nearby. But that is the short term. If newspapers do not whet an appetite among young people for real news, their future is as bleak as the pessimists predict.

Columnist Molly Ivins nailed the problem in her lovably blunt manner: "I don't so much mind that newspapers are dying—it's watching them commit suicide that pisses me off."[2]

We should mind that newspapers are dying. They are our common core, the equivalent of the village well where people gathered each morning to hear facts before drawing conclusions about the day ahead. Without them, we are lost in today's world. The Internet is a delivery system, not a source. It does not dispatch correspondents. Nor does it test facts, weave in context, or assign priority according to a clear sense of what is most important.

Elected leaders push limits; it is their nature. The Supreme Court and Congress impose some checks or balances. But newspapers are a constant, there when political terms begin and still there when they end. That is the origin of what is fast getting to be a misnomer: the Fourth Estate.

The Web can tell us about distant events that shape our lives. Or it can simply comfort our prejudices. If you set keyword filters finely enough, you will know each time Paris Hilton unzips her dress. If Germany invades Poland, however, someone will have to tell you about it.

In the end, our media watchdogs bark less because we pay so little attention when they do. Their owners keep them muzzled, and governments get away with swatting them across the snout.

In 2005, for instance, a brief "Periscope" item in *Newsweek* said an American guard stuffed a Koran into a toilet at Guantánamo Bay. Muslim zealots rioted in Afghanistan, leaving fifteen dead, triggering violence elsewhere. The origins of that outburst were complex, but *Newsweek* took the heat. It retracted the item.

A crowing White House used the incident to smear critical reporting from Iraq and Afghanistan. Laura Bush traveled to the Middle East to "repair the damage." Good reporters were maligned. For historians, the summary might be: Ill-considered U.S. foreign policy radicalizes Muslims, causing many to fear and loathe America. But that week's headline was: False *Newsweek* Report Sparks Deadly Riots.

The item was essentially correct. Its mistake was to say that U.S. authorities were investigating Koran abuse. *Newsweek* editors decided that rather than quibble, they would print a retraction. Spurred by the report, a U.S. military panel finally investigated. It confirmed well-sourced charges that had been circulating for two years. Among other incidents, one guard had splashed urine on the holy book. Another scrawled filthy words inside the cover.

Eventually, a larger truth emerged. We were abusing prisoners held for years on questionable grounds with no due process. Even after Americans force-fed hunger strikers, three prisoners managed to hang themselves. A senior Washington official sneered that such suicides were "good PR"; her heartless remark was flashed around a very small world. And Guantánamo was yet another item added to a bill we will someday have to settle.

Barring some happy miracle, we are stuck with filtering out the "fair-and-balanced" bigots, the guesswork Web logs, and the corporate cowards who pollute a mainstream that is still vital and sometimes noble.

We all love that scene in *Network* when a frustrated old newscaster stops reading and starts to rant. He sends people across the country to their windows to shout: "I'm mad as hell, and I'm not going to take it anymore." But nothing changes. In the movie, executives realize the potential and put the guy on air as a soothsaying clown.

Go ahead and rant, but don't expect much. CBS paid $75 million in 2006 for a perky morning-show anchor to read news off a prompter while it saved chump change by firing stringers who provided that news. On cable TV, you can read the script yourself on the crawl line on the bottom of the screen. But, as one comedian noted, it runs together so that you are not sure if it said the Lakers scored 88 points or 88 people died in Iraq.

Instead, try stepping back to see news as an index to reality. No one has time to stay atop every wrinkle on the planet. Even the best reporting can describe only part of a constantly changing picture. What matters is a deeper understanding of the larger human context so that events make sense when they happen. Once we get past meaningless collectives and pronouns—"the Muslims," "the Europeans," "the terrorists," "*they*"—the nuances are clearer.

The disparate crises we face are all part of this bigger picture. By reducing poverty, we dampen terrorism and stem illegal immigration. Wise foreign aid heads off hunger and blunts the impact of sudden disaster. Swift action contains plagues and pandemics. By holding a steady light on corporate greedheads, corrupt leaders, and crime lords, we can bring our legal system to bear. Prosecutions are often not even necessary; these people can only thrive in the dark. And if we do not protect our environment, none of this matters.

This comes down to basic common sense, the stuff of Forrest Gump and Chauncey Gardiner, the bowler-hatted hero of *Being There.* When Americans act nobly, addressing world problems with a larger view than our own narrow interests, reasonable people do not hate us. They may cease scorning us if we stop trying to "brand" America, selling ourselves like deodorant. What can we expect when, arriving at our gates, the world is seen as guilty until proven innocent?

Outsiders often miss the point. If America seems clueless and rudderless from a distance, it looks different up close. The society thrums with ideas, energy, and wisdom. Large numbers of people, young and old, know exactly what has gone off track and what challenges we face. They just cannot coalesce with one another into a critical mass that can change things.

The obvious question is whether these committed people are enough. A huge number of Americans, on the right and the left, just tune out. Dumb responses to questions about the world are funny as Jay Leno gags, but they reflect a harrowing state of complacent ignorance.

I put this question to James Hoge, the editor of *Foreign Affairs,* who has run perceptive newspapers since the 1960s. "For the most part," he said, "Americans follow the republican formula: I elected you; you take care of it. If things get really screwed up, I'll throw you out." The problem, he added, is that unless a functioning press makes clear how bad things screw up, we are condemned to wait for the final chapter before fear forces us to finally act.

I also went to Michael Getler, as close as anything foreign correspondents have to a rabbi-imam. After years abroad for the *Washington Post,* he was the paper's foreign editor. He edited the *International Herald Tribune* before returning to the *Post* as an ombudsman who took no prisoners. Now he is the conscience of PBS.

Getler excoriated American editors for missing the Downing Street tapes that revealed the Iraq invasion was based on sham. More than a smoking gun, this was a muzzle flash. Had we realized its meaning, 2004 elections might have come out differently. Yet when the *Sunday Times* of London broke the story during 2003, AP failed to relay it on the weekend.

On Monday, AP editors spiked it. Hardly anyone else took notice. Bloggers forced it into the mainstream. But time had passed; editors made it go away.

"The *Post* did not cover it," Getler said, his measured voice rising. Others did only marginally better. "It too easily adopted the knockdown view. It was astounding. Can you imagine if minutes of a National Security Council meeting were leaked and said that intelligence was manipulated, fixed, with all the principals of our closest ally in up to their necks with us in this war? Downing Street was the exact same thing. Editors did not sense the power of this dynamite. The head of British intelligence was talking to the prime minister right after he came back from a visit to Washington. This was fact. They don't make mistakes in these things."

Getler believes too many editors miss the significance of real news while squandering the resources they still have. This helps bad leaders shape their own truths. "The decision to invade Iraq may well be the worst decision in modern American history, with tremendous long-term effects," he said. "The administration presented a false certainty. They said they knew things. They knew where these weapons were. We said they were sure. They lied."

But, of course, governments lie. It is their nature. Journalism's job is to catch them at it. If editors cannot do it, citizens have to look out for themselves.

"America was, and is, a country that stands up and challenges wrongdoing, things that France and Germany and Japan see but look the other way," Getler concluded. "We have put into doubt what it is we stand for. It is a terrible, terrible potential loss if it remains. The kind of standards we used to have seem to be deteriorating, everything from Geneva conventions on torture, treatment of prisoners, to preemptive war, to environmental leadership, to health care, to education. This is diminishing a sense of aspiration that has always drawn people to America, sometimes in boats, sometimes just spiritually and intellectually. I think that has changed now. It may not be gone forever, but it has changed."

G etler, like Hoge and most other sensible thinkers, sees room for optimism. As he puts it, if you bet against America in the long term, you will likely lose. In every area where things are going wrong, people are seeking ways to do better. Bush père was right about those thousand points of light. The trick is to focus them into a single beam to illuminate the tunnel.

Broad solutions require a society's commitment: better schools that teach the world's true texture; public forums that focus on issues and action; environmental and energy polices with teeth; public-supported radio and television that need not pander for profit; corporations that add humanity to columns of numbers.

Yet much is within each individual's grasp. We can show our own children a wider world. We can vote, write letters, and make choices about where we put resources. We can combine what is best in the media with other tools to see our global setting as it really is.

The following chapters look by category at challenges we face. At the end, I suggest plans of action, relaying some of the wisdom that found its way into my stack of interview notes. But first, there are some basics.

Put aside any notion that simply scanning an array of untested sources amounts to a useful briefing. Taking news from the Net is like going after a steak with a knife and fork at the Chicago stockyards. With work, you can find a prime cut. But if you are not careful, you will end up with gristle and bull droppings.

Look for reporters who see things for themselves and say things as they see them. I loved it when Nicholas Kristof of the *New York Times* offered to take Bill O'Reilly to Darfur. O'Reilly said he was too busy interpreting the news to go out and see what he was talking about.

Later, Kristof confounded cynics who assert that young people no longer care. When he offered to take an aspiring correspondent on a road trip, nearly four thousand jumped at the chance to catch dengue fever out in the real world. The winner, Casey Parks, followed him to Equatorial Guinea in 2006. Now this is an annual event.

Famous names and faces are not necessarily the most reliable. Many of the best reporters work out of the limelight. Dana Priest of the *Washington Post* won a Pulitzer in 2006 for tracking down a story that began: "The CIA has been hiding and interrogating some of its most important Al Qaeda captives at a Soviet-era compound in Eastern Europe, according to U.S. and foreign officials familiar with the arrangement."[3]

Do not dismiss television, but use your remote more creatively. When Ted Koppel left ABC, we lamented an era's end. Yet Koppel went to the Discovery Channel and rose to new heights. Five years after 9/11, his calmly narrated but devastating report *The Price of Security* showed how we had upended our basic principles, to the point of trampling constitutional rights and torturing prisoners, for an illusion of more safety.

The hardest—and most important—part is to keep an open mind. While finishing this book, I went as a lecturer on a cruise of retired Americans to

cradles of Mediterranean civilization. We dined under the elaborately chis-
eled facade of the three-story library at Ephesus; it had held 300,000 works
etched on parchment two millennia ago, and much of that wisdom still applies today. As we steamed toward our final port, I talked about cave blindness.
Unlike the ancients, I said, we don't have to guess at what is beyond the hori-
zon, and yet many of us still close down our circuits and choose ignorance.

One woman, near tears, pinned back my ears. The United States, she
said, was the greatest country in four thousand years, the most generous, the
freest, the smartest, the biggest hearted. The *nicest*. I thanked her and moved
on. She believed what she said. As Getler had noted, we see ourselves as a
force for good, with the ability to deliver. But I thought of the Maltese,
Greeks, Italians, and Turks I had talked to while the group trooped after
guides. We once were all of those things and should be again. But for the
present, "they" worry at what they see: a strident dialogue of the deaf
among Americans who are forfeiting greatness and think no one is noticing.

With our own legwork, we can fill in missing pieces of a crucial mosaic. Take the case of Niger on a Dark Continent that figures so promi-
nently in world rhetoric. In 2005, after G-8 leaders praised themselves for
helping Africa, the Paris daily *Liberation* splashed a front-page photo of a
dying boy in Niger. With hollow, hopeless eyes, stick limbs, and distended
belly, he evoked the Biafran child Larry Burrows photographed forty years
earlier.

But Niger had already had its fifteen minutes of fame. To push for his
war, Bush declared that Niger had sold uranium to Iraq; this was irrefutable
proof. Saddam had to be stopped. When the information was debunked,
Niger dropped to its usual place in global geopolitics: nowhere.

Meanwhile, the landlocked nation was struck by locusts, a means of
mass destruction as old as the Bible. Swarms ate a meager crop that followed drought, an effect of climate change that vested interests continued
to minimize. Relief workers banged the alarm. More than a million might
starve. As usual, early action would have been cheap. By the time the story
made small headlines, the U.N. calculated, emergency aid would cost eighty
times more. Even at that, relief would amount to only twenty minutes of
world arms expenditure. It was slow in coming.

In an editorial entitled "The Indecency of Rich Nations," *Liberation*
noted that some countries require passersby to help endangered strangers. It
argued that international law ought to make the failure to help large populations in danger a crime against humanity.

Such stories pose a dilemma. How does one assign priority to any given calamity? If fanatics kill three thousand people by invading America. it is clear. But famine eludes news summaries, let alone a crawl at the bottom of a screen. The culprit is nature and faceless human apathy. To stricken families, however, dead is dead.

Victims react as any other humans would. They wonder why those who could have helped left them to suffer. They ask how a nation can consider spending a billion dollars to memorialize its own tragic loss when that money could save so many lives elsewhere. And they come up with explanations that approach the truth. This partly answers that redoubtable question: Why do they hate us?

Staying informed is easier than it seems. At the beginning, it requires commitment. And then you hit the zone. Keeping up with global currents takes no more time each week than aerobic exercise or watching a few old movies for the third time.

Getting involved is not much harder; it takes a broad, hopeful view. "Cynics say that real life is a choice between the failed revolution and the shabby deal—I don't know, maybe they're right," author Arundhati Roy mused in the *Nation*.[4] "But even they should know that there's no limit to just how shabby that shabby deal can be." As a novelist, Roy captures grand thoughts in microcosm. As a thinker, she warns of forgetting humans in any global equation.

She concludes: "What we need to search for and find, what we need to hone in and perfect into a magnificent, shining thing, is a new kind of politics. Not the politics of governance, but the politics of resistance. The politics of opposition. The politics of forcing accountability. The politics of slowing things down. The politics of joining hands across the world and preventing certain destruction."

There is really no option. We can no longer sit like Plato's metaphoric prisoners, backs to reality. We need to see what is out there—and do something. We have to see ourselves as others do, as equals facing challenges that demand common action. Far too many lives, perhaps our own or our children's, depend on it.

TWO

THAT FIVE-LETTER WORD

Flawed as it is, "the media" is our principal lens on reality beyond our direct line of vision. We each shape our own broad worldview. Internet postings add pointillist dabs of detail. But for a broad picture, with foreground subjects and backdrop motif, we rely on a twenty-first-century version of the venerable Press.

Today our trusty old watchdog of beloved metaphor has mutated into various hybrid species. Some "media" cowers in the shadows and growls at strange noises. Yet much of it ventures out to brave new dangers. I'd be happy for Ann Coulter to guard my junkyard but hardly the future of my planet. With, say, John Kifner of the *New York Times* sniffing outside the door, I'd sleep soundly.

The range is wide, even within the same organization. In 2006, French students protested a government plan to find more jobs for graduates. The idea was to exempt bosses from paying severance if they fired a young worker within two years. While Fox News's live coverage hyped "violence" it rarely found, Chris Burns of CNN related what he saw. Burns speaks French and had worked in Paris for AP. He noted that despite some scuffles, both police and organizers kept tight control. In Atlanta, an anchor added her own wisdom: "Sort of brings back memories of Tiananmen Square when you saw these activists in front of tanks." Burns, embarrassed, apologized to French authorities.

Some tyros evoked the 1968 Paris uprising that pushed Charles de Gaulle toward the door. Elaine Sciolino of the *New York Times,* who had also covered France for *Newsweek* decades earlier, made clear in a lead paragraph that this was not even close. "Our revolt is not to get more," a student leader told her. "It's to keep what we have."

This is why "the wires" are so essential. During four decades with the Associated Press, I never got over how little most people know about news agencies, which are vital to their lives. Some of their dispatches are signed. Often their content is used without credit in newspapers and on TV. Either way, they provide the bulk of what is reported in America, on the Web and everywhere else.

Small newspapers have only the wires. Larger ones with their own correspondents still rely on agencies for breaking news, background, and early word of far-flung ferment that could suddenly erupt onto front pages. No single newspaper staff can do more than sample world news.

The *New York Times* had thirty-five foreign correspondents at the beginning of 2007. The *Washington Post* was down to seventeen. Across the board, others closed bureaus and brought reporters home. Remaining correspondents write more and spend less. Instead of cultivating sources or following hunches, most stay at their keyboards all day to keep Web sites fresh. They do video feeds and chat with readers on interactive circuits. As young reporters replace veterans who take buyouts, living memory is lost.

This trend is dramatic with television. ABC, CBS, and NBC keep skeleton foreign staffs, mostly in London or Tokyo. If news breaks in West Malaria, someone can read a script in the bureau and still be technically abroad. When reporters parachute into a story, they often arrive without background or contacts. CNN does marginally better. But when you hear, "CNN has learned . . . ," you can often add the unspoken phrase "by reading the wires."

Since agencies provide wholesale reportage to news organizations of differing viewpoints all over the globe, they carry a heavy responsibility. They must be accurate and comprehensive but also (in actual fact) fair and balanced. Editors as well as reporters must learn to filter out their cultural or political bias. Everyone, including all the unpaid interns whom managers love, has to know the difference between noisy students in Europe and an uprising in China that is reshaping our world.

This chapter focuses on the AP and other primary news sources, as well as revisiting some news stories that have shaped the "media" that serves, or ill serves, us today. For seeing the world as it is, such context is crucial.

The Associated Press in New York and Reuters in London took shape in the mid-1800s in similar ways for the same reasons. Newspapers could afford to send reporters out in rowboats to meet incoming ships for a few hours' jump on the news. Samuel F. B. Morse's dots and dashes extended a correspondent's reach across oceans. But to keep up with distant war and peace, editors saw they had to share expenses to form cooperatives.

While Reuters thrived in Europe, AP distinguished itself in America. Mark Kellogg, an early star, never got to send the dispatch of his life. He took an arrow next to Custer at Little Big Horn. By 1900, when a New York newspaper publisher could start his own war in Cuba, the wires were as crucial as printing presses. A Serb zealot shot an Austrian archduke in Sarajevo, and the wires were there. With agencies to watch what happened next, Europe's Great War of 1914–18 is better known as World War I.

Over most of the twentieth century, AP had serious competition. Like AP, Hearst's International News Service and E. W. Scripps's United Press delivered news by teletype to papers under contract. But as businesses meant to make a profit, they had subscribers. AP, a cooperative, had members. In 1958, UP decided to merge with INS and became United Press International.

In Vietnam, the two New York–based rivals fought hard to outdo one another. Correspondents such as AP's Malcolm Browne and UPI's Neil Sheehan, who both moved on to the *New York Times,* set the tone for agency reporters, who took pride in calling themselves wire animals. Their dispatches in the early 1960s led daily papers and television newscasts across the world. Peter Arnett, not yet sullied by the exigencies of a media star system, was an AP wire animal of great skill and courage. Arnett once wrote about GIs looting after a victory. Wes Gallagher, the boss, had covered World War II. "American soldiers don't loot," he declared, and he killed the story. The desk revolted, and Gallagher relented. His reporter was there, and he knew from experience that he could trust his reporter.

Later, in Saigon, Richard Pyle liked to explain why he was the most important person on earth. As AP bureau chief, he oversaw the flow of information about the world's biggest story to every news organization on the planet. Pyle laughed at his boast, but I suspect he believed it.

Back then, as the cost of reporting soared, UPI suffered badly. The Scripps-Howard chain hung on until its pockets were empty. With short-cuts in quality, UPI lost customers. After a last gasp for the first Gulf War, it all but melted away. Helen Thomas at the White House stayed on through a succession of owners with dubious agendas, and then she finally quit.

Reuters continued as a newspaper-owned cooperative until the 1980s. Then it went corporate and listed on the London Stock Exchange. Reuters made billions supplying financial data; by comparison, its news service was a small dog wagged by a very large tail. Though it is still a solid news pur-veyor, many of its reporters say the company has lost its sense of mission. In 2006, executives decided to outsource some financial newsgathering to clerks in India. Reuters argued that this freed its experienced reporters from busywork. That businessman's rationale discomfited newspeople. By 2007, several thousand jobs had shifted to bargain-basement beginners in India.

Agence France-Presse, based in Paris, also calls itself a cooperative with roots that go deep into the nineteenth century. But official subsidies masked as subscriptions make up its deficit. Some of its work is excellent, but some is suspect. A news agency needs blanket credibility, with distance from any government or national allegiance. This is a much bigger problem with Xinhua, China's fast-expanding wire service, which often echoes Party propaganda.

Bloomberg, the product of a visionary businessman-politician who identified an important role to fill, may end up redefining the wire-service future. While other organizations cut back, it hires by the handful, stocking bureaus with correspondents across the world. Bloomberg, like its next-door Manhattan neighbor Bloomingdale's, is high-tech and high-fashion. Ten floors are linked by the world's first curved escalators, which deliver executives to fancy tables at Le Cirque on the ground floor.

Visitors are photographed for big flashy badges and then met at the ele-vator by peppy and preppy minions. It is serious future shock for anyone who remembers newsrooms where reporters hid pints of Jim Beam in their bottom drawer and enlivened dull mornings by flipping a glowing cigarette butt into a trash can full of paper.

With generous emoluments and free food, earnest employees beaver away in cubicles and do not smoke even on the outdoor terrace above Lex-ington Avenue. Rather than cranky journalists, they bring to mind con-tented cows attached to relentless milking machines. Their billionaire boss understands productivity.

Bloomberg is still mainly a financial news and data service. It earns close to $5 billion a year renting do-everything terminals to traders and business professionals. Revenue from news operations barely pays for the fresh flowers and tropical fish that decorate the open-plan hallways. That might change. But America must still depend mainly on AP.

In 1906, Mark Twain observed, "There are only two forces that can carry light to all corners of the globe—the sun in the heavens and the Associated Press down here." Later, Gandhi mused that if he ever reached those heavens, he expected to find an AP reporter asking him questions.

Today, new branders who make much of those encomiums have come up with a fresh slogan: "the essential global news source." When AP functions as designed, those words have never carried more truth. Yet America's only not-for-profit news cooperative is in the midst of metamorphosis.

Marketers boast of a "new AP." It is still owned cooperatively by every sizable newspaper and broadcaster in America, about 1,300 in all. It sells news to another ten thousand nonmember subscribers around the world. Its news digests, compiled throughout the day, set a broad agenda for everyone else. And its dispatches are cheerfully plundered; that is part of the deal.

But many publishers are reluctant to spend money on their essential raw material: news gathered up close and in person by professional reporters. Instead, resources are directed toward highly paid managers and editors who package words, pictures, and television footage into profit centers. In today's economy, this might make business sense. Yet the price is high to the rest of us.

Ex-employees are suspect sources. They are, however, well placed to see what may not be obvious from the outside. My purpose here is to find ways for us all to escape Plato's cave; understanding America's main source of world news is a large part of that. This is how I see it.

To raise its profile, the "new AP" pushes hard for dramatic scoops and stories people notice. This is good for any news organization. But to save money while feeding newspapers' nonstop Web updates, it cuts corners. The result is inconsistency, and far too much is missed.

When a stateless Hezbollah picked a fight with Israel in 2006, reality was blurred. As might be expected, there was no measured tit for tat. For me, the question was obvious: Could Israel silence the rockets and humble Hezbollah without handing a greater victory to a proxy Iranian militia because of a swaggering attempt at shock and awe? Middle East wars are about politics, and the spoils are measured in world sympathy.

Amid all the words and images in the first days of conflict, I saw a dispatch signed "By Kathy Gannon, Associated Press Writer." In a few paragraphs, I knew what I needed to know. Israel had lost a crucial part of the war. And, with the backlash sure to come, I pondered changing my name to O'Rosenblum. Gannon's dispatch from Tyre focused on an eight-year-old girl and what was left of her family. They had gone to see their new home in a southern village. Israeli planes demolished it and then hit their car as they fled. Her two sisters, teachers, were killed.

"Jawad Najem, a surgeon at the hospital, said patients admitted Sunday had burns from phosphorous incendiary weapons used by Israel," the report said.[1] "The Geneva Conventions ban using white phosphorous as an incendiary weapon against civilian populations and in air attacks against military forces in civilian areas. Israel said its weapons comply with international law." Phosphorous burns to the bone, with excruciating agony, unless a medic with copper sulfate extinguishes it. Armies drop phosphorous on troop concentrations to sow panic. Israelis would explain that the enemy was hiding among civilians. But that is no excuse. Unlike in past wars, anyone with an Internet link could see the effect. Lebanese bloggers, and Hezbollah propagandists, made sure of that.

AP did well in that case. But the crucial part of the byline was "By Kathy Gannon" and not "Associated Press Writer." I knew her to be a grand reporter, razor sharp, compassionate yet capable of calling things as she sees them. I know other AP writers who fit that description. I also know the opposite extreme—and the editorial structure in which they all work.

In AP's framework, people of far different competence levels contribute to the wire. Some comfortable old hands do not challenge editorial override. New hires are often eager to impress their bosses and move upward into emptied ranks. Since agencies want to appear to be present at every story, an "Associated Press Writer" might be an untested stringer reached by telephone. Some editors can help correct for this, drawing from their own experience abroad. But some recall a world that has since changed. Others, with only a cave-wall sense of the real world, would not know a phosphorous bomb from a book of matches.

The problem is partly structural. In earlier times, AP named foreign bureau chiefs who knew their territory, senior people who forged contacts with national leaders, newsmakers, ranking diplomats, and sectors of society. They directed reporters sent from New York and "locals," who worked in their own cultures under AP guidelines. The idea was a mix of skills, cultures, and energies.

AP reporters were hired only after five years' experience on a daily paper. After working in domestic bureaus, they trained on the foreign desk. Usually after years in New York, they were assigned abroad to chase news wherever they suspected it might be. When the bills came in, members paid. Newspaper owners who governed AP had a sense of mission; many worried less about balance sheets than about portraying the world as it was. People sometimes confused us with A&P, a large grocery chain of the time, and the name fit. It was a supermarket of news.

This structure softened over time, but the "old AP" spirit survived the millennium. Then, in stages, it began to change. When terrorists struck the Twin Towers, AP reporters swarmed to the scene. Readers got to know selfless firemen and workaday office drones who turned out to be heroes. Survivors told their stories. It was brave, skillful, evocative journalism. Bureaus added a nationwide perspective, detailing how Americans reacted to a modern-day Pearl Harbor. But an unanswered question, in a longer term the most important of all, still had to be answered after a hard look beyond our own borders: Why?

My own job, designed when I returned to AP in 1981 after two years as editor of the *International Herald Tribune* in Paris, was suited to the moment. As special correspondent, I was to take time with stories, cultivate sources, and, essentially, contribute to a fancy-food section of the AP supermarket. On major stories, I tried to add textured human backdrops for readers a world away.

I hurried to Afghanistan, where, with a wounded superpower raging like King Kong, there was much to be learned. I had help from a brilliant colleague: Kathy Gannon. "With satellite dishes snipped from tin cans, Afghans can sit back in the Middle Ages and keep tabs on the twenty-first century," I wrote from Kabul. "Their bad luck is that this optical miracle works only one way."

On a rich red rug inside old mud walls, an Afghani teacher poured me the inevitable glass of tea. "I'm afraid the world just doesn't understand us," Shahla Paryan told me, with a sad shake of her head. "It is wrong to believe that we were the same as those horrible people who brought terrorism to America. It is very wrong."

In the aftermath of 9/11, America and the world beyond relied heavily on AP. But during 2002, the 160-year-old cooperative began its self-reinvention. Wall Street had focused on "media properties"; twenty-first-century style yellow journalism was colorized with green. For a new sort of publisher, "nonprofit" was a dirty word.

A Wal-Mart can thrive on profit margins near 3 percent because it has room to grow. A family-owned newspaper can make it on not much more if it has a higher purpose beyond rapacity. When Ted Turner set up CNN, he accepted occasional losses if the network gained intrinsic public value. Faceless investors see things differently.

Newspapers grew used to annual profits ranging to 35 percent. But since most have saturated potential markets, growth is difficult. They can get better to attract more readers. Or they can plunder their assets, demanding more profit until the golden goose collapses of heart failure.

After 1989, with more of the world open, foreign coverage costs rocketed yearly, and new technology ate up capital. When big news broke, AP responded as usual. It deployed legions in all directions, stuffing bills into drawers to worry about later. Yet the AP board kept annual assessments—dues—at less than inflation. Key members pressed for new streams of income.

About the time Bush shifted his aim from Afghanistan to Iraq, AP's high command changed. Directors replaced the longtime president with the man who had run *USA Today*. He took the businesslike title of chief executive officer and hired a frequently changing phalanx of highly paid vice presidents.

A new executive editor, a product of Washington, reshaped AP's international desk according to her own worldview. Her desk editors, who were guided by TV monitors and goaded by orders from above, rained contradictory commands on foreign bureaus. Before long, she fired or forced into retirement a number of bureau chiefs and correspondents. Other seasoned hands quit or lapsed into discreet silence. Young talent who read writing on the wall moved elsewhere.

Some new people were excellent, learning quickly on the job. Some others were the opposite. We sent our stories to new regional desks, which worked them over before further handling in New York. The center of gravity shifted to the United States. A year after 9/11, AP's thick package of commemorative stories focused on how America had changed. One looked at Islamic attitudes, but that was it for the rest of the world. None attempted to answer that hanging question: Why?

Since bylines are perceived as reflecting credibility as well as physical presence at a story, desks stretched the limits. If you saw, say, Denis Gray's or Kathy Gannon's name atop a story, you could be confident. Some other names might be anything from a photographer who called in a few details he happened to notice to an untested local stringer hired by phone.

The emphasis was on showing the flag; that is, branding a new AP. Rather than simply speaking, sources "told the AP." New York made much of an early look one reporter got at Guantánamo. The story, however, suggested heavy compromise for access. The reporter saw selected interrogations through one-way glass, with no sound. She was forbidden to talk to prisoners, including one who yelled to her that he was an Al Jazeera reporter. The lead focused on a smiling captive playing chess with his interrogators and suggested prisoners were not unhappy because they were given such treats as Snickers bars.

AP correspondents got to be like those tiny cameras at the end of colonoscopy probes. We poked into the world's most distasteful places to relay raw data to distant editors in clean clothes who interpreted it according to their own assumptions and secondhand sources.

The baseball bat AP had given me was whittled down to a toothpick. New York knew what it wanted. When I tried to write about France's misgivings, one editor treated me to a Pepé Le Pew accent: "Who cares what ze French zink?"

We can only guess why Bush was so eager to assault Iraq. Saddam had tried to kill his father. A lot of oil was at stake. Perhaps it was a tempercentric notion that a righteous America could stamp its own image on a five-thousand-year-old multiethnic society that had never known democracy but, time and again, had united against foreign invaders.

Anyone near enough to see events take shape could see what was coming. If an unbalanced tyrant hid dangerous weapons, a multilateral attack might make sense. But that, certain to kill noncombatants and destabilize the Middle East, would require a clear reason based on evidence.

AP's Charles Hanley followed United Nations inspectors across Iraq. A Pulitzer Prize–winning reporter who works with elaborate care, he had covered nuclear, chemical, and biological weapons issues for years. Inspectors trusted him, respecting his sober skills. Hanley knew that invading forces were not likely to find forbidden weapons or evidence of programs to build them. He wrote two analytical pieces that would have led readers to question Bush's basis for war. Both were spiked in New York.

Meantime, in the months leading up to Colin Powell's U.N. speech, AP carried almost daily stories from Washington citing "intelligence sources" or "senior U.S. officials" on the presence of that hoary acronym: WMD. Several times, Hanley's Baghdad stories were stripped of lines saying the Bush administration claimed there were WMD but had offered no firm evidence.

On Feb. 4, Hanley got a leaked account of what Powell would say the next morning, including the audio intercepts and satellite photos. He sent a long dispatch that compared what Powell would assert to what was actually known on the ground. He also warned of the weakness of such evidence by gadgetry. AP killed that story, too. Instead of Hanley's vital exclusive, editors ran a story from George Gedda, their veteran State Department reporter. It began:

WASHINGTON (AP) _ It was the ear.

Decades ago, CIA photo sleuths determined that an elderly man swimming in the Yangtze River was not really Mao Zedong, as the Chinese regime had claimed, but a double.

The shape of Mao's ear differed from the swimmer's, something only a highly trained eye could have discerned. Though intriguing, that episode was a minor footnote to the history of spying compared with the war-versus-peace intelligence harvest on Iraq being presented Wednesday by Secretary of State Colin Powell.

Powell spoke, saying just what Hanley tried to signal he would. Like most news organizations, AP reported it uncritically. Hanley, on the spot in Baghdad, was too discouraged to try yet again to add reality to the glowing terms of AP's coverage. Six months later, when the national mood changed, he was able to write a piece that demolished Powell's case. By then, of course, we had already invaded, and there was no turning back.

While Hanley looked at the *casus belli,* I focused on the politics. In Amman, Jordanians and Palestinians who hated Saddam warned against a U.S.-led invasion. I phoned well-placed Saudis and other old sources from Morocco to Yemen. AP reporters from Arab capitals contributed to my notes. In Aqaba, I watched the news—live from Baghdad—as Jordanians muttered in anger. In Wadi Ram, I met Bedouins who saw current events in twenty-year cycles.

From the most radical to the most moderate, everyone saw folly in invading Iraq under an American flag without a wider mandate. They knew how Iraqis resent foreign incursion. Britain learned that the hard way only a few generations earlier. Most believed America could quickly push Humpty Dumpty off the wall. But then what?

Editors in New York added American think-tank remarks to my dispatch for "balance." Slashed in half, it read like any vox-pop piece, a string of pro and con opinions with no substance to explain why people shaped their views.

I had recalled Egypt's Gamal Abdel Nasser, whose secular nationalism swelled the ranks and hardened the line of the underground Muslim Brotherhood. The executive editor chided me for mentioning a name readers might not recognize. But that was the point. The essential global news source ought to remind people that history did not start each afternoon in the White House briefing room.

Vietnam parallels were unmistakable to anyone who had been there. Here was America intent on delivering freedom and democracy at gunpoint to a vastly different society. Blatant if unintended hypocrisy would turn others against us, foe and friend alike. When I quoted people saying this, editors cut it out. One told me, "We think it's too early to talk about Vietnam."

Some time afterward, I joined the AP roadkill.

I waited two years to watch a new AP take shape. Many of the best reporters were pinned to desks writing headline summaries and working by phone. Some veterans who resigned or were pushed into retirement were replaced with local hires who received few employee benefits and little of the basic training that once was required. Others were not replaced at all. Reporters with scant experience, or from AP television, took charge of major bureaus.

Such downsizing at operational levels had gotten to be routine among corporations. But with AP's fundamental mission in a troubled world, this was hardly an ordinary corporation. In fact, it was not a corporation at all.

Eventually, I wrote to Burl Osborne, chairman of the board. I recalled a letter I had written in 1990 in praise of an AP colleague, Mike Goldsmith, who died on the job at sixty-eight, the victim of a Liberian soldier's gun butt and a malarial mosquito.

"If his breed is not to die," I said then, "we must understand what fed the fires of a man who spent forty-five years working himself to death in AP service. He knew that all of the AP's fancy machines and systems are so much useless junk without the one thing at the heart of our being: the reporter's link to news."

My letter to Osborne was long, but the heart of it was summarized in this paragraph: "Inexperienced managers of a 'new AP' must understand that however they rearrange the furniture, the wire's integrity depends on the reporters who actually gather the news upon which billions of people shape their reality."

As large news organizations cut back their coverage or skimp on sending out tested reporters, the letter said, AP's role grows more crucial in direct proportion. It is the cornerstone of a professional correspondent corps we will need urgently as world crises get worse.

"No school can shape a seasoned correspondent," I wrote. "Young people must work with veterans. Background, vital to any story that matters, depends on long memories. Any eager neophyte can hop into a hairy situation. Then what? Danger is one thing. Experience saves more lives than flak vests or Centurion courses. But even in placid situations, it takes practice to find the program, let alone the players. Fresh reporters who prove themselves quickly must feel they have a solid future when they cost more and talk back. Walker Lundy, who edited the *Philadelphia Inquirer*, put it wisely: Newspapers are eating their seed corn."

D ecades ago, we lamented that American editors focused only on the top ten foreign stories at a time. In recent years, that rule of thumb was reduced to three. Now, essentially, we are down to one. The day's big story is covered. Important also-rans are sampled. The rest fit into the interstices.

Remember Afghanistan? Once attention shifted to Iraq, only the news agencies, the *Washington Post*, and the BBC stayed in Kabul. Carlotta Gall of the *New York Times*, with five years' experience, shuttled between Kabul and Islamabad. In February 2006, in Kandahar, Gall ran into what reporters call a shitstorm. As she watched, a suicide bomber killed thirteen people, including five policemen. Another thirteen were wounded. The Taliban quickly took credit.

The Taliban was back again in Kandahar where it all started. Once only the passive hosts to Osama bin Laden, now they had brought Al Qaeda's weapon of human sacrifice to the country that Americans were supposed to have pacified only three years earlier. This was news.

"What amazed me even more (than the explosion) was that editors weren't the least bit interested in the story, so I didn't write about it, even though I was right there," Gall told Sherry Ricchiardi of the *American Journalism Review*.[2] "Maybe I should have pushed harder. . . . It was more than blood and gore." But the story that day was reaction to Danish caricatures of the Prophet Mohammed. Gall had written about three deaths in Afghani riots, and the Kandahar bombing was folded into that.

Ricchiardi noted how Afghanistan dropped from sight. Television news, she said, was "shamefully inadequate." A count by the Tyndall Report found that in the last months of 2001, the three network newscasts devoted 1,288 minutes to Afghanistan. In all of 2005, the total was 147. From January to May in 2006, the number was 134; President Bush showed up for a surprise visit. Newspaper coverage was only marginally better. Mostly, papers used occasional AP and Reuters dispatches, cut to below five hundred words.

The three big newsmagazines went in every few months, but none had done a cover in nearly two years. Late in 2006, *Newsweek* finally did a solid job. A dramatic photo of resurgent Taliban fighters went on the cover of every international edition. In the United States, *Newsweek*'s cover was photographer Annie Leibovitz and her family.

By then, the Joint Coordination and Monitoring Board, made up of Afghan and international officials, was tallying six hundred insurgent attacks a month, four times the 2005 level. More than 3,700 people were killed during 2006, and the poppy crop sold for heroin increased by 59 percent.

Ironically enough, American indifference to events in Afghanistan is largely what led us toward 9/11 and its aftermath. And now a wise policy in South Asia is crucial to restoring world tranquility.

Ricchiardi's *American Journalism Review* survey drew its own conclusion: Although editors realized the story was important, their resources were too thin to cover it. Steve Coll, a *New Yorker* staff writer and former *Washington Post* managing editor who spent time in Afghanistan working on his book *Ghost Wars,* made the essential point: The media should be asking crucial questions about what Americans are doing right or wrong and about what has gone off track.

"When you break down the business models that can support long-term foreign coverage, editors no longer can afford to send people to Afghanistan to stay long enough to develop expertise and be valuable," Coll concluded. "It's not the kind of story you go over and do blogs on. You have to sit still and develop real engagement . . . and that costs money."

John Schidlovsky, a former *Baltimore Sun* correspondent who runs the International Reporting Project, summed up the piece with a point that ought to be blindingly obvious: "This is a hugely important story that we are ignoring at our own peril. When we're not given a good accounting of what is going on, it could lead to missteps in foreign policy, other misadventures and mistakes."

Some editors rail against these realities and do their best to push the edges. Others make excuses to themselves and answer criticism with hostility. Either way, that is a matter for personal conscience. What counts is the product they produce. If U.S. news organizations can't even scare up enough dog food to cover Afghanistan, it is time to stop expecting too much in the way of reliable barking.

By spring 2007, the Afghanistan story demanded to be told. The poppies bloomed in record numbers. Taliban fighters bedeviled American and coalition troops while building support among civilians. Washington added something near $10 billion to its Afghanistan war chest, but U.S. efforts focused on finding bin Laden before the 2008 elections. But, with a few exceptions, coverage was left to inexperienced if eager young reporters with no basis for comparing even the recent past to fast-changing realities.

Many U.S. commanders saw no reason for niceties toward a ragtag bunch of "media personnel." On March 4, a minivan rigged with explosives rammed a U.S. Marine convoy at Barikaw in eastern Afghanistan. In the frenzied aftermath, photographers pictured Americans spraying indiscriminate gunfire at civilian cars and pedestrians. Troops demanded their memory cards and left little room for argument. After a later ambush in Kabul, private American security confiscated cameras. Our system is not supposed to allow soldiers, let alone mercenaries, decide what gets covered in war. But without protest, who stops them?

During March, *Time* magazine did a full takeout on Afghanistan, as *Newsweek* had done months earlier. Time's cover photo, the bearded profile of an Afghan warrior against a stark landscape, was emblazoned with the headline: "Talibanistan." That was for international editions. Like *Newsweek,* *Time* decided Americans had other things on their minds. The U.S. edition featured an essay about teaching the Bible in American public schools.

A fghanistan is one example among many around a large globe, but nothing says it more plainly. We supported the bin Ladens because they served our purpose against the Soviets, and then we did not bother to look as they transformed into our worst enemies. We paid heavily to learn that was not smart. And now, already, we have stopped bothering to look.

Whatever editors may feel in their gut about the news beyond American borders, they are tightly constrained not only by budgets and staff levels but also by what they call the news hole: physical space in the paper or time on the air. This is dominated by whichever single story obsesses America at the moment. Editors answer to executives who focus blindly on circulation or ratings. They must guess at what uninterested and easily distracted audiences think they want. Creating new tastes is out of the question.

Then there is the problem of experience and ability all along the line.

Even when circumstances come together and a seasoned reporter gets to the scene for a close look at important news, an anchor or editor back home still might confuse rowdy kids in Paris with Tiananmen Square.

News organizations protect themselves with parachute journalism. Correspondents base in large bureaus and race for the airport when a story breaks elsewhere. This almost guarantees skewed reporting. Getting to a story and covering it are worlds apart.

What about the world beyond Afghanistan? We need to know about a lot of places. Is Hugo Chávez in Venezuela a dangerous leftist lunatic to isolate? Or is he a crucial player, not to speak of an oil supplier, to whom we should be listening for possible good sense amid all his bombast? However you answer, what's your source?

If this voluntary defection by the Fourth Estate can be fixed in time, it might be during the run-up to the Vietnam War, which is now often cited as a high point. Fred W. Friendly, a pioneer at CBS along with Edward R. Murrow at CBS, quit in disgust as head of CBS News. He watched live NBC coverage of George Kennan testifying to the Senate Foreign Relations Committee why war might be a very bad idea. On the CBS monitor, he saw *I Love Lucy,* a rerun on its seventh time around.

Friendly's book title is part of a phrase he nearly put on the air in protest: *Due to Circumstances Beyond Our Control.* . . . Its frontispiece adds a remark made in 1958, soon to be prophetic, by Dorothy Greene Friendly, his wife: "What the American people don't know can kill them."

Congress debated at length President John F. Kennedy's gradual "incursion" in Vietnam. Senate hearings examined evidence and heard expert dissent; such legislative checks are designed to keep a trigger-happy chief executive from folly. Friendly argues that had Americans watched live testimony as they did a few years earlier during the Army-McCarthy hearings, rather than a few minutes of summary on the evening news, we might have avoided an unwinnable war that crippled our nation. He is probably right. Back then, there were only three networks, each trying hard to avoid cant. Viewers tended to follow what news executives thought was important.

In its early days, television joined newspapers to set a national agenda, just as morning chatter around village wells still does in remote villages. Without this global agenda, defined by professionals who are rooted in a reality they observe up close, we are all lost.

Dwell on this thought for a moment with a metaphor from Homer, who predated Plato by a few centuries. It does not matter how big the Cyclops or how all-seeing the eye. A hot poker can strike it blind.

E. B. White offered a prophecy in 1938: "I believe television is going to be the test of the modern world, and that in this new opportunity to see beyond the range of our vision we shall discover either a new and unbearable disturbance of the general peace or a saving radiance in the sky. We shall stand or fall by television—of that I am quite sure."[3]

In the glory days that followed, television went to World War II, and it curtailed Sen. Joseph McCarthy's witch hunt. Yet clear warning signals flashed. In 1958, Murrow spoke now-familiar words: "This instrument can teach, it can illuminate; yes, and it can even inspire. But it can do so only to the extent that humans are determined to use it to those ends. Otherwise it is merely wires and lights in a box."

Two years later, Friendly had an exchange with CBS president James Aubrey that foreshadowed a different age. "Look, Fred, I have regard for what Murrow and you have accomplished, but in this adversary system you and I are always going to be at each other's throats," he quoted Aubrey as saying. "They say to me (he meant the system, not any specific individual), 'Take your soiled little hands, get the ratings, and make as much money as you can'; they say to you, 'Take your lily-white hands, do your best, go the high road and bring us prestige.' "[4]

The rest, alas, is history. For all its stunning exceptions, the value of live coverage at monumental moments, and the visual backdrop it still provides, television has badly failed the E. B. White test. Had we been wiser, we might have combined the skills of reporters who cover a world they now only sample with camera crews to show us undistorted reality as it happens.

Today, there is a wide choice on television but no solid center. C-SPAN bores, Fox skews, CNN confuses, and the big networks mostly skim the surface. Raw footage needs editing by people who understand its context and analysis by seasoned journalists who have seen news for themselves. The bulwark of our news media remains written words on paper—or perhaps, now, on a computer screen.

To escape the cave, many more of us will have to demand much better. We need to understand this.

For me, the turning point came in the mid-1980s, with a string of shameful episodes known collectively by a misnomer, Iran-Contra. At the start, many editors chose not to notice serial outrage by Washington warlords, out-of-control spooks, shadow warriors, careerist bureaucrats, greedy outsiders, intriguing foreign governments, drug smugglers, and Central American killers whom Ronald Reagan called "the moral equivalent of our Founding Fathers."

Theodore Draper documents this period in a masterful work, *A Very Thin Line,* based on his perusal of fifty thousand pages of documents and uncounted months of testimony. But even in scrupulous hindsight, much is left unclear. Those who excuse inattention or censorship like to say truth emerges over time. It seldom does and, in any case, is always too late.

By the 1960s, U.S. policy in Central America was already making people hate us. Viron Vaky, deputy chief of mission at the U.S. embassy in Guatemala, noted in a secret memo in 1968 that police squads tortured Communist suspects and mutilated their bodies. He wrote: "In the minds of many in Latin America, and tragically, especially in the sensitive, articulate youth, we are believed to have condoned these tactics, if not actually encouraged them."[5]

This undercut our demand for just societies, Vaky said, and suggested that a "twisted adversary concept of politics" rationalized atrocities to achieve our purposes. "Is it possible," he asked, "that a nation which so reveres the principle of due process of law has so easily acquiesced in this sort of terror tactic?"

At the time, Guatemala was a sideshow; we were busy with Vietnam. By the mid-1980s, however, Central America was a main event. The Somozas' three decades of corrupt dynasty in Nicaragua had collapsed, giving way to the left-wing Sandinista government of Daniel Ortega. Although U.S. presidents had dealt happily with Somoza dictators, Reagan and Vice President George H. W. Bush called for democracy. Since Ortega had friends in Havana and Moscow, they wanted a democracy of their own choosing.

Reagan avoided detail, protecting himself in a cocoon of deniability, while top aides and unsavory intermediaries thwarted Ortega. Foreign agents and private U.S. citizens armed proxy armies in exchange for White House access. United States funds could not be used, but Saudi Arabia gave $32 million, and Taiwan kicked in another $2 million. Neither cared much about Nicaragua, but they wanted friends in Washington. CIA contractors, unburdened by legal or human rights constraints, trained the *contrarevolucionarios* known as Contras. American coordinators enlisted Argentine officers, fresh from torturing to death thousands in their dirty war. Honduras was deeply involved. Hard-line generals lent logistic support. In exchange, Washington overlooked corrupt dealings and depredations against opponents.

The mess in America's backyard was one thing, but the same White House back office involved a volatile Middle East. A firm U.S. policy of not dealing with terrorists was secretly scrapped. Iran released U.S. hostages one by one, as ransom demands escalated. Secretary of State George Shultz and Defense Secretary Caspar Weinberger objected vehemently. Even the shadowy Iranian émigré who arranged the deals warned the United States was becoming a hostage to hostages. Michael Ledeen, a freelance operative who negotiated for Washington, expressed similar doubts. But the dealing went on, steadily more damaging.

If we ever needed canine snuffling and howling, it was then. Some reporters dug hard. The *New York Times,* the *Washington Post,* and the *Miami Herald*, among others, broke important pieces of the story. But the full picture emerged only after the harm was done. The Reagan administration ventured far beyond what one operative termed a very thin line. The message it delivered would poison U.S. foreign policy for decades to come: Never mind what we say in public; use the backdoor.

My interest was cocaine smuggling. This was at the height of a "war on drugs." The Drug Enforcement Agency infiltrated cartels, losing agents to torture. At every occasion, Nancy Reagan pleaded: "Just say no." Yet some of our Contra allies shipped cocaine to Florida in the same U.S. transports that flew arms south. Central American governments were implicated. CIA handlers said nothing.

Robert Parry, a dogged AP Washington reporter, got a first bite of the story in December 1985. He wrote that Contras were smuggling cocaine into the United States under the averted gaze of CIA handlers. As AP editors wrung their hands over the story in New York, someone on AP's Latin America desk mistakenly put it on the Spanish-language wire. When reaction started coming in, main wires sent it to all U.S. members and worldwide subscribers.

Few newspapers paid much attention, and Parry's follow-up stories met resistance from AP Washington editors. In 1987, Parry went to *Newsweek,* where, he said later, executives up to Katharine Graham steered him off the story. Washington insiders were loath to jeopardize their access to power. And, after all, it was preposterous to think official Americans might cover for drug smugglers.

But that first AP dispatch intrigued John Kerry, the freshman senator from Massachusetts, who pursued an investigation within the Senate Committee on Foreign Relations. Republicans and even fellow Democrats resisted his work. The CIA monitored his proceedings. During two years of probing, Kerry's subcommittee produced fat bundles of firsthand testimony and clear evidence. Yet few editors backed reporters who wanted to dig into the story.

In Paris, American sources and French intelligence contacts told me about complex drug networks. Between the cocaine and the money, the traffic involved not only Contras but also Colombian growers and drug cartels, Manuel Noriega in Panama, Central American generals, U.S. bankers, and a legion of sleazoids in Miami. Political activists, freelance journalists, and former CIA agents had much to say. But little of this reached print or airwaves.

American papers that set a national agenda stayed clear of the drug connection. The *San Francisco Chronicle* reported part of the story. Silence followed. The *Miami Herald* experienced the same reaction. Editors focused instead on the larger aspects of Iran-Contra.

As an AP special correspondent with a mandate to travel widely, I decided to pick up where Parry left off in Washington and then follow leads into Central America. Despite sneers from colleagues, I spent hours at the Christic Institute. Its directors sometimes made unsubstantiated claims. But their files were stuffed not only with original documents, congressional findings, and background but also with phone numbers and addresses.

Along Miami's Calle Ocho and in shabby neighborhoods near the airport, I collected bits of the mosaic. When people in shadowy worlds get a chance to talk and they are confident of anonymity, some amazing things emerge. Drug mules told me their experiences; dates and places checked out. Frustrated U.S. attorneys were eager to talk, with transcripts and quashed indictments to make their point.

In Costa Rica, I found an airstrip where weapons were unloaded and cocaine was put aboard in their place. I talked to CIA contractors who had left the network but still kept in touch. After months of reporting, I sent my story to New York. Despite more months of transatlantic discourse, it sat there. It was like a snake that had crawled onto the desk. If it did not slither away, someone would have to chop it to pieces. The designated editor tried to convince our bosses. He urged me to excise a link to the White House. "Look," he said, "just sacrifice this on the altar of getting the story on the wire."

Eventually, Lt. Col. Oliver North was hauled before Congress, and my story was definitively spiked. I took vacation time, went to Honduras, and wrote a different version for *Vanity Fair*. Working undercover, DEA agents in Lubbock, Texas, arrested a Honduran businessman at the trunk of his car as he produced bricks of cocaine he had driven from Miami. Video of the bust joined a fat file of tapes and other irrefutable evidence. Then the U.S. attorney's office dropped the charges—for lack of evidence. The CIA had phoned to say he was one of theirs.

No one disputed the *Vanity Fair* story, neither the case in question nor the larger picture I described after a week in Honduras. More details came in from several directions, including accounts from pilots who said they flew drugs into Homestead Air Force Base in Florida and walked away from the aircraft while someone else unloaded. By then, though, we had all moved on from Central America. The Berlin Wall had collapsed, and the story was Europe.

North, if reviled by some, was nearly elected senator from Virginia in 1994. Just before the vote, Nancy Reagan said he had lied to her husband. Now, North is "the media," a regular commentator on Fox News.

Two decades after his AP scoop failed to impact history, Parry drew the larger lessons. Writing for Slate.com in 2004, he recounted how Kerry tried hard to rout out taint in U.S. Central American policy. And later, on his own site, www.consortiumnews.com, he told the tragic tale of Gary Webb at the *San Jose Mercury News*.

In 1996, Webb's three-part series "Dark Alliance" finally nailed the story hard. Though late, it was a clear account of how two Nicaraguan Contras linked to the CIA funneled crack cocaine into black neighborhoods of Los Angeles. His stories forced CIA Inspector General Frederick Hitz to take a hard look. In 1998, Hitz named more than fifty Contras and Contra-related groups that were implicated in drug smuggling. He detailed how Reagan administration officials and CIA agents thwarted U.S. Drug Enforcement Agency efforts to pursue them.

By then, Webb had left the paper in disgrace. And on December 10, 2004, divorced and unable to find work, he shot himself.

Rather than pick up on Webb's story, national dailies slimed it. The *Los Angeles Times* put seventeen reporters on what amounted to a three-day, twenty-thousand-word rebuttal. Like the *New York Times* and the *Washington Post*, it debunked a claim Webb did not make, that the CIA purposely fostered a crack epidemic on black Americans. The *New York Times* tarred Webb as reckless, a description colleagues ridiculed.

Nick Schou, an editor of *OC Weekly,* whose book *Kill the Messenger* defends Webb, acknowledged that critics were right on one count. The series had "major flaws of hyperbole that were both encouraged and ignored" by editors who "saw the story as a chance to win a Pulitzer Prize, according to

Mercury News staffers [Schou] interviewed." But in an *L.A. Times* op-ed piece he called the episode "one of the most bizarre, unseemly and ultimately tragic scandals in the annals of American journalism."

When Webb died, Parry wrote, "The full scope of the Iraq disaster was still not evident, nor was the major press corps ready to acknowledge that its cowardice in the 1980s and its fecklessness in the 1990s were the direct antecedents to its complicity in the illegal invasion of Iraq." Had we reflected on the substance of Webb's reporting, he said, we would have seen "warnings about grave dangers that, if left ignored, would wreak even worse havoc on the United States and the world."

In a conversation late in 2006, Parry was more specific. "We see now that Iran-Contra was a test run for what happened later," he told me. "The executive decided what Congress should pass as laws. The press was intimidated or manipulated, and the public was fed scare stories so they didn't respond in any rational way."

As Iraq unfolded, I went to Jack Blum, the bulldog attorney who had been Kerry's chief investigator. He saw then the implications of a White House that systematically lied to Congress, dealt illegally with hostile states, and employed under a veil of deniability people who belonged in prison. Americans were in the dark. But foreign leaders, freedom-fighter criminals, and thugs on the taxpayers' payroll saw our hypocrisy up close. When truth surfaced, as it would, America would pay heavily. Blum noted that credibility, like virginity, does not come in degrees.

Kerry's final report in 1989 concluded that security concerns had overridden efforts to police drug trafficking from Nicaragua, Panama, and Honduras, from which the Contra rebels operated. With lengthy testimony and hard data, it implicated senior Contras and official Americans. There was much more. But Republicans picked at the report or ignored it, and Democrats were not eager to rock any boats. Reporters did little with it. And not much happened.

Looking back, Blum reached the same conclusion as Bob Parry. Conservatives in office then, including the freshly named secretary of defense, Dick Cheney, learned a crucial lesson: Simply brazen it out. Neither legislators nor the press nor the public will confront the Big Lie.

"All of the things the government did in secret back in those days, it now does in the open," Blum concluded. "Now these guys don't even bother to hide it. They don't have to. We catch them lying, making things up, doing secret deals, and nobody seems to care. No one is accountable for anything."

As for journalism, those Iran-Contra years entrenched what is now a basic approach. When an unwelcome story breaks, editors and officials and lawyers parse it with magnifying glasses. Any single defect disqualifies the rest. In practice, honest mistakes happen, even if they are stupid honest mistakes. Rather than working from what is solid in order to carry the story further, it is easier and safer to discredit the entirety.

Dan Rather, for one, learned this the hard way. Because of a still-unresolved controversy about a detail, CBS's story of George W. Bush's military nonrecord was smeared. A long career ended in ignominy. And we still do not know how Bush slipped out of the Texas National Guard.

As for that historical continuum on which foreign reporting so heavily depends, forget about it. After the 2006 elections, a chastened George W. Bush replaced Donald Rumsfeld with a man few reporters remembered, Robert Gates. Whoever he was, most Americans thought, he had to be an improvement. In fact, Bush had reached into the past to pick the CIA deputy director who had insulated his father, then vice president, from Iran-Contra tarnish.

And, of course, there was a final irony. The whole thing began because Washington wanted Daniel Ortega out of office. In their 2006 elections, Nicaraguans resurrected Ortega from the past and made him, again, their president.

The trends are not hopeful. Commerce is eating up newspaper icons at a dangerous pace. Knight Ridder, America's second-largest newspaper company, was created in 1974, a merger of John S. Knight's empire with papers in the Ridder family since the 1890s. By 2006, its thirty-two newspapers, with eighteen thousand employees, had a combined circulation of 3.7 million and a trophy case of eighty-five Pulitzer Prizes. Its last annual profit increase was 16.4 percent, better than ExxonMobil but lower than its usual 20 percent because of profit declines at the *Philadelphia Inquirer* and the *San Jose Mercury News*.

P. Anthony Ridder, the chief executive officer, told Wall Street analysts in June 2005: "The newspaper industry generally, and Knight Ridder specifically, are strong, healthy businesses with a bright future."[6] He neglected to mention that for three months a group of shareholders headed by Bruce S. Sherman of Private Capital Management had been pushing him to sell the company.

In the spring of 2006, with other investors joining the chorus, he did.

The McClatchy chain paid $4.5 billion and took over $2 billion in debt. Until then, McClatchy was still a family-dominated chain based in Sacramento, California, with a reputation among its editors for trying hard to maintain quality in journalism.

Gary Pruitt, head of McClatchy, dumped twelve of the papers. But, as industry analyst Peter Appert of Goldman Sachs told the *New York Times*, "Financial restructuring is not the answer to what ails the newspaper industry."[7] Over the year since the purchase in March 2006, the newspaper industry followed the S & P on an uphill curve. McClatchy stock dropped from a $50 range to near $30.

James Naughton, a solid reporter who once edited the *Philadelphia Inquirer* before becoming director of the Poynter Institute for Media Studies, blamed Ridder and a generalized new mentality. He told the *New York Times*: "It's the notion that you can continue whittling and paring and reducing and degrading the quality of your product and not pay any price. Tony's legacy is that he destroyed a great company."[8]

One Knight Ridder orphan was the *Akron Beacon Journal*, Knight's original flagship. David Black bought it and fired a quarter of the 161 editorial people. "I don't really believe that the quality of a newspaper is a direct function of body count in the newsroom," he told Reuters.[9] "I walk through way too many newsrooms where I see people just talking or looking on the Internet and having fun." Hard to imagine: reporters communicating with others, researching online, or, God forbid, enjoying their work.

Old hands at the *Beacon Journal* still speak in awe of "the shrine," a plaque in the trophy room that recalls the founder. It is a quote from the old days: "We believe in profitability but do not sacrifice either principle or quality on the altar of the countinghouse." Modern printing presses run more quietly now. That rumbling you might hear walking along Exchange Street in Akron is just Jack Knight doing backflips in his grave.

Knight Ridder, if a chilling example, is hardly alone. Pick up your local paper and count the foreign datelines. Deduct purely American stories reflected abroad. This will not take you long. But all is not lost, by a long shot.

The hard truth is that our traditional "press" is emperiled as a definable collective. Yet plenty of information-gatherers and truth-tellers thrive, with tools their predecessors never dreamed might exist. Excellent reporting can be found in the old familiar places. Just don't count on it. Keeping up with reality now takes more work. We can help committed mainstream editors to fend off short-sighted managers.

Our flagship dailies can be formidable when news people defend their principles. The *Chicago Tribune* owners who swallowed the *Los Angeles Times*, for instance, ended up choking on it.

Over seven years, Chicago executives cut the *Times'* newsroom staff from 1,250 to 920, with more to follow. Two good executive editors left, sickened at the sight of such needless bloodshed. In a PBS *Frontline* documentary, one investor aiming to dumb down the paper opined that *Times'* readers could get foreign news elsewhere; they wanted features on style and the movies. Eventually, the Tribune Company decided to sell.

A top tier of old pros, notably Managing Editor Doug Frantz, had quietly held the line. Despite the layoffs and buyouts, the paper kept its crew of 30 correspondents abroad. Three staff reporters and 45 Iraqis cover Baghdad; in 2007, they won three Overseas Press Club awards.

When I met Frantz in Quetta, Pakistan, it took about four minutes to see why colleagues regarded him so highly. With avuncular gray whiskers softening his substrata steel, he senses what is important, hones in on it, and pins it down hard. Good reporters do that as a matter of course. Frantz, however, is an investigator, digging deep to the roots of complex news. And he can tell a story, making real-life humans of characters who people his dispatches.

Back then, he was based in Istanbul for the *New York Times*, which later brought him home to be editor of its investigations unit. Soon after, he returned to the paper where he had made his name: the *LA Times*.

"We have worked hard, sometimes against long odds, on our commitment to foreign news," Frantz told me in 2007, after the Tribune Company had put its papers up for sale. "We have a great tradition of correspondents who interpret other cultures. We are not always driven by events. This has never been more important to our readers than it is today."

One problem, he said, is that few Americans understand how vital it is to keep sharp eyes close to distant complexities. Those few Americans often do not include the top editors of leading news organizations. Many have never reported from abroad, Frantz said, and they do not understand how differently other societies see things. After September 11, this insularity could be virulent.

The *Columbia Journalism Review* of September/October 2006 quoted Frantz on a battle at the *New York Times*. Carlotta Gall was at its center, but this time her problem was not editorial indifference, but rather the opposite.

In December 2002, Gall was intrigued by military press releases about

Afghani prisoner deaths at Bagram Air Base. Officers stonewalled her, re-
fusing to release names or produce bodies. Assiduous reporting led her to
the family of a victim identified as Dilawar. They had a death certificate,
which she later confirmed was authentic, that declared: "homicide." Dilawar, at 22, died from "blunt force injuries to lower extremities complicat-
ing coronary artery disease." Gall wrote the story in February 2003 and
waited as it sat on the desk for two weeks. Foreign editor Roger Cohen said
he pitched the story four times, sometimes laying awake at night in frustration, but senior editors resisted.

Frantz told the *CJR* that Howell Raines, then the Times' executive editor, and his deputies "insisted that it was improbable; it was just hard to get
their minds around . . . Compare Judy Miller's WMD stories to Carlotta's
story. On a scale of one to ten, Carlotta's story was nailed down to ten. And
if it had run on the front page, it would have sent a strong signal not just to
the Bush administration but to other news organizations."

The story eventually ran on page fourteen under a headline saying the
U.S. military was investigating mysterious deaths. The point, of course, was
that Gall's reporting forced the investigation.

Gall, who is British, told the *CJR*, "There was a sense of patriotism, and
you felt it in every question from every editor and copy editor. I remember
a foreign-desk editor telling me, 'Remember where we are—we can smell
the debris from 9/11.' "

Journalists, being human, are allowed to love their country. But patriotism means reflecting reality as accurately as they can. That is crucial to any
free and democratic society.

There are plenty of others like Doug Frantz, and they need help. I'll offer some specific ideas in chapter 10. One is dead obvious right off the bat:
When a newspaper is worth buying, buy it and make sure other people do
as well. In the end it is up to each of us to do our own snuffling around and
bark as loud as we can when something smells bad. Plenty of odiferous issues confront us all.

THREE

WHY *DO* "THEY" HATE US?

One evening in 2005, via satellite across one of the oceans that insulate America, I watched some riveting reality TV. A student pilot and his teacher veered into closed airspace over the White House. Jets scrambled, ready to do what they must in extremis. Government workers fled their offices for safety, sensibly enough. They had seen terrorism from the air only a few years before.

As the cameras rolled, order broke down. The seat of world power was in blind panic. Officials whose decisions affect millions ran for dear life, herded by security men bellowing contemptuous commands. It was as if, in the face of unknown danger, authority had been heedlessly handed to anyone wearing a uniform. Logic had vanished. Not much fits into a two-seat Cessna, but if it had carried a dirty bomb, or anthrax spores, surely there were better options than running outside and gulping air.

The threat of sneak attack is real enough. Yet such a terrorized response was unsettling in a country where flag-bedecked bumper stickers boast, "These colors don't run." Evacuation is one thing, but senseless stampede is another. Was this the very heart of "the land of the free and the home of the brave"?

Watching from a distance, I thought again of Plato. Without warning, something terrifying had appeared at the cave's mouth and was about to come inside. Panicked people, with a thin grip on reality blurred by distorted reflections, did not pause for rational thought. An instinctual alarm sounded: "They" might be attacking. From half a world away, I saw Americans who had forgotten the watchwords of Franklin Roosevelt, who eventually defied the isolationists and saved Europe's collective butt: The only thing we have to fear is fear itself.

Such incidents evoke that recurring question: Why do "they" hate us? In fact, not everyone does. A fanatic fringe will despise a powerful nation no matter what. A broader group resents us in direct proportion to how long we point guns at them, how much we lump them together as no more than population units to buy our stuff and do our work cheaply, or to what extent we demand special rules because we are somehow a superior exception.

More often, allies and enemies alike see that we are losing what once made us great. We ignore the wisdom of Roosevelt's cousin Theodore: If we carry a big stick, we need to speak softly. When we boast that we are the model for less-enlightened peoples, others are less convinced. Perhaps worse than hatred, this evokes scorn. Or pity.

Cedric Judicis, a mild-mannered Parisian coiffeur in his early fifties, is a revealing case in point. I talked with him before the 2004 U.S. presidential election. He hates ketchup, he told me. But, having read about the Democratic candidate's wife, he poured Heinz on his *steak-frites*. "That," he explained with a rueful snort, "is my only way to help Kerry beat Bush."

Judicis typifies Europeans who say that although they do not qualify for absentee ballots, U.S. elections impact heavily on their lives. "To us," he explained, "America was always the gold standard. It made mistakes but always meant well. We were like pupils who admired the master. It gave us moral guidance, inspiration. No longer."

He had made six trips to the United States and, unlike many others, he was still eager to go back. "But America is different now," he concluded. "It rules by force and not by the weight of respect. There is a sense of 'do what I say and not what I do.' It was always so liberal. Now it seems so totalitarian."

A Pew Global Attitudes Project survey in 2006 quantified a broad-based change that Judicis represents. Dramatic results came from Turkey, the southeast corner of NATO and a bridge linking Europe to Asia. In 2005, according to Pew, 23 percent of Turkish respondents approved of America. Within a year, that number plummeted to 12 percent.

Understandable, perhaps, since largely Muslim Turkey is wary of our crusader mentality. But other statistics were even more troubling. Spain's prime minister joined Bush's invasion in 2003. But Spanish positive opinions went from 41 percent in 2005 to 23 percent in 2006. In Britain, approval ratings went from 75 percent in 2002 to only 56 percent in 2006. And if anyone gives these anonymous numbers a human face, it is my friend James Talbot, whom we met briefly earlier.

Talbot is an always-amused, shaken-not-stirred character that Noël Coward and Ian Fleming might have dreamed up in tandem. Though Irish, he went to school in England before working in America. He also mined coal and restored Bentleys. Today he is a gentleman farmer in Provence and a Londoner, happy in black tie or bathing trunks, a dashing bon vivant sought out for dinner tables.

Talbot learned early to look beyond stereotype and simplification. Take that blurred line between freedom fighter and terrorist. His uncle, a British army officer who spent seven years in a Nazi prison camp, was in the detail that arrested Menachem Begin in 1946 after his band of zealots blew up the King David Hotel in Jerusalem, killing ninety-one. Do such means justify the end? Some things are a personal call.

Despite close American friends, Talbot's fondness for America chilled to freezing in the aftermath of 9/11. He feels Tony Blair had blunted his own ability to lead by following Bush into dubious battle. He worries when a disenchanted United Kingdom rethinks its cornerstone alliance with the United States.

He is disgusted by excesses in Iraq and Guantánamo. He chaffs at a bullying, jingoistic tone in speeches. He is baffled at how a nation that consumes so much can refuse environmental treaties. Like many Europeans, he has horror stories of friends flying to America to be arbitrarily jailed, mistreated, or bundled onto the next plane.

"That is not," he concluded, "the America I knew."

People like James Talbot and Cedric Judicis might chuckle when self-styled patriots rail at foreigners and rename deep-fried potatoes that are Belgian in origin. They are dismayed to hear that U.S. officials plant stories in the foreign press and pay journalists to distort; this, they know, flouts America's own vaunted principles.

But they are insulted to the core when official pitchmen tell them how to think about America when they see the opposite for themselves. Orwellian-style doublespeak may sway an inattentive American public, but it feeds visceral scorn, if not hatred, when directed abroad.

It is chilling today to watch Terry Gilliam's film *Brazil,* made in 1985 when computer printers were like IBM typewriters. A falling swatted fly changes a keystroke, making Tuttle, a suspected "terrorist," into Buttle, a blameless workaday drone. Hooded SWAT teams blast Buttle's house to toothpicks, with him inside. His widow fruitlessly seeks information from faceless bureaucrats while leaders explain on television how they are keeping the nation safe. These days, *Brazil* is a lot less amusing than it was.

"They" know better when Karen Hughes, George W. Bush's head cheerleader, explains how warmly we welcome others. Promising students are denied visas. Others who earn degrees are forced to work elsewhere. At our borders, thinly educated officials with long mysterious lists turn back distinguished academics, artists, journalists, businessmen, and simple tourists. Routinely, European papers tell of people who were held for hours, flexi-cuffed, and put back on a plane because of some mistake.

Karen Hughes, a former Texas TV newscaster long close to Bush, paints a public happy face on the opaque White House depredations that have done us so much harm. Her job is to brand America, which is a preposterous notion. People draw opinions from what they perceive for themselves.

When Hughes was named undersecretary of state for public diplomacy and public affairs in 2005, she went on the road. She assured a roomful of Saudi women that they, too, will someday drive cars. They told her to butt out; they were actually happy right now. In Turkey, a group of women active in politics told her she has no credibility as long as U.S. troops occupy Iraq.

In Indonesia, the world's largest Muslim country, Hughes held a public debate with sixteen students, mostly women. One said America should take September 11 as a warning not to interfere in other countries' affairs. Another compared Bush to Hitler. A third said: "Your policies are creating hostilities among Muslims. It's Bush in Iraq, Afghanistan, Palestine, and maybe it's going to be in Indonesia, I don't know. Who's the terrorist? Bush or us Muslims?"[1]

In arguing America's case, Hughes evoked Saddam Hussein's 1988 poison gas attack on Kurds in the Iraqi border town of Halabja. She said hundreds of thousands died. The actual toll of five thousand was bad enough. Such wild exaggeration undercuts any credibility.

Back home and abroad, columnists roasted her. Sidney Blumenthal, a former adviser to Bill Clinton, wrote: "Hughes appeared as one of the pilgrims satirised by Mark Twain in his 1869 book *Innocents Abroad,* on his trip on 'The Grand Holy Land Pleasure Excursion.' 'None of us had ever been anywhere before; we all hailed from the interior; travel was a wild novelty. . . . We always took care to make it understood that we were Americans—Americans!' "[2] With simplistic, well-meant arguments, he said, Hughes provided proof for bin Laden's claims about American motives.

Fred Kaplan, on Slate.com ridiculed the casting: "Wouldn't it be better to find someone who—oh, I don't know—speaks the language, knows the culture, lived there for a while, was maybe born there? Put the shoe on the other foot. Let's say some Muslim leader wanted to improve Americans' image of Islam. It's doubtful that he would send as his emissary a woman in a black chador who had spent no time in the United States, possessed no knowledge of our history or movies or pop music, and spoke no English beyond a heavily accented 'Good morning.' Yet this would be the clueless counterpart to Karen Hughes, with her lame attempts at bonding ('I'm a working mom') and her tin-eared assurances that President Bush is a man of God (you can almost hear the Muslim women thinking, 'Yes, we know, that's why he's relaunched the Crusades')."[3]

Beyond Hughes's office, American officials sometimes resort to blatant fakery to shape our image. Late in 2005, the *Los Angeles Times* and then the *New York Times* exposed a multimillion-dollar Pentagon program for the Lincoln Group, a private contractor, to plant articles in the Iraqi press. Willem Marx later described in *Harpers* how, as a 22-year-old intern for Lincoln, he paid Iraqi editors up to $2,000 to run fake stories. Television producers earned more.

Bogus commentaries sometimes smeared real journalists. One began: "Western press and frequently those self-styled 'objective' observers of Iraq are often critics of how we, the people of Iraq, are proceeding down the path in determining what is best for our nation." Other items faked news about Al Qaeda and Iraqi politics. Apart from creating blowback that ends up misleading Americans, such hypocrisy blackens our image.[4]

Looking in from the outside, a larger point is clear. In the United States, we have grown used to the term "spin" and its various derivatives. Such euphemisms suggest playful banter among people entrusted to run the government and those who inform the public on how they do it. For many people across the world, much of that vocabulary boils down to a three-letter synonym: "lie."

It is not as though America had been universally loved before George W. Bush arrived in Washington. Our secret double-dealing goes back a long way, but let's start with 1953. With allies in a true coalition, Harry Truman had just gotten us through the Korean War. But in Persia, we were not happy with a democratically chosen prime minister, Mohammed Mossadegh. In a CIA coup masterminded by Teddy Roosevelt's grandson Kermit, the shah was restored to his Peacock Throne. Mossadegh was hanged. Ask any Iranian, a half century later, for an opinion on that. Not long after, we helped murder Patrice Lumumba in the newly independent Congo, bringing in our kind of tyrant, Joseph-Désiré Mobutu. And so on.

During the 1950s, two best-selling novels focused attention on our way of reshaping the world. Eugene Burdick and William Lederer's *The Ugly American* made anti-Communist blunders in a fictional Asian nation called Sarkhan. Graham Greene's American was Quiet and operated in the realities of an imminent war in Vietnam. Greene's naively pure young American spook ended up bringing violent death to people he meant to save.

Greene was an old lefty with tortured thoughts about Catholicism, not an easy fit for mainstream America in the mid-twentieth century. But back then, he believed us to be well-meaning simpletons whose blindness to reality was no brake on our mission to remake the world. By the time I first met him in the 1980s, he was in another place entirely.

He had watched his prophetic fiction become prescient war reporting. Having grown fond of Omar Torrijos in Panama, he followed our Central American intrigues with contempt. Greene was not welcome in the United States, and that suited him fine. We were not simply naive, he had decided. We were self-obsessed bullies. And I knew from my own travels that Greene was hardly alone.

Foreign adventures, in rapid succession, muddied our image. On the tiny island of Grenada, in 1983, our elite 82nd Airborne took nine days to rout Cuban bulldozer drivers at the airport and travel a distance to the capital that American medical students jog in a few hours. American commanders sequestered American journalists on a warship and bombed mental patients because of sloppy sighting. Happily enough, no Internet flashed images around the world, sparing us from derisive laughter. Other fiascos followed.

When terror struck America in 2001, however, an overwhelming majority across the world rallied in support. The often-caustic Paris daily *Le Monde* pronounced on its front page: "We are all Americans." President Jacques Chirac flew west to show solidarity and discuss what world leaders might do to blunt a threat they faced in common. Atlantic allies went off together after Al Qaeda and the Taliban. Even in a frustrated Third World, only hardcore zealots celebrated our humiliation.

This was our chance to wipe our ugly past clean and seek some common sense in a perilous world. But this outpouring of goodwill was quickly squandered. Sympathy for America soured almost everywhere. The French, particularly, were a revealing bellwether. Hardly anything in world affairs fascinates like the centuries-old love-hate sentiment between the United States and France.

C ultures seldom fit comfortably into generalities; certainly not the French. No other people I know separate into such distant extremes. The worst—self-obsessed, pigheaded, shallow, and rapacious—can be beyond odious. Many more are the opposite: generous in spirit and substance, outward looking, and loyal friends for life.

Yet all societies are defined by dominant traits. Each approaches consensus according to its own collective experience. Artful diplomacy is crucial to find compromise among overlapping national interests. Sensitive reporting, up close, is equally vital to explain why similar-seeming peoples can view things so differently.

Most of our moss-covered beliefs about France went out with Bob Hope. No one I can name thinks much of Jerry Lewis, but lots of Frenchmen know that Bree, rather than misspelled cheese, is a desperate Wisteria Lane housewife.

The French can be duplicitous about foreign policy, and, unlike some nations, they cheerfully admit it; France is not hypocritical about its hypocrisy. They can be insufferable about food. Many are murderous behind the wheel and worse in ski lift lines. But they are not a cowardly people. They just know a lot about war.

All those white crosses and six-pointed stars at American cemeteries in Normandy still bring tears to French eyes, veterans and kids alike. Yet septuagenarians, while grateful to allies who delivered them, recall how many of their own countrymen risked German firing squads to help the Resistance prepare the ground for invasion.

An earlier generation remembers the sacrifice of U.S. doughboys at

Verdun. By the time American troops came to help, as welcome as they were, France had been bled white. The smallest of hamlets has its monument listing the local boys who died in two world wars in less than one long lifetime. They number well into the millions.

A miniature Statue of Liberty on an island in the Seine marks an earlier debt of a different sort. Had it not been for Lafayette and a French fleet at Yorktown, Americans would be drinking tea each day at five o'clock.

Today, France is still ready for a fight, which is why Washington has turned to the French for dirty work in Africa and the Balkans. Not long ago, as rebels threatened Americans, among others, deep in Ivory Coast, U.S. troops waited safely at a distance as French commandos hurried in to save them. When crisis erupts, the routine is for U.S. Air Force transports to fly French troops to an airbase nearby. Then they leave before any shooting starts.

French forces went to Afghanistan. Once U.N. inspectors made their report, they likely would have joined a real coalition in Iraq as they did in 1991. But the French know war always produces something unexpected. Before signing on, they want to know why. In 2006, when someone had to separate Israelis from Hezbollah, Washington had the usual answer: Send the French.

Chirac sent two hundred engineers to repair bridges and strategic spots until officers had a clearer mandate to protect a larger force from high casualties suffered in past U.N. forays. That came, and he sent two thousand more. Meantime, he was roundly reviled. There are always plenty of reasons to rag on France. But America, which would not spare a few thousand token troops and was seen as far too one-sided to do the job, was in no position to criticize.

The French can laugh at themselves these days. Many do not need subtitles when Bart Simpson, on their satellite English-language Canal Jimmy, jibes at "cheese-eating surrender monkeys." But if people in France chuckled at freedom fries, American invective against their ingratitude brought a reaction that went far beyond the usual ups and downs of a historic relationship.

In such circumstances, we badly need balanced, seasoned journalists on the ground to sift out jingoistic taint from both sides of diplomatic issues. Instead, we listen to pundit clowns who stay home to define complex truth by yelling at those who disagree with them, offering no more than silly circus. When actual reporters take notice, it is often with a slant.

Soon after Colin Powell delivered his spurious evidence to the U.N. Security Council, I got a call on a Friday from a writer I knew on the *New York Daily News*, an old hand at Fleet Street–style sensation. He was flying in for the weekend and wanted an interview with Chirac. After all, it was the *Daily News*. Suddenly, I caught on.

"You're not headed for Normandy," I said.

He waffled. Obviously, he was.

The *Daily News* front page appeared exactly as I had imagined. A stark photo showed those rows of American war graves that still choke up the French. The headline was along the lines of "France to U.S.: Drop Dead."

During 2006, long after Bush and Chirac feigned friendly reconciliation and the war took its course, I interviewed a range of young French people unencumbered by the Charles de Gaulle era. My question was simple enough: What do you think of America and Americans?

Pierre-Charles Torno, the seventeen-year-old son of my dentist, grew up hearing his parents extol the United States. Laurence, his mother, exhibits her paintings in New York. Now she has changed her mind. "We no longer feel much sentiment for America," she told me. Her husband, a soft-spoken, gentle man, added his own view: "It is too aggressive, too full of itself."

Pierre-Charles had saved for years for a post-high-school grand tour, from Florida to New York—but too many of his friends came home from their own grand tours having been pushed around and insulted for being French. When he was graduated in 2004, he went to Australia.

But there was also Fanny Boyer, a bilingual international affairs graduate with an easy laugh and an agile mind. She had just returned home reluctantly after two semesters at Wesleyan University in Connecticut. She knew the differences between red and blue America.

"I came back a virulent pro-American," she said. "Of course, I was in a microcosm. In one year, I didn't find a single person who was for Bush. Wesleyan is Michael Moore country. Students are motivated, educated. A lot of them have spent a year in Europe or somewhere else. They're interested in the rest of the world. Most read the *New York Times* every day. I get mad at French people who tell you that all you'll find in America are idiots. They're just as bad. Half of them think the capital is New York."

For Fanny, the question is not about nationality. It is about ignorance and arrogance wherever she finds it. She doesn't hate us any more than she hates her own society. She just wishes more people in both countries would stick their heads out of the cave and look around.

Some Frenchmen snickered with ugly I-told-you-so glee when Iraq fell apart. But my friend G., who had told me so in no uncertain terms, was simply sad and worried. G. prefers anonymity; he commanded a nuclear-powered French warship and reports for work at the Defense Ministry. He admires the United States, and he wants to see it stronger.

"Americans always look at things in terms of good and bad," G. said.

"In reality, the good are sometimes bad, and the bad can have their aspects of good. You can't use simple thinking and blind force in complex situations. In the end, that always makes things worse for everybody."

G. understands the nuances. Ranking U.S. Army and Navy officers tell him of their frustrations in carrying out American foreign policy. In the thick of it, they see things as they are. But orders are orders.

"What amazes me, what I cannot understand," he concludes, "is why Americans won't see how their policies turn people against them. It doesn't matter if their intentions are good. Everyone else looks at the results."

It is hardly only the French who are ambiguous about America. During two years of research for this book, I heard variations on these themes from every corner of the globe. Yet for all the range of opinion, a common thread ties them together: negative reaction to temper-centric thinking. Australians, South Africans, and Argentines across the bottom respond like Estonians, Icelanders, and Canadians across the top. By seeing the world with narrow vision, by not understanding others and assuming vastly disparate societies will react to sticks and carrots as it would, America as a nation has lost its ability to inspire.

The snubbing of Kyoto did far more damage than most of us realize. Smart people know their planet is dying, and they know why. There are other reasons. Many were flabbergasted when we reelected Bush by a greater margin than in 2000. It did not matter whether it was blindness to reality or an agreement with his America-first swagger; either is bad enough. Yet another source of scorn is our lack of political accountability. Neither failure nor fraud nor foolishness seems to exact a price.

Reasonable critics know that plenty of individual Americans confound this bleak judgment. People everywhere still look to the United States for fresh ideas, cutting-edge culture, and the rest. But that is not enough. A world in trouble needs a strong center with leaders committed to the principles for which we purport to stand.

For Americans tired of hearing complaints from foreigners, there is always Kosovo. A few million Albanian Kosovars in their autonomous province of Serbia admire the United States in the cockle-warming way so many nations used to do. Kosovo may not be much of an example, in the grand scheme of things. But it is instructive.

In March 1999, President Clinton finally had enough of Slobodan Milosevic's depredations of Albanians, who made up 90 percent of Kosovo's population. He pushed reluctant NATO allies into action. Warplanes pounded Serb military units. After a final flurry of terror, Serbs fled north.

Clinton had waited four years to take action in Bosnia, despite a campaign promise to thwart Serb assaults. In Kosovo, air strikes were too late to save thousands from beatings, rape, or death. Yet he finally acted.

"We will never forget the Americans for what they did," Lutfi Haziri, Kosovo's minister for local government, told me in Priština during 2005. Six years after liberation, Kosovo was still nominally part of Serbia. Investors shunned it, waiting for status talks to unscramble an insoluble ethnic puzzle. But Americans are still remembered as saviors.

Government offices perch along a broad thoroughfare named Bill Clinton Boulevard. Bookstalls do a brisk business in an Albanian translation of Madeleine Albright's memoirs. In scattered villages, some Muslim kids are proud of names they were given at birth: Bill and Madeleine.

Nearly all Albanian Kosovars are Muslim, but many of them find ways to defend America's policy in Iraq. Why, I asked the minister, were people so generous on the subject of George W. Bush? "Because," he replied, with a broad smile, "he is American."

Among the young people who will shape Kosovo's future, the outlook is less heartwarming. Like their elders, many revere an America that set them free. They are reluctant to find fault with military intervention for high purpose; that is what saved them. Yet many see their saviors evolving into something decidedly different.

Albanian Kosovars, as a rule, are about as relaxed and secular as Muslims get. Yet fallout from Iraq and Afghanistan quickly eroded much of their goodwill. Extremists among them harp ever more insistently on America's changed role in the world. Radical imams attract ever larger audiences. Young men head off to holy war.

Small as it is, Kosovo makes a telling point. It does not take much to win a nation's gratitude. A single fair-minded and courageous decision can do it. Once implanted, loyalty can remain firmly rooted. Yet nations are no more than collectives of the people who make them up. It is foolish to take them for granted.

To see why foreigners eye America with coolness, it helps to look at reality through outsiders' eyes. These days, a visit to the United States can do less to dispel nasty misconceptions than to reinforce them. Often, hackles are raised at the first port of entry.

Every country needs security measures, but America is prone to overdo things. Agents in Washington pore over passenger lists of every flight bound for the United States. When in doubt, they act. This discomfits many, including infants, who are denied boarding because they share names with those on very long watch lists. At times, it provokes transatlantic fury.

On a December 23, I checked in for an Air France flight to Los Angeles. It was delayed, and desk agents were oddly mysterious. Three hours later, after departure was announced and then "suspended" for the third time, we were told the plane would not go. No reason was given.

I found a seat on the next flight, which was canceled. Air France got me on the last plane of the day. That, too, was grounded, as were all three flights the next day. I made it for cold Christmas turkey on December 26.

Our plane landed in Los Angeles without incident, and passengers were bused to a distant hangar. As I stood in line for an hour to await a body search, airport police officers filmed us continuously. Each wore his or her best welcome-to-Guantánamo thousand-mile stare.

Considering that I would have been aboard one of those aircraft had it blown up in midair, I was appreciative of careful security. But this smelled bad. Later in Paris, the chief executive of Air France told me what happened.

Screening the manifests, someone in Washington saw the name Mohammed, or Ahmed, or something similar, and sounded the alarm. French police studied the alert and found no basis for it. They probed the plane, and the passengers, from nose to tail. Paris cleared the flight for takeoff; Washington denied permission to land. This happened to six flights in a row. Air France took the blame and ate the cost. Meantime, three British-carrier flights out of London were also canceled.

After similar instances since, foreign airline executives privately describe themselves as livid. At one point, two pilots were fired. Incensed at overofficious screeners at American airports, they flung themselves onto the conveyor belt to ride through the X-ray machine.

Upon arrival in America, agents use a more thorough way to screen potentially dangerous foreigners. Each is fingerprinted and subjected to an eyeball scan. All too often, people are turned around, or detained, against all reason. Recently, just as one example, a wealthy Israeli woman with a valid visa was denied entry upon landing in New York, where her daughter owns an apartment. Her passport noted she was born in Iraq, from where she moved to Tel Aviv at the age of six months. Such stories are a dime a dozen.

The process alone is a national shame. At a Kennedy Airport security check, I watched two beefy officers order a frail woman in a wheelchair to stand and walk to a rubber mat so they could prod at her. She was perhaps eighty.

As the woman tried to walk on her cane, she grimaced and then moaned. "I'm in pain," she said in a thick German accent. "Don't you understand pain?" An obese woman security guard chuckled, "Oh, I know pain." Some people in line seemed amused. Others clucked their tongues; why was this old woman holding up progress?

After the search, the woman collapsed in a chair and wept. I walked over and asked if I could help. She looked up, like a fox cornered by hounds, and snapped, "Leave me alone!" Do not expect to see her in America anytime soon.

Over time, such human indifference has gotten to be the rule. We accept it meekly, fearful of ending up in some government computer. Early in 2007, as my friend Gary Knight waited in a stalled foreign arrivals line at Kennedy Airport, an Asian teenager lay on the ground for hours. He had fainted, likely from stress. Passengers shouted for help, but no one would touch him. Border authorities refused to let him into the terminal for treatment; that would mean an admission to America. Other officials did not want to risk legal action should anything go wrong. Terrorists are a threat. But no group is likely to take over the United States or any firmly rooted democracy. Their success depends on scaring free people, taking the fun out of simple pleasures, and forcing them to live in ways they would not choose. Elsewhere, by not overreacting to terrorists, leaders thwart their purpose. For some reason, the most powerful nation on Earth cannot manage that.

A recent trip to New York went without incident, except for the confiscation of a minuscule cigar guillotine with which I might have been able to circumcise a cockroach. The Paris airport cop chuckled and explained: "It's an American carrier." The next morning, up at 5:00 A.M. with jet lag, I switched on CNN. Terrorists in London had bombed three subway trains and a bus.

For ninety minutes, I fingered the remote like a mad pianist. Each time I returned to CNN, someone told me that London's subway system was called the Underground and Scotland Yard was the cops. Not much else. Several hundred available channels did not include the BBC. I tried radio, recalling the old WINS slogan: "All news all the time" and "Give us ten minutes, and we'll give you the world." They gave me traffic on the Tappan Zee Bridge.

When I got finally got the story, its impact was clear. Bombers struck just as G-8 leaders met in Scotland behind barriers to compare notes on their security successes. European Union partners were urging Britain to open its borders for freer movement. London had just been picked for the 2012 Olympics. Even before the cheering stopped, its vulnerability was plain to the world.

Tony Blair, shaken nearly to tears, declared the British would not alter their way of life. That, he said, would give victory to terrorism. One after the other, people in the street said things like "Well, we'll just have to get on with it," that phlegmatic phrase that marks British society. There was much for Americans to learn by watching closely that day. Most people, though, seemed to drift quickly on to something else.

Perhaps this is unfair, but I sensed a near unanimous reaction in New York: That was nothing compared to 9/11.

Just before that trip, I came across a remark made well before either Gulf War. I might have skipped over it had it been made by some sourpuss Frog, or a foreigner who unreasonably hates us. But it was attributed to George Kennan. Our culture produces few like him, a man wise enough to have foreseen the Cold War and its eventual thaw. I met him in 1980 and have yet to find a better-placed quintessential American patriot rooted solidly in world reality.

Kennan decried "the flag-waving, the sententious oratory, the endless reminders of the country's greatness, the pious incantations of the oath of allegiance, and the hushed, pseudo-religious atmosphere of national ceremony, the self-righteous intolerance towards those who decline to share in these various ritualistic enactments."

This hardly describes all Americans. There is, for instance, George Kennan. And there is you, if you have managed to read this far. But he captured a dominant trait that defines American society. People in every country pay far more attention to their immediate line of sight than they do to foreign affairs. Yet nowhere else do so many take such pride in ignorance and boast that they neither know nor care about the rest of the world. Why should they? We are, after all, the big dogs.

When this nationalistic ceremony is added to a propensity to attach shorthand labels to matters of dizzying complexity, our society seen from the outside can look downright silly—and also threatening. "Radical" and "moderate" applied to Islam takes us no further than dividing a world between good and evil.

It was no fluke that a sizable poll in 2006 found many foreigners believed the United States was a greater threat to security than Iran.

When Harold Pinter accepted his Nobel Prize in 2005, most of his speech oozed venom. "The crimes of the United States have been systematic, constant, vicious, remorseless, but very few people have actually talked about them," he said. "You have to hand it to America. It has exercised a quite clinical manipulation of power worldwide while masquerading as a force for universal good. It's a brilliant, even witty, highly successful act of hypnosis. I put to you that the United States is without doubt the greatest show on the road. Brutal, indifferent, scornful and ruthless it may be but it is also very clever. As a salesman it is out on its own and its most saleable commodity is self love."[5]

There is a lot more, but you get the idea. Pinter can get a little cranky. Still, there is some truth in his bile. Too many of us settle back on pillows of fatuous words that keep us from hard analysis. Rather than listening to understand others' reality, we tune out. Beyond foreign affairs, this also applies to affairs at home.

True, we excel in a lot of categories. We are also the number one jailers. The Justice Department tallies 7 million Americans imprisoned, on probation, or on parole. Of those, 2.2 million were behind bars. China, with four times our population, has 1.5 million prisoners. A study at King's College in London finds the U.S. incarceration rate of 737 per 100,000 is the world's highest, followed by 611 per 100,000 in Russia. For most industrial nations, the rate is near 100 per 100,000.

"We send more people to prison, for more different offences, for longer periods of time than anybody else," Ryan King told Reuters.[6] King, a policy analyst at the Sentencing Project advocacy group, pointed out that Americans often jail drug violators when other countries would provide treatment; failures in education, poverty relief, urban development, health care, and child care all add to the toll. When the society fails to deliver, he said, people end up in the criminal system.

Increasingly, law officers and private rent-a-cops use muscle at the slightest pretext. After a while, I stopped collecting reports of ordinary people arrested for wearing the wrong T-shirt or committing some silly breach. Though often minor, such incidents are poison to our way of life.

First Amendment or not, our vaunted freedom of the press is not exactly number one. On a per capita basis, we lock up journalists on a par with the worse totalitarian states. In 2006, Reporters Without Borders ranked the United States at 53 in press freedom among 168 nations; we were 17 on the list in 2002. The index is based on responses to fifty questions asked of journalists, free press organizations, human rights activists, and others.

"Relations between the media and the Bush administration sharply deteriorated after the president used the pretext of 'national security' to regard as suspicious any journalist who questioned his 'war on terrorism,'" the worldwide group said. "The zeal of federal courts which, unlike those in 33 US states, refuse to recognise the media's right not to reveal its sources, even threatens journalists whose investigations have no connection at all with terrorism."[7]

We, as a people, seldom get worked up about such things. Remember all those people who marched in freezing Ukraine streets, day after day in 2004, until Viktor Yushchenko was declared winner of a presidential election they said had been stolen by his Moscow-backed opponent? As Jon Stewart might say, "Hmmmm."

Overwhelmed with mountains of stuff to process, we simplify our lives with sweeping generalities. Our richly layered nation of 300 million people, of every possible political shade, somehow breaks down into two meaningless catch-all nouns: "conservative" and "liberal." To take issue is to whine. To firmly state an opinion is to rant. You are with or against us. A penchant for shortcuts, which seems to permeate every segment of society, prevents intelligent discourse. People jump immediately to extremes, often with obscenities in place of thought. It is one thing to buy precooked pasta to save a little time. It is another to eviscerate news and comment into meaningless snippets.

One-line executive summaries can amuse, alert, or anger, but they seldom convey the story. Try telling a sports lover traveling beyond reach of CNN that "an American football team won a Super-something by a score of 21–20." My bet is that he will want to know more.

Many people shrug this off as an immutable fact of life. The world is too big to watch. We elect and hire leaders to do that for us. But, of course, that raises the obvious question. On what bases do we choose them? Even before he was reelected, George W. Bush boasted that he did not bother reading newspapers; he had superior sources.

In a sensible democracy, it should be easy enough for people to elect leaders who care more about the wider world than their own personal situations. A good leader could expect to win another term for effective work done without sacrificing too much time campaigning.

But the key word is "sensible." An involved electorate must take an interest. We can't throw the bums out of office unless we can recognize a bum.

My Parisian friend Cedric Judicis made a point I hear often abroad. The president of the United States, in essence, is their leader, too. If they do not have a say in who that is, they expect Americans to make an intelligent choice.

Say, for instance, a group of twisted lunatics strike terror into America's heart. Does a reasonable society really want someone who whips up raw emotion, blinding citizens to more productive, and safer, responses?

Fighting terror does not take a world war or widespread spying on people's money transfer. Mostly, terrorists are ordinary humans whose anger at perceived injustice is fanned to a murderous degree by frustration and humiliation. Networks recruit foot soldiers and leaders from alienated classes that grow proportionately with perceived injustice. Theirs is not a costly endeavor. Anyone can wreak havoc with tenpenny nails and a few pounds of explosives. Al Qaeda brought down the Twin Towers for less than a half million dollars.

Bill Clinton had failed to capture Osama bin Laden, using Cruise missiles against dubious targets rather than tracking down the terrorist mastermind before he could strike harder at America. After 9/11, Bush responded quickly in Afghanistan, rousting the Taliban who protected bin Laden and chasing Al Qaeda into the hills.

Then Bush waged a quixotic "war" on terror that no one could define, let alone win. By November 2004, we were on our way to squandering our first trillion dollars in Iraq, with no end in sight. That was only money. No one was counting the Iraqi dead. By then, the figure was likely near 200,000. Even a low estimate of 100,000 was proportionally equivalent to a million Americans. That sort of casualty level would likely upset us, as well. No wonder those who cheered the fall of Saddam are beseeching Allah for deliverance from us. Meanwhile, the Taliban was streaming back into Afghanistan, this time murdering people rather than only making their lives miserable. Opium poppies, like terrorist enlistment, flourished as never before.

And yet more people voted for Bush in 2004 than in 2000. Were we just not paying attention?

The Americans most people see in troubled places have arrived in C-130 aircraft with flak vests and M-16s. Intentions may be noble, but this normally ends badly, leaving a lingering price to pay. Unlike ours, most cultures have a long attention span and longer memories.

At a distance, many of us see the military in simplistic terms: "good" or "bad." As a collective of humans, it is both. If its failings are not brought to light and corrected in a way that matters, its tactical victories usually degrade to lasting strategic defeats.

Having covered U.S. forces in most major conflicts since Vietnam, I am still amazed at the extremes. From grunts on up, I've seen some of our best and brightest. From generals on down, I've seen others we ought to trade to the North Koreans. When they go to work in our name, we have to keep an eye on them.

In 1992, Somalia warlords slugged it out, leaving millions without food. Bill Clinton sent troops to deliver the groceries. Generals ignored expert civilian advice from the field to first secure interior towns where people were starving. They staged a dramatic Navy SEALs landing at Mogadishu and seized the city's snake pit of a seaport.

I watched marines occupy the port and search workers as they showed up at dawn. One Louisiana private with a shaved bullet head and a bright red neck patted a man's ankle. He found a small steel blade. It was the customary knife every Somali male carries from his teens, like those daggers so beloved to Yemenis. The marine held it aloft and pranced around bellowing as though he had just found a concealed canister of weaponized Ebola.

Just then, I exchanged glances with the soldier's captain, a cool dude I had come to admire after a brief conversation. He rolled his eyes skyward and smacked the heel of his hand against his forehead. Both of us knew then what lay ahead.

Within twenty-four hours, Mogadishu street kids caught onto the game. The Americans who had impressed them so much the first day proved to be muscle-bound Goliaths with no more real force than Gulliver on his travels. As foot patrols passed, they darted out of shadows to steal canteens off the marines' backpacks. It suddenly got complicated.

In the end, it wasn't warlords who beat us but rather Somalis stirred up by a military trained to kill enemies but not to make friends. We lost a skirmish, as happens in military situations. Crowds got hold of a dead American soldier and dragged his body through the streets before cameramen from a dozen nations. Faced with stunned reaction at home, Clinton ordered the Americans out.

The fallout spread far beyond Somalia in an inexorable chain reaction. Fresh memories of that humiliation stopped Clinton from sending troops to save Rwanda. He apologized later. But in the hundred days that we stood by, using the Security Council to block others from beefing up a pathetic U.N. presence, 800,000 Tutsis were hacked to death.

Later, on separate occasions, bin Laden and Saddam made it plain that

Somalia had impacted on their thinking. When pressed, they believed, Americans would cut and run.

Perhaps nothing galvanized loathing of this dark side of America more than Guantánamo. It showed, in microcosm, not only what happens when overarmed, undertrained young Americans are let loose but also the price we pay when a U.S. administration ignores our basic values.

Reporters were kept away or given guided tours without interviewing prisoners. Secondhand stories revealed how troops force-fed hunger strikers. Then three prisoners managed to hang themselves. Our closest European allies expressed outrage. And our official response, via Colleen Graffy, whose title is deputy assistant secretary of state for public diplomacy, made headlines across the world: The suicides were "certainly a good PR move."

The few details we had were sanitized. Carol Williams of the *Los Angeles Times* got to Guantánamo to report on the suicides. American officials strapped her into an available seat on a military transport, a toilet as it turned out, and expelled her to Miami.

"In the best of times, covering Guantanamo means wrangling with a Kafkaesque bureaucracy, with logistics so nonsensical that they turn two hours of reporting into an 18-hour day, with hostile escorts who seem to think you're in league with Al Qaeda, and with the dispiriting reality that you're sure to encounter more iguanas than war-on-terror suspects," Williams wrote later.[8]

In this case, she added, "I ended up on that plane, on that seat, because of a baffling move by Defense Secretary Donald Rumsfeld's office, in which the only three newspaper reporters who managed to surmount Pentagon obstacles to covering the first deaths at Guantanamo were ordered off the base. Rumsfeld's office said the decision was made 'to be fair and impartial' to the rest of the media, which the government had refused to let in."

This was us, the American good guys. In the vacuum, reality was defined by fiction and guesswork. For instance, audiences around the world saw a film called *The Road to Guantánamo,* about four young Britons—three ethnic Pakistanis and an Indian Bengali—who spent more than two years in Cuba before they were cleared. Three had gone to Pakistan for the fourth's wedding. They said they went to Afghanistan for some adventure tourism.

The four were played by actors, and so were their American captors. Some footage was real, such as a clip of Bush defending Guantánamo, with a half-amused smirk, because "these people's values are different from ours." And Donald Rumsfeld explained that everyone was treated well, according to the Geneva Conventions.

Watching the film, I felt a harrowing ring of truth in the bullying humiliation and physical abuse. A soldier-actor smacked one of prisoner-actors as he was praying and shouted: "Fucking British traitor. Are you a Muslim? What about your queen?" A fanatic for hard sources, I distrust dramatizations. Yet I found myself caught up in the fiction as if I were watching fact. I could only imagine the reaction of others who were already prone to believe the worst. If it was not a fair portrayal, why didn't American authorities show reporters the reality?

Real or not, ten minutes of *The Road to Guantánamo* did more to shape America's image abroad than a football stadium full of Karen Hughes–type salesmanship.

At one point, AP's battery of lawyers dislodged a heavily edited transcript of detainees' pleadings at Guantánamo. *New York Times* reporters used it to look into the names. Some were hardcore combatants determined to fight infidels. Many more were like the Pakistani chicken farmer who was not, as accused, a ranking Taliban official. He told his interrogators, fruitlessly: "My name is Abdur Sayed Rahman. Abdur Zahid Rahman was the deputy foreign minister of the Taliban."[9]

In other cases, prisoners were arrested for wearing a particular type of cheap watch supposedly popular with Al Qaeda. One Afghan, accused of being a former Taliban provincial governor, explained he was someone else entirely. When he asked captors to verify his story with the current governor, he was told to produce his own evidence. He pointed out that he was incommunicado at the edge of Cuba, not allowed to make a call. The presiding officer told him to write a letter; his case would not be reviewed for a year.

In an editorial, "They Came for the Chicken Farmer," the *Times* said: "A case of mistaken identity's turning an innocent person into a prisoner-for-life was supposed to be impossible. President Bush told Americans to trust his judgment after he arrogated the right to arrest anyone, anywhere in the world, and people into indefinite detention. (Rumsfeld) infamously proclaimed that the men at Guantánamo Bay were 'the worst of the worst.'"

At times, our brazen hypocrisy is beyond laughable. A chicken farmer stays locked in hell without due process. Meantime, Abdul Qadeer Khan swans around the world in a style to make a Saudi prince blush, selling nuclear components to anyone with a checkbook. President Pervez Musharraf himself said in 2005 that he believed Khan exported a dozen centrifuges to

North Korea to make nuclear weapons. He has done lucrative private deals elsewhere. But A. Q., as he is known and loved at home, is the father of Pakistan's bomb, a national hero beyond reproach. Now he has cancer and is under house arrest. Americans probably would not bother him if Musharraf would let them. After all, you can't embarrass an ally.

During 2006, as world reaction raged on, the Supreme Court ordered the Pentagon to apply Geneva Conventions protection to all U.S. military prisoners. This was soundly cheered by a lot of Americans. But few read those conventions. Degrading treatment, humiliation, and all the rest continued out of reporters' sight.

Late in the year, Cheney made clear to what depths we had sunk. Scott Hennen, a conservative talk show host in Fargo, North Dakota, asked him: "Would you agree a dunk in water is a no-brainer if it can save lives?" The vice president replied: "Well, it's a no-brainer for me, but for a while there, I was criticized as being the vice president for torture. We don't torture."[10]

In fact, conceptualizing torture takes a brain, not to speak of a heart and a human soul. Even without those last two, it must be clearly understood: Torture turns mere opponents into embittered foes who hate with every fiber of their being. Ayman al-Zawahiri writes convincingly that torture at the hands of Egyptian police turned him toward terrorism. I have seen, and heard, enough torture to hear his ring of truth.

"Water boarding" is no Club Med sport. Few forms of abuse are worse than simulated drowning for sheer physical and mental terror. Victims are held underwater until they are certain their lungs will burst. On occasion, torturers get it wrong; lungs do burst.

In 2006, photographer Gary Knight and I took Tufts University students to Argentina to study a theme: the politics of fear. I helped one young woman find victims of the Dirty War; it was an easy search. An engineer with haunted eyes and halting manner described with fresh memory *el submarino,* water boarding that he barely survived. More than the torture, he remembers the torturers.

Later, I was on a panel at Tufts for a conference on the politics of fear. One speaker, a former South African police colonel, had spent twenty-five years using torture to force suspects to talk. A second, an African National Congress leader who was with Nelson Mandela at Robben Island, was one of his repeated victims. Torture doesn't work, both asserted. It only brutalizes the torturers and hardens the victims.

Never mind whether useful intelligence emerges from brutal methods. Forget that it all but guarantees future terrorism. Our elected officials defend inhumane treatment in our name. Even among foreign leaders who torture at home, this defines us. For a nation that flaunts its flag and its freedoms at every occasion, such hypocrisy is a point of convergence for vague hatreds of widely disparate origins. And if we cannot see that, we are pathetically naive in the eyes of people we expect to admire us.

We cannot say no one tells us these things. Among others, Jane Mayer showed in the *New Yorker* how cruel abuse, neither isolated nor rare, was embraced as official policy over objections by senior officers who knew better. She profiled Alberto J. Mora, general counsel of the U.S. Navy, who spent three years in the losing battle.[11]

George W. Bush declared in 2002 that detainees should be treated "humanely" in accordance with the Geneva Conventions. Later, he said, "Any activity we conduct is within the law. We do not torture."

But Mora, whose rank was equivalent to four-star general, assembled a twenty-two-page internal document outlining his efforts to stop prisoner abuse. The memo, Mayer wrote, "shows that almost from the start of the Administration's war on terror the White House, the Justice Department, and the Department of Defense, intent upon having greater flexibility, charted a legally questionable course despite sustained objections from some of it own lawyers."

Mora spoke with Mayer cautiously, declining comment on Defense Department matters beyond his memo. A conservative who admired Reagan and served in both Bush administrations, he supported the war on terror, Iraq included. But he worried that America was on a dangerous course and, he said, "It's my Administration, too."

Naval investigators at Guantánamo told Mora that poorly trained intelligence officers vented their frustration with escalating physical and psychological abuse. One man had been in isolation for 160 days under floodlight, interrogated for eighteen to twenty hours a day on forty-eight of fifty-four days. He had been stripped naked, straddled by taunting female guards, threatened by dogs, and told his mother was a whore. Then he was subjected to phony kidnapping and filled with intravenous liquid without access to a toilet.

The harder Mora dug, the worse abuses he found. Mora was born in Boston to a Hungarian mother and a Cuban father; his family knew that this was no abstraction. A great-uncle was hanged by Nazis after torture. As a four-year-old child, he saw his mother crying as Russian tanks, on TV, crushed the 1956 anti-Communist Hungarian uprising. The family, in Havana when Castro seized power, barely escaped jail when a servant said they planned to flee to America. They got away. "People who went through things like that tend to have very strong views about the rule of law, totalitarianism, and America," Mora told Mayer.

Mora said reporters focus too much on defining torture; cruelty is equally unlawful. If it is applied as a matter of policy, he said, "It alters the fundamental relationship of man to government. It destroys the whole notion of individual rights. . . . If you make this exception the whole Constitution crumbles. . . . The debate here isn't only how to protect the country. It's how to protect our values."

At Guantánamo, Mora found that commanders had called for tougher tactics. The senior legal adviser noted that soldiers had been court-martialed for such methods as water boarding in past conflicts. But she offered a remedy: troops could be given advance immunity from the Uniform Code of Military Justice. Mora was outraged.

Back in Washington, Mora told William Haynes, the Pentagon general counsel, that a recent Rumsfeld memo had condoned torture. He expected Haynes to get the secretary to revoke it. Instead, things got worse. On January 15, Mora showed Haynes a document he planned to circulate describing Guantánamo interrogations as "at a minimum cruel and unusual treatment, and, at worst, torture."

Haynes called back to say Rumsfeld would rescind his memo. But a week later, Haynes outflanked Mora. He got a superseding opinion from the Office of Legal Counsel at the Justice Department. This was the later-famous John Yoo memo, which essentially left the door wide open to abuse.

The door had long been open. In January 2002, Alberto Gonzales, then White House counsel, sent Bush an opinion that a new situation "renders obsolete" limits in the Geneva Conventions on questioning enemy prisoners. In August, the Justice Department's Office of Legal Counsel issued a secret memo—called the Torture Memo after it was leaked in 2004—authorizing the CIA to inflict pain up to the level caused by "organ failure." Under a doctrine of necessity, it said the president could ignore national and international laws against torture.

Over those three years, administration officials publicly denied using cruel and unusual treatment, let alone torture. Mora knew better.

"These were enormously hardworking, patriotic individuals," he told the *New Yorker* in hindsight. "When you put together the pieces, it's all so sad. To preserve flexibility, they were willing to throw away our values."

With the CIA's policy of "extraordinary rendition," legal niceties had no place at all. Suspects were simply put on a plane and sent to the Middle East to be tortured. But unless these people somehow die in captivity, they offer to others plenty of reasons to hate our guts.

Maher Arar, for instance, is a Syrian-born engineer whose family took him to Canada when he was a teenager. He was arrested in New York while changing planes on the way home from a Tunisian vacation. His name was on a watch list, linked with a suspected terrorist he says he barely knew. Without being charged, he was placed in leg irons and put on an executive jet to Syria. For a year, he was repeatedly whipped with electrical cables, among other torture, and kept in a grave-like underground cell. With help from the Canadian government, he was released, and the Syrians said they found no connection to terrorism. Now Arar is suing the U.S. government.[12]

By now, we know he was just another among many. Suspects were sent to Egypt, which the State Department condemns repeatedly for practicing torture. Others went to Syria. Then we found friendly thugs in Romania and Turkey and elsewhere to whom we could outsource our dirty work.

Human considerations aside, how exactly do we exercise future diplomacy with such states as Syria? We stand on our hypocritical high ground, but they know us much better than that. This is shameful, yes. It is also stupid.

If much of America was deceived, the world outside the cave only had to look at the evidence. Abu Ghraib made this plain to all. But it hardly stopped there. As the war dragged on, military recruiters scraped the bottom of barrels. At the peak of Guantánamo scandal, five soldiers were accused of an elaborately planned rape of an Iraqi woman whose body was burned to hide evidence. The alleged ringleader had been in prison as a civilian. Apologists blame a few "bad apples." Few Iraqis see it that way. Late in 2006, military prosecutors finally indicted four marines for the premeditated murder of twenty-four civilians, including a dozen women and children, at the Iraqi village of Haditha in November 2005. Four officers, including a lieutenant colonel, were accused of covering up the facts. A roadside bomb killed a marine, the charges said, and the others spewed fire. They riddled a car with bullets and systematically stormed three houses, killing civilians.

The *New York Times* account carried a color photo of Staff Sgt. Frank

Wuterich, twenty-six, who faces thirteen counts of murder. He is the absolute picture of young America, rosy cheeks, shy smile, and wise eyes. War, yet again, is hell.[13]

Beyond what reporters can see, soldiers' firsthand accounts sketch a general mood in Iraq. Along with his M-16, John Crawford carried a pen. *The Last True Story I'll Ever Tell* recounts a war he reluctantly fought in the duty-bound way that marks America's spirit.

Crawford sketches in low-key but vivid terms how soldiers interacted with Iraqis. The nobility of a rescue mission quickly morphed into something else. Stung by what they saw as ingratitude, baffled by strange customs, and scared by a very real threat, they grew bitter.

Iraqis were all "hajjis," a different generation's "gooks." Homes were stormed, cars were commandeered, and families were brutalized. When in doubt, troops sprayed machine-gun fire before asking questions. Men were humiliated in ways people with long memories never forget.

Describing a raid on one house Crawford remarks on a "shit-brown BMW" in the driveway. He writes: "'Who picked that fucking color? Fucking hajjis got no fucking taste,' Ramirez commented, and I smiled. My desert boots trampled the flowers in their well-manicured lawn, something that gave me rare pleasure."

There is not much hope for warming hearts or impressing minds in the frank, often ugly, account. But Crawford steps back to add wise context, far beyond Iraq. As an epigraph to one chapter, he cites words from the grand psychiatrist Karl Menninger: "The voice of intelligence . . . is drowned by the roar of fear. It is ignored by the voice of desire. It is contradicted by the voice of shame. It is biased by hate and extinguished by anger. Most of all, it is silenced by ignorance."

And we wonder why they hate us?

FOUR

TERRACIDE

Tropical splendor gets no richer than on a mountaintop in Tobago, where hibiscus flames deep crimson among a dozen shades of green. I climbed up one morning and looked south to admire a turquoise Caribbean seascape. The water was muddy brown. "Ah, that," explained an islander friend, "is silt from the Orinoco River." When I looked up, the pristine air I expected was darkened with smoggy haze. "That," my friend added, "is dust blowing from Africa."

No one paid much attention. Divers in search of beautiful coral went instead to Tobago Cay, somewhere else entirely to the north in the Caribbean. And you can get used to a little dust. Bob Marley had the answer years ago: Don't worry. Be happy.

It is too late for ifs. We have already poisoned our planet, and we are fast tapping out irreplaceable stores of groundwater and oil. The only questions left are how much we can still save, and what damage we might manage to repair. That many of us still do not realize this should be no surprise. Try putting a headline on news that moves so slowly you cannot see it until it has already happened. Yet we need to know these facts, and we need to act—decisively and rapidly. It *is* ten minutes to midnight.

Among the worst crises is polluting energy. Yet the federal government is spending less than half of what it spent twenty-five years ago for all energy research and development. According to studies analyzed by the *New York Times*, the total sank to $3 billion in 2006—what we waste in a few afternoons in Iraq. That is for all energy research, not only technologies to help protect the climate. The total in 1979, adjusted for inflation, was $7.7 billion.

Every crisis is linked to the others. This is no Chinese menu where one picks two from column A and three from column B. If any of the multiple challenges we face gets out of hand, we are finished. This is no hyperbole.

Start with the oceans. Perhaps not during a Super Bowl, but people might get off the sofa at a headline crawl reading, "Oceans to rise 80 feet by next month." At the rate we are now going, that might be accurate if it said "by next century." Some may take comfort from this distant future date—but children alive today may see much of their world sink from sight.

Eighty feet reaches to what once were the tenth-floor windows of the World Trade Center. It is as tall as fifteen Los Angeles Lakers standing on one another's heads. Waters rise in increments, so hundreds of millions of people will have moved to higher ground that cannot feed them all.

The figure of eighty feet is no wild guess from some alarmist flake. It comes from Dr. James E. Hansen, perhaps our most eminent climatologist, who directs NASA's Goddard Institute for Space Studies. In a measured piece in the *New York Review of Books* of July 13, 2006, he sketched realities we cannot ignore. He simply reported a fact: "The last time that the Earth was five degrees warmer was three million years ago, when sea level was about eighty feet higher."[1]

Jim Hansen, balding, courtly, and slightly rumpled, is a hero to those who understand what is at stake. Cutting through the formulations and equations, his message is dead clear: without firm action at the highest government levels, people will die in unimaginable numbers.

Even though China may soon surpass the United States as the worst polluter, he says, the threat is from cumulative emissions; ours are three times greater than anyone else's and will be for decades. The Chinese insist that they are only following our example of putting national interests first. We delay action that we say would give Beijing an advantage. But, of course, we share only one planet.

Hansen's science is harrowing enough. But there are also the politics he has the courage to expose. The Bush administration masked hard evidence, muzzles experts, and willfully confuses the public for the clear purpose of helping private interests amass short-term profit. Reflect on this a moment in light of the potential consequences.

In March 2007, Hansen told the House Committee on Oversight and Government Reform: "In my more than three decades in government, I have never seen anything approaching the degree to which information flow from scientists to the public has been screened and controlled as it has now. The effect of the filtering of climate change science during the current Administration has been to make the reality of climate change less certain than the facts indicate and to reduce concern about the relation of climate change to human-made greenhouse gas emissions."[2]

For example, he said, one of his staff members reported that the ocean was found to be less effective at removing human-made CO_2 than had previously been estimated. The NASA Public Affairs office decided that information should not go to the media. Another staff member, at an imposed "practice" press conference, was asked what could be done to stem accelerating loss of sea ice. "When he suggested 'we could reduce emissions of greenhouse gases,' he was told sternly 'that's unacceptable!'" Hansen testified. Scientists were not to say anything that related to policy.

Hansen said that NASA press releases on global warming science have gone to the White House for review, approval or disapproval, and editing. "That this practice is inappropriate, if not illegal, is indicated by the response from NASA Public Affairs when I made note of this practice in a public talk," he said. "The NASA Assistant Administrator for Public Affairs traveled from Headquarters to Goddard Space Flight Center to deliver an oral 'dressing down' of the professional writer at Goddard Public Affairs who had informed me about this practice. The writer was admonished to 'mind his own business.' This dressing down was delivered in front of the writer's boss. Such reprimands and instructions are delivered orally. If NASA Headquarters Public Affairs is queried by media about such abuses, they respond 'that's hearsay!', a legal term that seems to frighten the media."

He had much more to say on how science was thwarted by high-level interference. He was kept from interviews on NPR. Worse, strategic budget cuts blunted the data flow from small satellites which had found that the Greenland mass and West Antarctica are each decreasing by about 150 cubic kilometers a year. "One way to avoid bad news: stop the measurements!" he testified. "Only hitch: the first line of the NASA mission is 'to understand and protect our home planet.' Maybe that can be changed to '. . . protect special interests' backside.' I should say that the mission statement *used* to read 'to understand and protect our home planet.' That part has been deleted—a shocking loss to me, as I had been using that phrase to justify speaking out about the dangers of global warming."

Hansen got to the nitty gritty:

I believe that the gap between scientific understanding of climate change and public knowledge about the status of that understanding probably is due more to the impact of special interests on public discourse, especially fossil fuel special interests, rather than political interference with climate change science. I have no knowledge of whether special interests have had a role in political interference with climate change science. Nevertheless, it is my personal opinion that the most fundamental government reform that could be taken to address climate change and government accountability in general would be effective campaign finance reform.

And he went on to a higher plane:

The American Revolution launched the radical proposition that the commonest of man should have a vote of equal weight to that of the richest, most powerful citizen. Our forefathers devised a remarkable Constitution, with checks and balances, to guard against the return of despotic governance and subversion of the democratic principle for the sake of the powerful few with special interests. They were well aware of the difficulties that would be faced, however, placing their hopes in the presumption of an educated informed citizenry, an honestly informed public.

Benjamin Franklin, who divined the future crisis with his own crude tools, would have been dumbstruck by the satellites and supercomputers we have today, Hansen said. But what, he asked, would Thomas Jefferson have thought of "recent tendencies in America, specifically increasing power of special interests in our government, concerted efforts to deceive the public, and arbitrary actions of government executives that arise from increasing concentration of authority in a unitary executive, in defiance of the aims of our Constitution's framers?"

But, mainly, he stuck with science. Our delay in acting has already cost us immeasurably, making the challenge far greater. And we have only a few more years to get it right. If we reach a tipping point, it will be too late to do anything but suffer the calamitous damage.

Hansen's testimony lifted only a corner of the carpet. The House committee released documents showing hundreds of cases in which a Bush administration official softened wording on climate change. Philip A. Cooney was chief of staff of the White House Council on Environmental Quality, hired from his previous job as "climate team leader" for the American Petroleum Institute, the industry's main lobby group. Cooney left in 2005 soon after the *New York Times* exposed frequent editing that cast doubt about human impact on climate change.[3] He quickly found work—at ExxonMobil.

Cooney, who had no background in science, told Congress that his judgments were based on "the most authoritative and current views of the state of scientific knowledge." His past work had no influence, he testified. "When I came to the White House, my sole loyalties were to the president and the administration."

Earlier testimony hammered at the theme. Rick Piltz, who resigned from the government's Climate Change Science Program, said: "If you know what you are writing has to go through a White House clearance . . . people start writing for the class. An anticipatory kind of self-censorship sets in." Other scientists said that even titles of reports were changed to blunt their impact.

While hearings continued on Capitol Hill, Britain became the first national government to propose binding laws to cut greenhouse gases. Tony Blair's Climate Change Bill would reduce carbon emission by 60 percent before 2050. In April 2007, by coincidence of timing, the U.S. Supreme Court essentially ordered Bush to follow suit.

The landmark decision ruled that the Environmental Protection Agency had the right to regulate gases in auto exhaust. In fact, the court said, the EPA was required to take action unless it could provide a scientific basic for not complying. The Bush administration had insisted that the EPA was not authorized to limit heat-trapping gases and, even if was, it would not use that authority.

Viewed from a distance, this meddling with science and law is stupefying. That a president of all Americans might favor narrow interests is shameful, but that is not new. It is different if by favoring those narrow interests he abets irreparable damage to the future of an entire planet.

Countless experts, from every field of science across the world, add to the irrefutable evidence. Do some sound too apocalyptic? Ask James Lovelock, among our grandest of earth scientists, who is now in his eighties.

Lovelock's invention of an electron capture device enabled others to understand how chlorofluorocarbons (CFCs) were eating away the ozone layer. He advanced the idea that the planet might be seen as a single organism—he calls it Gaia—that is striving desperately to keep itself in balance. And in discussing his book *The Revenge of Gaia: Earth's Climate Crisis and the Fate of Humanity,* he declares it is too late for most of us.

Lovelock says processes now at work will raise temperatures by perhaps eight degrees Centigrade in temperate zones. He calculates that only about 200 million people will survive—one-thirtieth of the world's population—if leaders can shape a new society up near the Arctic Circle. Surely, Lovelock must be at least a tiny bit right.

Within the coming century, however high the waters go, much of the world may be starving to death. We are running out of water. With money and electricity, we can desalinate enough to drink for people living near an ocean. But a ton of wheat requires a thousand tons of water, and the world is already falling short of grain.

As China and India boom, they eat more and grow less. When food becomes scarce, it will most likely go to those who can pay rising prices. Then what? If people are ready to kill because of religious beliefs, what might happen when they see their children going hungry? Survival of the fittest, in extremis, is not about wealth.

Our methadone for oil addiction is to use plants, and corn offers the most profit for industry. But if we cannot feed ourselves, how will we feed our Nissans? What about those who can't pay the rising prices? Corn viots in Mexico are not a comforting sign.

Clear evidence says we will destroy 90 percent of the oceans' fish by midcentury, as well as 60 percent of their life-supporting coral. Commercial fleets use space-age technology to find the last great blue-fin tuna and sweep up entire schools of smaller species. Worse, carbon dioxide is acidifying the seas, killing our essential food chain from the bottom up. Melting ice is altering the precarious balance of ocean currents.

Sir Nicholas Stern, in a seven-hundred-page report for Prime Minister Tony Blair released late in 2006, put a price tag on global warming. If carbon emissions are controlled, he said, savings to the world economy would range near $2.5 trillion a year. And if not, he added, the progressive damage will be irreversible.

Future projections, in any instance, are nightmare guesswork. The present that we blissfully and insanely ignore is bad enough.

Once environmental calamities happen, they are hard to miss. Pacific atolls disappear. Great gashes of raw earth and endless rolling dunes obliterate African farmland. Ice floes calve, leaving polar bears, then people, to fight for their lives. Each calamity, separate but linked to the others, worsens toward a point beyond our ability to affect it. And new ones emerge at a fast-growing pace.

Swift, intelligent world action helped reduce the gasses that opened holes in our ozone layer. Nations sat down in Montreal and figured it out. Even so, an ozone threat remains. These broader new challenges, far more complex, impact on corporate strategies, trade, and a lot of people's jobs. World action has been neither swift nor intelligent.

It is pointless now to debate culpability. At this stage, any delay because of economic haggling is, beyond obscenity, a crime against humanity. Nature has no regard for lines on a map or anyone's narrow interests. This is about our survival. If we pollute and plunder to a tipping point, nothing else will matter. What counts is what all inhabitants of a single planet can do together—and how fast we can do it. We have only a few years left to act.

In March 2005, a Millennium Ecosystem Assessment prepared by 1,360 experts reported on twenty-four major ecosystems. Convened by Kofi Annan, it carried the moral weight of U.N. agencies, the World Bank, and a broad range of others. Food was the good news, it said. Agricultural advances would keep most of us fed for the time being. Otherwise, it concluded, "Human activity is putting such strain on the natural functions of Earth that the ability of the planet's ecosystems to sustain future generations can no longer be taken for granted." For scientists, those are tough words.

Unless we set actual values on "ecosystem services" we have regarded as free and unlimited, the report said, we will not make it. It urged an end to subsidies on agriculture, fisheries, and energy producers that encourage waste. A score of other recommendations, in sum, called for the Earth's inhabitants to take charge of the elements they need to survive. Rich societies must help poor ones manage dwindling resources. The principle ought to be clear: No one nation, let alone private interests, can be allowed to plunder what belongs to everyone.

P lato was an ecologist. Although the comfortable classes have ignored the obvious for millennia, thinkers since early antiquity recognized inevitable consequences. The Greeks had earth sciences down cold. Here is how Plato, in his *Critias*, saw soil erosion at Attica:

"What now remains compared with what then existed is like the skeleton of a sick man, all the fat and soft earth having wasted away and the bare framework of the land being left. But at that epoch, the country was unimpaired, and for its mountains had high arable hills . . . and it had much forest land in its mountains, of which there are visible signs even to this day; for there are some mountains which now have nothing but food for bees, but they had trees no very long time ago, and the rafters from those felled there to roof the largest buildings are still sound. . . . Moreover, it was enriched by the yearly rains from Zeus, which were not lost to it, as now, by flowing from the bare land into the sea; but the soil it had was deep and therein it received the water, storing it up in the retentive loamy soil; . . . it provided all the various districts with abundance of spring waters and streams."

We have thrived all these centuries since on a fallacy. We believed we could outsmart nature. Surface water was squandered and replaced from deep wells. When land eroded, machines pushed aside forests to clear new fields. We dammed rivers, flooded canyons, and built giant aqueducts. As technology advanced, we dug deeper not only for water but also for oil. Now, as carbon dioxide overheats the planet and delicate balances collapse, nature is letting us know we were not that smart.

To take action at this late date, we must first realize the enormity, and the urgency, of what we face. Environmental stories have finally reached the American mainstream. *Time* and *Newsweek* hammer the broad themes with long cover articles. *Vanity Fair* puts out a fat green issue. Newspapers make front-page space for global warming. After each flurry of attention, the subject drops back out of sight until some editor notices again. If alarm bells are clanged too hard or too often, people tune them out as media hype. Once the subject is covered, and silence follows, many assume that the problem has been solved simply by defining it.

News stories focus on the effect at its most dramatic. But the real issue is in the cause, sometimes barely measurable change in places we do not see. That corner of the Caribbean is a fragment of the bigger problem. Winds today carry dirt and microbes from one continent to another. Coral beds bleach and die in almost every sea on earth. The list, already long, is growing fast.

If we care, we must follow the stage-by-stage murder of our environment by our own devices. Waiting for some epiphany in print to command our attention is like drinking hemlock to see if it is dangerous. By the time we are convinced, it is too late to matter.

This is a strength of the Internet. Facts, graphics, photos, and projections are abundant enough to choke up any decent computer's memory. Official bodies and voluntary groups study every aspect. Fresh data is easy to find, with more coming in by the month.

Magazines have shown their strength. The *New Yorker* and the *New York Review of Books* have offered thoughtful, solid coverage over recent years. Elizabeth Kolbert expanded her three-part *New Yorker* series on global warming into a hair-raising book. There is much more, in periodicals and books, on every phase of the calamity.

Still, it is one thing to keep track of climate change, water shortage, ocean rise, spreading desert, melting ice, dying reefs, ozone levels, and the rest. It is another to rally critical masses of public opinion to take action.

Beyond simple inattention, there is flat denial. Many block out the truth as inconvenient. Action means doing things differently. Convincing economic studies show that measures to protect the environment need not dampen anyone's gross national product. But money might come out of— and end up in—different sets of pockets.

The inconvenient truth that Al Gore laid out in his film and book already falls short of reality. When first dropped, his bombshell was a muffled rumble. Partisans dismissed it as pre-campaign propaganda. Others thought about it, worried a little, and then drove their SUVs to the store for more barbecue charcoal. But as the message sank in and momentum built, the Goracle got our attention.

In March 2007, our should-have-been president swept back into Washington with all the hoo-hah of a Rolling Stones revival. He had won an Oscar, and his groupies ranged from hard-nosed scientists to teenagers who care about the future.

Our "planetary emergency" is growing geometrically, Gore told

Congress. Fresh evidence rolls in by the week. For instance, he said, scientists now say methane gas under Arctic permafrost is leaking five times faster than they had predicted. Methane is 23 times more potent a greenhouse gas than carbon dioxide; billions of tons remain under the ice. Already, Gore said, 420 American mayors were applying Kyoto guidelines. But effective action must come from Washington and other world capitals.

"This is not ultimately about any scientific discussion or political dialogue," he said. "It is about who we are as human beings and our capacity to transcend our limitations and rise to meet this challenge."

The jury is out on whether we are up to it.

During Gore's testimony, James Inhofe, the Republican senator from Oklahoma who pronounces global warming the greatest hoax perpetrated on mankind, made a ham-handed lunge for the jugular. Would Gore pledge to use no more energy at his Nashville home than the "average" American household, yes or no? Gore tried to explain that he used green energy—wind and solar—which did not pollute but, since Congress had not worked out subsidies, cost more. But Inhofe wanted embarrassment, not answers. Why do we vote for people like that?

Gore faces so many self-interested hecklers that one wag came up with a mock caption for pictures of him holding his Oscar: Gore is seen with a small naked man.

Even Gore's disciples often miss the message. Academy Awards organizers declared the ceremony as "green," and everyone made the right noises. Then, one by one and two by two, people climbed into their limousines. Many later blasted off in private jets.

A big aircraft uses as much fuel on a transcontinental flight as a hybrid car consumes in a million miles. Private aircraft sales rose by 20 percent during the first nine months of 2006. A celebrity wedding in Italy can burn enough fuel to illuminate a small county.

This gets to the heart of our problem. Faced with rising prices and a mania to be free of "foreign oil," we seek alternatives. Whatever we burn, however, impacts increasingly fragile ecosystems. Farm economies are out of whack. Forced production hammers diminishing aquifers and depletes fields. Droughts bring catastrophic shortages.

Lester Brown of Worldwatch offers some context. Each 25 gallons of corn ethanol that are pumped into an SUV could instead feed someone for a year. If we simply increased mileage by 20 percent, to European standards, we would save as much fuel as our entire corn crop can produce.

The answer is not in science, of course, it is in politics and economics.

Archer Daniels Midland and Cargill do not make much money if we burn switchgrass or wood chips. They make less if we reduce the demand.

S till, we go deeper and farther to find more oil with little thought to using less. And we consume as if there is no tomorrow. Ships that parade out of Miami for Caribbean cruises, for instance, can each gulp up to thirty tons of fuel a day. Bright lights in big cities exact a cost.

"Oil independence" means little with such a fungible commodity. The country of extraction has political implications. But petroleum flows to where it is needed, propelled by whatever price buyers are willing to pay. It all comes from the bowels of Lovelock's overstressed Gaia.

As Gore points out, newspaper and television stories are often "balanced" in the maddening new style imposed by managers afraid to offend. A scientist presents elaborate findings of a study, with an explanation of methodology and related uncertainties. Then some industry flack gives an opposing view based on intentional denial.

For many Americans, all of this is a side issue. Well into 2006, the Pew Research Center asked 1,501 adults across America to rank nineteen issues in order of importance. The results were horrifying. For Republicans, terrorism came first at 84 percent. Flag burning was up there at 60 percent, ahead of energy policy. Global warming was last at 23 percent, just after government surveillance and minimum wage. Gay marriage outranked an overheating planet by two to one. It was well ahead of the less specific category, environment.[4]

Democrats worried most about health care and education. Global warming came in only thirteenth, at 56 percent. Environment was eleventh. Independents put education and health care at the head of their list. Global warming also ranked thirteenth; only 49 percent of independents gave it top priority.

The survey found Democrats outnumbered Republicans—81 percent to 58 percent—in the belief that clear data showed temperatures rising. Twice as many Democrats as Republicans saw humans as the root cause. Together, only 41 percent blamed fossil fuels and other human-related causes. Twenty percent saw no solid evidence of a problem.

In a Pew Global Attitudes survey a month earlier, of fifteen nationalities questioned, Americans were the least troubled. Only 19 percent were concerned "a great deal"; 47 percent worried "only a little (or) not at all." In Japan, the tally was 66 percent and 7 percent. In Nigeria, where few people read the papers but instead look out their doors, 45 percent saw a critical problem.

Among Americans, 39 percent of those who believed in global warming thought major sacrifices would help, and 23 percent expected some technological solution would make them unnecessary. The rest said it was out of our hands, or they had no opinion.

W e are finally recognizing hard data from the Intergovernmental Panel on Climate Change, which has tried to alert us for seventeen years. In 2003, when I visited John Church at the World Meteorological Organization in Geneva, I could sense global warming under his collar. A plainspoken Australian climatologist, he was then executive secretary for the thousand contributors behind the IPCC report that appears every five years. The panel had just banged the alarm yet again to a largely indifferent world.

The IPCC assessment is a climatologists' baseline, the lowest common denominator of what widely diverse experts can agree on. As a U.N. document, the draft spends many months circulating in each state, where scientists, officials, and various kibitzing specialists attempt to blunt edges and soften language. Still, the science emerges. For politicians, it is a troubling jolt of inconvenient truth. Before the 2007 report, most people just ignored it.

Climate scientists have known since the panel's first study in 1990 that the world had limited time to deal with impending calamity. Countless calculations later, those early projections are essentially the same. If we do not reduce greenhouse gases, we can expect a 5.5 degree Fahrenheit (3 degrees C.) temperature increase by the end of the century.

It was Jim Hansen, in fact, who said in 1988 that he was almost certain that humans were behind climate change. British Prime Minister Margaret Thatcher, among others, was intrigued, and the IPCC went to work.

The 2002 version contained nearly as much evidence as the 2007 report. The difference is that scientists now agree overwhelmingly with Hansen's original hunch. The crisis was largely manmade.

When the latest findings were released, IPCC chairman Rajendra Pachauri lamented to reporters that 17 years had been squandered during which the blanket of greenhouse gases had thickened by 7 percent. Using projections of what they call the radiative forcing potential of those gases, scientists say the warming capacity of emissions since 1990 has increased by 30 percent.

After the April release of the second part of the report—a 1,400-page survey of expected effects of warming—European Union officials excoriated the United States and Australia for ducking the Kyoto Treaty and not doing enough since. Stavros Dimas, EU environment commissioner, told a meeting in Brussels that U.S. emissions were 60 percent above their 1990 levels.

"We expect the United States to come closer and not to continue with a negative attitude in international negotiations," he said. "It is absolutely necessary that they move."

However the numbers are interpreted, the main point is clear. Only cranks, or people with an interest to protect, could continue to argue that we face unstoppable natural forces.

There were, of course, plenty of skeptics from each of those categories. The American Heritage Institute, funded partly by ExxonMobil, immediately offered $10,000 for scientists who could write a "policy critique" of the IPCC report.

With an often artificial sense of balance, media reporting has tended to "balance" expert warnings with opinions from people who would prefer not to have a crisis. And there are serious scientists who argue that the threat is overblown—not not nearly as critical as the mainstream believes.

But in the end, we have no choice but to act, urgently and decisively.

By the time the television says, "World Ends; Details at 11," we will be out of options. It comes down to reversing that refrain: You can't worry about what you can't change. If we worry enough, we can change just about anything. And we had better start now.

Our environmental nightmare—global warming, rising seas, dwindling water supply, dying coral, grain deficits, fish crashes—is already in full bloom. Only its future pace and scope are in question. No counterargument makes any sense. Even if only natural forces were at play and man's role were minor, we have to protect a future. Yet we are hardly bit players in this tragedy. Whatever else is going wrong, man is speeding up the process. When past ice ages came and went, they took their own sweet time about it. God, mysterious ways notwithstanding, is not driving all those Hummers stuck in freeway traffic.

We hear this ratio often: Americans make up less than 5 percent of the world's population but consume nearly half of its resources. If we see nothing wrong in those numbers, the other 95 percent does. We will hear more from them.

People who see what is happening must help others to understand the threat. Individual efforts help, but they will be nowhere near enough. Citizens have to demand that elected or hired civil servants—the president and

Congress, for instance—do something significant. We have to think in the long term, at whatever the cost.

Big stories capture our attention on their own, particularly if they involve high rain-charged winds that ruffle TV correspondents' hair. Less evident developments, like grueling drought and the growing resentment of dispossessed peoples, get smaller type. That is human nature, which is not likely to change. In either case, we can only observe the effects. We have to start thinking about the causes—and start doing something about them.

We all know about that figurative frog in his pot of slowly heating water, blissfully unaware that before long his boiled legs will be someone's lunch. But small amphibians are not especially suited to thinking through such predicaments. What is our excuse?

We probably won't get down to the last drop of oil. More likely, as the price of light sweet crude rockets, we will find something more useful to do with it than splashing it into cars. And if we did use up our oil, ingenuity might possibly provide. Water is another matter entirely. Try living even a day without it.

The Earth's fresh water supply, a closed hydrological cycle with evaporation and precipitation, has stayed constant for millennia. Melting ice turns salty when it reaches the sea, but we are more likely to have drowned en masse before that alters the balance. The problem is that abundant fresh water is usually too far from the places where most people choose to live.

Near Palm Desert, California, a place so dry that they have to irrigate the saguaro cacti they steal from southern Arizona, I found a miraculous body of water called Shadow Lake. Developers had just gouged it out of the sand. They were building forty-two home sites in their $70 million project, each with a dock for water-ski boats. It was a great idea. All they had to do was add water.

This was in 2001, when people were realizing the Colorado River could not possibly supply the water that nine states and Mexico demanded from it. Tom Levy, head of the Coachella Water District, told Shadow Lake developer Kevin Loder he could not tap the imperiled aquifer. Loder insisted it was his right as a property owner, and it was. Levy appealed twice to Sacramento and was told to stop being a pest. To protect the aquifer, he allowed Loder to use scarce Colorado water. At agricultural rates, water to fill the lake, twelve feet deep and forty-two acres, cost $3,400.

From Palm Desert, I went to El Mayor, in Baja, California, the pathetic remnants of a Cucapa Indian village that thrived next to a Colorado River that ran into the Sea of Cortez. Now only a salty trickle reaches the little settlement before sinking out of sight.

"Our river is gone," Chief Onesimo Gonzales told me. "No more fishing. Trees are dead. No one plants. The wells are dry." El Mayor had forty-five families left, as many as would live around Shadow Lake. They can coax enough murky sludge from a distant borehole for washing. But for drinking and cooking, they buy five-gallon jugs at seven pesos (sixty-five cents) each from a truck that sometimes passes.

For the same amount of Colorado River water that Shadow Lake bought for $3,400, the desperately poor Cucapa Indians would have to pay $13 million.

I wrote about this as part of an AP series that was widely used.[5] The *Los Angeles Times* put it on the front page. *Time* magazine sent a reporter to Palm Desert to do its own version of the story. The series won a Harry Chapin Award. And since it was about California, not Swaziland, I waited for some resonance. So much for the power of the press. Nothing, in essence, changed.

Five years later, the Shadow Lake Web site displays a toothy golden-skinned family frolicking in the water. Those million-dollar homes are listed at $2.5 million, for starters, and the up-from-nowhere community has spread into the desert. When I talked to Loder in 2001, he admitted his plan looked like a waste of water—but he urged me to consider how much his project would contribute in taxes.

This is the same reasoning beyond the colossal consumption in Las Vegas, where a take-no-prisoners water czar named Pat Mulroy demands a growing share of the Colorado. True, the city is a bit overopulent with its towering fountains, uncounted pools and golf courses, and lush tropical gardens. But Mulroy points to the city's $60 billion annual economy to argue that water features pay off.

Considering that only four hundred farms in California's Imperial Valley were getting as much Colorado River water as all of Nevada and Arizona combined, Mulroy makes a strong case. But that misses the point. Fresh water is a wasting resource, with no alternative. In the Southwest, groundwater dates back more than 100,000 years. Little recharges even when new droughts do not slow the rains. This is not about money, in any amount. It is survival.

My main water story was datelined Palm Springs. The city's quarter million residents used an average of 375 gallons a day at home, twice the national average. That cost a household only half as much as cable TV. At the Palm Desert Marriott resort, boats ferried diners from the lobby across a twenty-three-acre artificial lake to waterside tables. A brochure boasted, "It took over 50 million gallons of water to fill the indoor lake and waterfalls."

At outdoor cafés, sprays of droplets just over the heads of patrons delivered a cooling mist in the day's heat. Palm Springs was air-conditioning the outdoors.

"People today are selfish, thoughtless, and don't seem to care about anyone's future," Pat Finlay fumed at the time. A good friend, she is a retired actress and self-described water Nazi. She badgered her neighbors to save every drop they could.

I stopped off to see Pat in her new condo in a development laced with wide canals. She was still badgering away, but no one was listening. Early in the morning I walked outside in a jungle of flowers and dense vegetation on a small lagoon. Gushing irrigation hoses and lawn sprays sounded like a storm in a rain forest. This is a guess, but in a minute or two those hoses sprayed more water than Pat had saved in a lifetime of turning off the tap while brushing her teeth.

But the shock was worst closer to home. When I grew up in Tucson, water was precious because you somehow knew it was. We beat the summer with swamp coolers, water droplets falling on aspen pads that perfumed the house with a damp forest scent. When steering wheels and car seats got hot, we had a remedy; we yelled, "Ouch." If some rich guy had a pool, we all befriended him, at least in summer.

Lawns were reasonably sized with Bermuda grass that survived the heat. Eucalyptus trees, palms, and indigenous palo verdes sank roots to the water table. Cacti such as our noble saguaros looked after themselves. Greasewoods and mesquite smelled wonderful after the rain.

In fact, I like air-conditioning and swimming pools as much as the next guy. But there are limits, and Arizona today shows just how far shortsighted and thoughtless people can blast past them.

During 2006, I asked Tom Maddock how long Tucson could continue its rate of water use before the aquifer tapped out. "Oh," he replied, "about five years."

I nearly choked on my tuna sandwich. Maddock heads the University of Arizona hydrology department, which is respected across the world. He has studied Arizona groundwater for decades. Measuring tools have gotten sophisticated, and he has access to the best of them.

Many disagree with that pessimistic prediction, but Maddock explained some facts of life that most people overlook. You can map the extent of an aquifer, but it is almost impossible to judge the usable water it contains. Developers, seeking the best case, divide the estimated volume by the projected usage. The problem is that water quality changes as aquifers diminish.

At lower levels, greater heat dissolves mineral deposits that pollute the water. Salts and natural poisons increase. Below certain depths, even at the higher cost of pumping, the water is too contaminated for use. Desalting and other treatment might satisfy the 10 percent demand for household use, but that cannot cope with agriculture.

When scientists estimate the capacity of an aquifer, planners take that as a safe minimum. The true figure, in fact, is much less; it can be very much less. Even before years of drought, rainfall came nowhere near to recharging southern Arizona groundwater. That leaves only the Central Arizona Project, which distributes dwindling amounts from interstate rivers. Increasing that supply means arm-wrestling not only with the water-wasters in Phoenix but also with Pat Mulroys in eight other states.

Despite all this uncertainty, Tucson carried on as if there were no day after tomorrow. Vast tracts of the treasured Sonora Desert were bulldozed. When Pima County imposed sensible limits on development, with careful thought to conservation, large out-of-state developers built huge communities just across the county lines.

In Tucson's wealthy enclave of El Encanto, 40 percent of homeowners draw water from private wells sunk to the aquifer. That allows them to pump as much as they want for free. Near the University of Arizona, cafés spray mists to air-condition the outside just like in Palm Springs.

By 2006, the richly varied Sonora Desert was already dying. Water tables dropped below deep root systems, and the green palo verdes were turning brown. Barrel cacti that store water from one season to the next grew thin. Prickly pear cacti, which spread lateral roots to catch any drop of surface moisture, shriveled to dead brown pads.

Tucson's hundred-plus golf courses, however, were a rich, lush green. People who moved from the East and California brought their exotic plants with them and poured on water each morning to keep them in bloom.

Huge new spa resorts spill across desert land ripped up by dozer blades. Retirees seeking the sun build new homes with pools and fancy gardens. For all the debate, the winning argument is what it is in Las Vegas: money. Think of the income.

On a drive to what used to be rich virgin growth in the northern

foothills where trails wind up the Catalina Mountains, I found a gated enclave of dazzling ugliness. An old couple strolled by a waterfall spilling
down a fake rock formation. I asked them if they did not worry about future water supply. "Oh," the man said, before his wife trundled him off,
"there'll be enough for our lifetime."

Southern Arizona is hardly an isolated microcosm. Point anywhere on
the map, and you will find a different set of serious problems. And water is
only part of it.

Most of Maddock's work has been along the San Pedro River, to the
southeast of Tucson near the old Apache country, a lovely riparian habitat
that has been protected and partly restored. These days, it is under extreme
pressure because of Fort Huachuca. Since America's wars are now mostly in
deserts, the old army post is expanding geometrically. Scores of thousands
of new homes need gardens and pools.

When Maddock reported that groundwater levels were dropping dan-
gerously, he said, local politicians had him declared persona non grata. It is
simple enough, he said. They will commission a new study, which can take
years. Meantime, water is drawn off as fast as people can pump it.

As the baking summer heat approached in 2007, I went back to Maddock to see if his views had changed. Did he still think Tucson's aquifer
would fail in five years?

"I don't know if we have even that long," he said. "People here have no
concept of the danger. They're being warned and warned and warned.
Soon they will simply have to start squeezing people, rationing the newcomers. It's absolutely unbelievable."

I saw Jonathan Overpeck, director of the university's Institute for the
Study of Planet Earth, who had drafted sections of the IPCC report. He
had no doubts at all. Desert regions like Arizona would be among the first
victims, with worsening drought, along with coastal areas exposed to more
frequent, more devastating hurricanes. It was already happening.

Robert Strom, retired professor at the Lunar and Planetary Laboratory,
had just finished a book on drastic climate changes he had watched since
the 1980s. "I cannot understand why so few people care," he told me.
"Don't they have families who will have to live with this?"

Heading toward Los Angeles, at Yuma, I drove across the pathetic stream
that had once been the broad Colorado. By then, hydrologists had already
declared the river to be so hopelessly oversubscribed that new water sources
must be found. The problem is that there aren't any. Meantime, Arizona is
the nation's fastest growing state.

In Las Vegas, the nation's fastest growing city, inhabitants average 180 gallons a day, twice Tucson's level. Hotel casinos with lavish fountains and water parks produce tons of cash. Las Vegas seeks to slake its unquenchable thirst with water from upstate. In northern Nevada, however, ranchers are not selling. They fought hard to settle their land, and they know water is at the heart of it.

"To make an environmental disaster out of this area is not the solution for Las Vegas," rancher Dean Baker told ABC News in April 2007. He and his neighbors refused to sell. "It'll be a pipeline that doesn't have enough water to justify it. . . . It's a Band-aid that'll be more costly in the end than seeking a better plan."[6]

In the end, wherever water is scarce the choices are fast narrowing down to one: use a great deal less of it.

Compared to most of the world, Americans are still rich in water. At the other extreme, vicious fights over drying wells already take lives in parts of South Asia and Africa. Years back, when he was foreign minister of Egypt, Boutros Boutros Ghali predicted that the world's next war would be over water. Other sorts of skirmishes have muscled in first, but he is not far off.

At a meeting in Cairo on Middle East resources, I cornered Turkey's minister for water. His government was racing ahead with the Southern Anatolia Project, known by its Turkish initials, GAP. A series of massive dams would give Turkey the possibility of shutting off the Tigris and Euphrates rivers before they reached Iraq or Syria. This was in 2000, when Mesopotamia was still off world policy makers' maps.

I asked the minister what would happen if the Turks reduced water flow to their southern neighbors. He grinned broadly and replied, "Let them drink their oil."

Gulf states do drink their oil—by using it to pay for desalination plants—but they can't eat it. Saudis squandered their ancient aquifer in the 1990s in an effort to be self-sufficient in wheat. They learned what any farmer could have told them: growing grain demands a lot of water. Tourists in Dubai splash around in a giant water park. But desalting is an option only for thinly populated countries near an ocean, with money to spend and no crops to grow.

As an Israeli engineer once told me, when water supplies run low, there are only three options: You can use less; you can make more; or you can steal it from your neighbor. The intended joke is not so funny.

Israel manages water well, but it also needs a lot. The Sea of Galilee, which should supply a third of the demand, is sometimes so low that Jesus could walk across it without a miracle. Other water comes from sources shared with Arab neighbors. The rest is from aquifers under the West Bank but drawn from pipes within Israel. Palestinians get a relative trickle. The Gaza aquifer is badly polluted by infiltrating saltwater and chemical waste.

Sooner or later, there must be a reckoning. And there will be others, in a lot of places.

The physical state of our world is humanity's first great test of its ability to save itself. Old piecemeal half-measures cannot work. The intricately linked challenges we face transcend borders and blame.

We need something similar to an antilitter campaign on a grand scale. It requires clear laws across jurisdictions and frontiers, stiff fines, assiduous monitoring, and rigorous enforcement. We need tough new treaties and a worldwide consensus that national sovereignty cannot allow any one government to plunder everyone else's future.

We might have headed off the worst of it had enough people cared a generation ago; it is pointless to lament about that now. Today we need action that is broad-based and multinational, steered by scientists with no interest in protecting anyone's economic advantage. This is now less about ecology than about poverty and greed. And it is beyond anyone's party politics.

Governments and industries must be held as accountable as individuals; their scale of pollution and ecological destruction is far higher. If the Kyoto accords do not suit Washington, we urgently need something else with our signature at the bottom. China may eventually surpass us as the planet's worst perpetrator, but that is hardly comfort. We have to lead the way to a better environment.

The notion of sovereignty is sacrosanct. Yet in Iraq, Washington invoked the principle of preventive as well as preemptive invasion to depose a tyrant who had dabbled in weapons of mass destruction. A nation's willful damage to global ecology is also an instrument of mass destruction. This is no stretch. The effect of plundered watersheds, unchecked fires, devastated rain forests, or thoughtless overuse of fossil fuel does far more deadly and long-term harm than Scud missiles laced with pathogens.

This concept falls apart when powers that seek to protect global ecology are themselves guilty. Developing nations make a compelling case. Why shouldn't they get to pollute up to world-class levels? Few have resources beyond land to exploit and minerals to extract. Much of their industry is inherited from colonial systems geared to one-way flow. Raw materials are kept to low price levels.

Some of this argument is baseless, yet much of it is not. What we call the world community needs hard rules that apply across the board, and Americans have to set the example. No government should have the right to plunder a collective future. But unless action is perceived as fair, we face another problem: A lot more people will hate us.

These grand themes are not beyond individual reach if we pay more attention to unreported reality. We can elect and hire leaders who say they care. By watching them, we can ensure they keep their promises. Here is where "think globally, act locally" makes an impact. States, cities, and communities are taking their own action while waiting for the federal government to admit there is a crisis.

The heavy work must be done in Washington. Ever since Ronald Reagan had Jimmy Carter's solar panels taken off the White House roof, the environment has suffered from avaricious turf war. Robert F. Kennedy Jr., born into a patrician family whose young men habitually head toward the Senate or beyond, decided to work from the outside, looking into an opaque system he knows well.

As counsel for the Natural Resources Defense Council (NRDC), Kennedy helps an energetic agency hold governments and companies to account. For decades, I have admired how NRDC digs in, collects solid data, and stays the course.

Crimes Against Nature is the title Kennedy chose for a crucial little book that began as pieces in *Rolling Stone.* The subtitle makes its point: *How George W. Bush and His Corporate Pals Are Plundering the Country and Hijacking Our Democracy.* When Kennedy speaks in the Republican heartland, he notes in a foreword, applause is just as loud as among Democrats. Sensible people from all sides care about the real legacy they leave behind.

When self-interested politicians subsidize polluters and exonerate them from cleaning up their own mess, he argues, everyone else pays. "The fact is, free-market capitalism is the best thing that could happen to our environment . . . ," he writes. "In a real free-market economy, when you make yourself rich, you enrich your community. But polluters make themselves rich by making everybody else poor."

Kennedy writes, "The coal-burning utilities that acidify the Adirondack lakes, poison our waterways with mercury, provoke 120,000 asthma attacks, and kill 30,000 of our neighbors every year are imposing costs on the rest of us that should, in a free-market economy, be reflected in the price of the energy when they bring it to the marketplace. By avoiding these costs, the utilities are able to enrich their shareholders and put their more conscientious and efficient competitors out of business. But these costs don't disappear. The American people pay for them downstream—with poisoned fish, sickened children, and a diminished quality of life."

During George W. Bush's first term, his administration set in motion more than three hundred major rollbacks of federal laws to protect air, water, public lands, and wildlife, Kennedy notes. In 2003, by failing to renew an environmental tax on oil and chemical companies, Bush bankrupted the Super Fund. One in four Americans lives near a toxic site that may never be cleaned up.

That year, Republican pollster Frank Luntz told party leaders that they were vulnerable on the issue. The public, Kennedy quoted him as writing, tended to view them as "in the pockets of corporate fat cats who rub their hands together and chuckle maniacally as they plot to pollute America for fun and profit." Kennedy summed up Luntz's advice: "In essence, he recommended that Republicans don the sheep's clothing of environmental rhetoric while continuing to wolf down our environmental laws."

An initiative that would destroy healthy old-growth trees was named Healthy Forests. The Clean Air Act was gutted and called Clear Skies. "Cloaked in this meticulously crafted language that is designed to deceive the public," Kennedy wrote, "the administration—often unwittingly abetted by a toothless and negligent press—intends to effectively eliminate the nation's most important environmental laws by the end of the term." This, he notes later, is part of a larger pattern:

"The free market has been all but eliminated in an energy sector dominated by cartels and monopolies and distorted by obscene subsidies to the filthiest polluters. Our once vibrant agricultural markets are now controlled by multinational monopolies with no demonstrated loyalty to our country and its laws. Media consolidation is transforming journalism into a forum of ideas into a marketplace exclusively for commerce."

For diehard news professionals, that last point hurts, more so because Kennedy is dead right. Equally disturbing is the final paragraph of *Crimes Against Nature:* "If they knew the truth, most Americans would share my fury that this president is allowing his corporate cronies to steal America from our own children."

Why don't most Americans know the truth? This is not exactly classified material. Some reporters do write it, and it gets past their editors into print. But it is all over cyberspace, starting with the NRDC Web site. The point of a democracy, as of a real free-market economy, is that is takes watching by people who benefit from it.

Washington is only the starting point, and not the worst of it. Beyond our line of sight, these same corporate despoilers are joined by worse perpetrators with almost no oversight at all. The NRDC and other groups have challenged some of the worst depredations, sometimes with success. Even so, willful, avaricious exploitation is speeding the planet toward ecological overwhelm.

What else matters more than the shape of the planet we leave to our children? True, a new kind of China is reshaping the world, politically, economically, socially. It is rapidly getting to be a security issue. Yet the back story to China's headlong growth is man-made environmental damage such as the earth has never seen. As the Chinese rapidly catch up, trading bicycles for family sedans and consuming at First World levels, an overexploited Earth will have to supply the raw materials. Already, China's old hardwood tropical forests are being cut down for packing crates and pallets. And then there is India, and all the rest. The impact is everywhere.

Go back for a moment to that high bluff in Tobago. Silt in the Orinoco comes largely from uncontrolled logging upriver. By now, no one needs reminding of damage caused to the Earth's atmosphere by raping the Amazon rain forest. Stopping that is beyond conservationists. That requires developmental economists and armed troops.

Dust from Africa is topsoil that desperate families need to grow millet. It blows away because people cut down the last trees they can find for firewood. Telling them to desist is pointless. Without some alternative cooking fuel, they will starve. Each year, the crisis worsens because we have diminished their rainfall. The Niger River and other rare waterways run lower. And the deserts inexorably grow. Many people quietly die. A lot hold out against indescribable odds. Others join warlords or religious zealots who give them a gun.

In the mid-1980s, I interviewed a frustrated Malian official whose repeated pleas for European aid were ignored. "Maybe when the dust starts blowing north they'll take notice," he told me. Now it does blow north, but aid money is still tight. With famine, locusts, and war, more urgent problems take precedence. Besides, Europeans now have deserts of their own.

Much of southern Spain and Italy today looks like the West Africa I saw decades ago. I can watch the northern Mediterranean coast wither from my own hillside perch in southern France. Smoke columns start each spring, forest fires sparked by man but fueled by nature. Ancient olive trees, the last to go in a stressed climate, are dying. Rains come too hard at the wrong time or not at all.

The phenomenon is everywhere. Global warming really means drastic extremes, hot and cold. While northern summers rise into triple-digit temperatures, southern winters might freeze hard. And this has a multiplier effect. Air-conditioning and heating consume yet more energy, which turns wasting resources into greenhouse gases. Melting ice exposes trapped solids that release yet more harmful gas.

Kennedy's example of acidifying lakes is an important one, but that is a fraction of the problem. Among the greatest threats we face is chemical change in our oceans, caused by carbon dioxide. Late in 2006, a comprehensive British study warned we could lose 90 percent of marine life by midcentury. One CNN anchor, adding the item to a newscast, burbled: "I guess our kids won't know about fish sticks." The damage will be a little worse than that.

Scientists have warned us about all of this for generations, but their complex formulas made little sense and their projections seemed far-fetched. Now we only have to step out of the cave and look around for ourselves.

In the 1970s, after I quite literally watched the Sahara moving south while based in West Africa, I made a sideline of reporting on deserts, oceans, climate, and wildlife. It was a tough sell. Once I raised the subject with Ben Bradlee, who replied with a characteristic snort. He would put an environment story on his *Washington Post* front page, he said, when water flooded the newsroom.

(When I mentioned this to a *Post* editor late in 2006, he rolled his eyes. Things have hardly changed. With tight space, Washington's hometown paper has decided to focus on community news, national politics, and only certain sorts of foreign stories. The environment, covered elsewhere in specialized publications, is not one of them.)

In the 1980s, I met a Croatian scientist named Stjepan Keckes, a U.N. Environment Program oceans expert. With charts and figures, he laid out the future. Seas rise in irregular increments, he explained. One year may show no perceptible change. The next, Staten Island could be bailing water. Oceans were rising. But anyone with an interest in pooh-poohing the real threat need only point to a year of no change. My AP foreign editor ran my story, with a snicker, after I bent his arm for an hour. Hardly any newspaper printed it.

Regularly, Keckes updated his data and added more detail as he saw the seas change. He wrote scholarly works for the like-minded, and then he quietly retired.

My files from back then bulge with other such ignored alarms. Jacques-Yves Cousteau campaigned fiercely to protect Antarctica. He saw in the 1980s how quickly ice would melt when man altered the precarious balance.

Today, reporting on the environment is still difficult, even with editors' best intentions. During 2000, the old-version AP gave me free rein to circle the world to report on water crises. I ranged from the southwestern United States and Mexico to the Middle East and India. But I did not get to the biggest story: China.

Playing by the rules, my press visa application mentioned interest in how China manages water. This was so that I could ask for essential official interviews. But it was like waving a giant red flag, which by then was no longer such a popular fashion in China.

Officials had reason to be wary. They were building the Three Gorges Dam, the largest retooling of nature anyone had ever attempted. The social impact of flooding hundreds of thousands out of their ancestral homes was one thing. The danger posed by a monster man-made structure holding back so much devastating power was another. But even in terms of its stated purpose—flood control and a water supply for farming—experts I had learned to trust described it as a very risky venture.

Not only the dam, but the whole reason that something was necessary, was one of the great stories of our time. The Yangtze River feeds innumerable waterways that wind through farmland China needs badly. The Yellow River up north, once broad and deep, runs dry before it reaches its mouth for much of every year.

Writers with access had to be careful what they wrote. Some did splendid work, nonetheless. Critics marshaled a convincing case. Satellite photos and scientific studies were revealing. But I wanted more old-style journalism. This was a story you had to see up close, balancing official comment and data with the observations of people who had lived with their waterways for millennia. One American colleague dealt with the subject in his own way. Describing life in Beijing, he noted that in outdoor cafés grit blew into his contact lens. His problem could be solved with saline solution. What about that grit?

Even from a distance, the picture is clear enough. Emphasis on industry, power, and raw materials carries a huge ecological cost. Great swaths of productive land are turning to desert, blowing that dust far beyond Beijing. Spiraling demands for ever scarcer water limit food crops.

As a sovereign nation, China can ignore outside meddling just as the United States can reject a Kyoto treaty that it says harms its short-term economic interests. But in the end, lines on a map mean nothing to nature.

For years, this has been a main theme for Lester Brown, whose respected Worldwatch Institute in Washington keeps track of such things. With tonnage and consumption figures he updates each year, he shows an inexorable pattern. Variables make such calculations imprecise. A year of good rain might fortify the optimists. But it is no more than a question of time before China and India need to buy grain. When Lester Brown gets to say "I told you so," we are all in trouble.

Even when environmental stories land on front pages, nothing significant happens. We have sounded the alarm loudly over the Amazon, as one example, with world summits and grand promises. Chico Mendes died trying to protect the disappearing rain forests that amount to a planetary lung that allows us to breathe. Indian tribes deep within the Amazon have held the line, moving from blowpipes and arrows to appearing on world stages to plead their case.

Still the devastation churns on, despite proclaimed measures of protection. In the Proceedings of the National Academy of Sciences in 2005, specialists studied high-resolution satellite images of four Brazilian states. From 1999 to 2005, 16 percent of selectively logged areas were deforested within a year after cutting. In four years, 32 percent of the logged areas were laid bare. The annual loss in those four states was seventeen thousand square kilometers.

Most of this was within twenty-five kilometers of major roads. Regulated areas and indigenous reserves showed less damage, suggesting that tough conservation measures bear results. The Amazon, of course, is only part of it. Look anywhere that interests you. Just spin a globe and point.

These various calamities—it cannot be repeated often enough—are linked, and each worsens the other. Mostly, they are part of a large pattern that is getting worse. Katrina killed 1,300 people and did $80 billion in damage. It was only one of twenty-eight hurricanes and tropical storms in 2005; that broke the record of twenty-one, set in 1933. Four were Category 5, the strongest on the Saffir-Simpson scale. Wilma was the worst ever seen in the Atlantic. There were fewer storms in 2006, but a pattern remains.

James Elsner of Florida State University compared 135 years of air and sea temperatures with hurricane intensity. "It appears that atmospheric warming comes before sea warming," he reported. That is, increased green-house gases are likely to produce storms of growing severity. Elsner said a natural fluctuation called the Atlantic Multi-Decadal Oscillation has some effect.[7]

Politics dampen optimism. In the United States, strategists for both par-ties are convinced that tough action to protect the environment will cost votes. In light of those Pew findings, they are probably right. Many Americans believe that God gave our society the right to live as we choose at whatever the impact on benighted lesser peoples. Still, a democracy can head in any direction a majority chooses, and a public groundswell is building.

In 2006, the Sierra Club produced a pack of "knowledge cards" enti-tled *Save the Planet*. Each of the forty-seven cards had a tip for protecting the environment. The most useful said only "Get Connected!" On the back, it gave the number of the U.S. Capitol switchboard: (202) 224-3121. The White House is (202) 456-1414. (For mail, just use a title, a name, and Washington, D.C. The post office works.)

One card noted that a TV picture tube contains four to eight pounds of lead, which pollutes water and poisons fish. Consumer electronics account for 40 percent of lead—along with mercury and barium—in landfills. A flat-panel TV is better, says the Sierra Club, but not as good as reading a book or taking a hike.

My favorite notes that if you traded an average car for a 13 mpg SUV, you would use as much extra energy as leaving a refrigerator door open for six years—or burning a bathroom light for thirty years. SUVs emit 43 per-cent more greenhouse gases and 47 percent more pollution than cars. If cars averaged 45 mpg and light trucks managed 34—both possible with ex-isting technology—America would save 1,507 gallons of gas every second.

It actually helps to switch off a car stuck in traffic; after thirty seconds, that saves gas. Public transportation would help a lot more.

More than combined small savings, we need the sort of mentality change that comes from parents and schools. This certainly works with tobacco. Try lighting a cigarette in sight of a sixth-grader who cares about you.

We have to curb our appetites. Just take electricity. Do we really need housefuls of plugged-in stuff on pointless standby? Air-conditioning is es-sential now that we have freaked up our climate. But how much do we need, at what temperature? Ceiling fans are great.

If demand were lowered, we could supply much of our need from the

sun, the wind, and ocean currents. Of course, that will not be enough. Oil-
and coal-powered turbines produce greenhouse gases and deplete finite resources. Hydroelectric current needs dams that impact on our land and our
rivers. A sensible alternative is nuclear plants cooled by saltwater—and if
that does not scare you silly, do some more research.

My friend L. writes computer programs for nuclear power reactors.
Her specialty is trying to keep them safe. She is a free thinking, spiritual-
minded nondrinker who in broad terms is lumped in with liberals. L.
knows the good and bad of all alternatives. She believes reluctantly that nuclear power is the only way to meet rising demands with the least collateral
damage to the environment. That is, as long as everything works like it is
supposed to.

Recently, L. and I chatted about the nuclear business. It seems that one
result of the Soviet collapse is a lot of excess weapons-grade plutonium
hanging around in America. Being practical and profit-minded, we put this
to use in reactor plants in the place of the normal stuff. In the event of catastrophe, however, it is twice as deadly.

Among L.'s tasks is to whip up hypothetical kill rates on her computer.
For one reactor in Charlotte, North Carolina, engineers figure that an un-
toward "incident" with its plutonium would take 150,000 lives. Normal
fuel would kill only half as many, which seems like cold comfort.

One can take these things personally. As it happens, I have a beloved
nephew in Charlotte, whose older daughter is heading toward marriage-
and-kids age. That hypothetical "incident" hovers over the head of three
generations of my own family. But then everyone is similarly involved at
personal levels on a planet that is facing terracide.

The good news is that by looking closely, we can find plenty of instances
where intelligent action can make a significant difference, even if it is
late in coming. If enough people are resolved to do something, the picture
is not so bleak. A great deal of promising scientific and engineering work is
already under way. The hang-ups, as usual, are largely politics and greed.

As the National Resources Defense Council saw in California, solutions
can take no more than demonstrating simple interest. Barry Nelson, the
NRDC resident wise man in San Francisco, is one of those housebroken
zealots on whom our survival will depend. Though passionate and intimately informed on the basics, he speaks gently. And he listens carefully to
the other side.

"Our energy team persuaded utilities that conservation is the smart strategy not because of global warming, not because of air quality, but because it was the cheapest, fastest approach," he told me. With a process called decoupling, utilities no longer have to sell more power to increase profits. Instead, they cut demand 20 percent by pricing to encourage less use. They need fewer new generating plants and use less fossil fuel.

"It was an incredibly rational conversation," Nelson added. "We're a remarkably innovative species. You only need to recognize the problem and see what is in the way. If you just made the economically rational decisions you'd make the right decisions ninety percent of the time on environmental issues."

That energy approach could work with water, Nelson said, but only if voters forced authorities to take sensible action. Eighty percent of California water is used by agriculture at such ludicrously cheap rates that it is not cost-effective to save it. Because big farmers lobby hard and contribute generously to political campaigns, legislators ignore the obvious imbalances.

Agriculture pumps $32 billion into the state's economy, but much of it is on life support from subsidies, and farmers are fast losing market share to China. By comparison, Nelson said, Intel alone contributes $38 million to the California economy. Dairies and feedlots add to the crisis. Beyond all the farmland devoted to pasture and alfalfa, Nelson calculates, California cows slurp more water than all the people and all the industry in the state.

In the Central Valley, he said, farmers who pay $30 for an acre foot of water lobbied for a dam on the San Joaquin that would add more water at a new cost of $3,000 per acre foot. Farms above 960 acres are not supposed to receive subsidies, but families simply divide up holdings among their sons and daughters or nieces and nephews. "Urban water users need to think about how to meet their needs," he concluded. "Essentially, they let agriculture drive the bus. We're paying agriculture to waste water when we live in a water-short state. That's just crazy."

Like so many other environmental lobbyists, Nelson focuses on small triumphs that suggested a changing mentality. The NDRC was in the process of restoring the San Joaquin River outside of Sacramento. The state's second-longest river has been essentially dry for fifty years. By moving back levees and undoing past damage, it will flow again.

"Benefits of this will reach across the state," Nelson said, dismissing critics who say the plan favors fish over people. "This will restore salmon at Sacramento and bring drinking water to Los Angeles. We now have farmers standing by our side to save salmon." Ironically, he added, large-scale farms were the easiest to win over. "These are tough business decisions, and the ones who find them the hardest are small guys, the guys we like. The big ones are business people. They understand. It's not a question of protecting fish. It is protecting the world."

California can be an innovative laboratory. In the Chino area, the world's densest concentration of cattle has poisoned the groundwater. Aquifers are too contaminated to store surplus runoff. Faced with this, the Inland Empire Utilities Agency treats water with a process akin to desalination. And the fuel used is methane—cow shit.

"The public 'gets' climate change in California, and there is an enormous amount of activity in western states and the Northeast," Nelson concluded, citing NRDC monitoring reports. "Outside the Beltway, things are changing at a staggering rate. But without a national policy framework, we won't win this. And the planet will not win this without the United States."

That policy framework is an essential cornerstone, and interconnected action depends on legislators who think beyond their campaign war chests. To ensure Congress and federal officials do their job, we have to understand the basics for ourselves. This is not as hard as it seems.

The End of Oil, a wise energy primer by Paul Roberts, explores options that more research can perfect, such as hydrogen fuel cells and, eventually, nuclear fusion. Meantime, renewable sources—wind, solar, hydropower, biomass, as well as others like geothermal and tidal—provide less than 9 percent of total world supply. The two most obvious options, power from wind and the sun, add up to one-half of 1 percent. Their combined output of about two thousand megawatts barely matches two coal-fired power plants.

"Why, after three decades of effort, do alternatives claim such a tiny fraction of the energy market?" Roberts asks, although that is hardly a tough question. "The industries that profit from hydrocarbons (and the politicians who profit from those industries) have zero interest in seeing the emergence of competing technologies or the new, more decentralized energy system these new technologies may make possible."

While we develop new sources, Roberts advises, we can make far better use of liquid natural gas, which adds less to the greenhouse that is cooking us. But the easiest and most effective way to ease away from petroleum addiction is simple behavior change. If we consumed the fuel we actually need, as opposed to what we mindlessly squander, we would slash consumption substantially. But business is business.

The other day I saw a full-page newspaper ad from an oil company pleading for Congress to give them billions of our tax dollars so they could suck the remaining oil from under the Gulf of Mexico and grow yet richer while passing the inevitable end of oil to a later generation.

Just exactly how blind *are* we?

Finding smart scientists and inspired thinkers is not the problem. One morning I sat down for breakfast at a permanent floating coffee klatch in Boulder, Colorado. By lunchtime, I had enough answers in my notebook to save Earth from terracide with a minimum of muss and fuss. But like the people around the table, I just didn't know who to call to get us started.

I was with my old high school pal Binx Selby, an inspired loony whose inventions include a prototype portable computer. He had bogged down in Boulder with a car full of honeybees en route to Alaska, where he planned to supply distilleries in a booze-happy town with natural sugar. His idea for a mountain cabin that made fresh water from the septic tank found little popular enthusiasm. But he had just built a well-lighted 45,000-square-foot house, with a nineteen-car garage, that operates totally off the grid. In the dead of winter, it is no colder than forty degrees. With a little solar heat, it is positively toasty.

Binx figures that if we could just find a way to get energy production out of private hands in order to supply free juice from natural, rechargeable sources, we would be halfway toward solving the rest of our problems. But human logic based on simple physics is no match for self-interested politics.

Whatever we do and however we do it, the crisis is now. Plato warned us 2,300 years ago. The soil erosion he saw turning fat land into bare bones is emblematic of far worse damage we cannot see. It is (for now, we can still use our favorite metaphor) the tip of the iceberg. Do not wait for more headlines.

FIVE

PLAGUES UPON US ALL

K inshasa needed no more bad news in the early 1980s. Mobutu Sese Seko, having squandered stolen billions, lived isolated in a jungle Versailles up the Congo River while mineral wealth that could feed all of Africa streamed into his European bank accounts. People dropped dead on the streets in the broken remnants of a capital city that once sparkled with life and light. Deep in the rain forests and savannahs, cut off by roads eroded with neglect, outsiders could only guess at the misery.

Down a reeking corridor of Mama Yemo Hospital, I met a young American doctor named Jonathan Mann who had a great deal of bad news. He puzzled over a mysterious virus believed linked to a small green monkey. It rendered the body vulnerable to just about any infection it encountered. And in Africa, there were plenty. Doctors called this autoimmune deficiency syndrome. Or, for short, AIDS.

Over the next quarter century, I watched this scourge move out of remote pockets of the Congolese hinterland to every part of the planet. We can explain away our difficulty at grasping terracide. AIDS is different. Nothing in human experience so far illustrates better our collective inability to confront the clear and present calamity of something we can see in front of us.

The word "plague" goes to back to antiquity. So does "epidemic" (*epi*, on, and *demos*, people). Plato used both terms often. Back then, rampant mysterious death was part of life. The Athens plague during the Peloponnesian Wars killed tens of thousands in a fairly small city. We might have learned since then how to curtail such contagion. Yet HIV/AIDS, after fast muscling past the epidemic stage, is a world pandemic. After a death toll near 30 million and so many words and promises, HIV/AIDS rages on, out of control.

Within a generation, deaths may reach 100 million. Each casualty comes with family suffering and societal cost. Haunting orphanages that TV cameras show us are only part of it. In Africa, the virus nullifies decades of foreign aid. China and Russia, for all their economic promise, are just beginning to feel the impact. America and Europe are plagued by recurring outbreaks. Yet we still do far too little—and often the wrong things.

Scientists have made important headway since the 1980s. Antiretroviral drugs can dramatically slow the advance in victims lucky enough to get hold of them. But, as Mann saw from the first, this is about much more than medicine. World leaders including, honorably, George W. Bush pledge to unite against AIDS, but promise outstrips delivery. Ideology and religion get in the way. Damage already done by ignorance, pride, avarice, apathy, political feuding, and obstinate tunnel vision has crippled whole societies.

Some African life expectancies have dropped to thirty-three years, far below their 1960 levels and forty-six years lower than Norway or Sweden. Death takes productive people in their twenties and thirties. Elsewhere, the patterns are clear. Whenever energetic prevention campaigns ebb, yet more sexually active young people and drug users fall victim.

Depredations aside, we had better take note of the larger lesson for humanity. HIV/AIDS shows with chilling clarity how inattention to the obvious can kill us.

For all that Mann's team did not know, they quickly saw that the most common vector was blood passed between humans during sexual intercourse. Condom use would contain it. Contaminated hypodermic injections were equally dangerous. Clean needles would fix that.

Before long, Mann saw something else. Because the disease had no symptoms of its own, it remained a fearful mystery among people who put great store in bad juju and unexplainable phenomena. If it could be demystified— if people did not give up in the face of a curse that was spread by an evil eye—families could care for their victims while containing the virus.

That would require large investments, with mobile teams traveling among vulnerable villages to counsel victims and educate their families and friends. National governments and local elders would have to be enlisted and enlightened. Yet little of that happened.

Mann moved from the laboratory to whatever public forums he could find. Eventually, he believed, doctors would find a way to treat HIV/AIDS, but he knew that was a long way off. Meantime, the only option was to control its spread. This was a public awareness challenge as much as a medical mystery. People everywhere had to know how to deal with it in their midst. Mostly, we ignored the threat.

Some of the blame falls on the press. Reporters did not fully understand what we were seeing. Few editors supplied the resources for us to dig harder. Yet every manner of human frailty contributed.

The virus divided those who sought to understand it. A French scientist in Montpellier and an American at the National Institutes of Health each made credible claims to its discovery. Rather than join forces, they worked separately, each barely concealing scorn for the other. Neither governments nor international agencies came up with sufficient funds. Though quick to respond to such definable outbreaks as cholera, they were stymied by a disease for which there was neither vaccine nor treatment. Most stricken nations denied its existence. Some, like Kenya, feared scaring tourists. Others, like India, said their cultures not did condone promiscuity or prostitution. An indifferent public found reasons not to give a damn.

Many people shrugged off the strange virus as yet another curse of the Dark Continent. The more callous remarked it would help control population. When it moved out of Africa, most victims were homosexual men. Anal sex easily tears tissue, causing an exchange of infected blood. The virus was a problem of deviates, perhaps even divine punishment. It reached Haiti, and yet another myth spread. This was a black man's affliction.

When AIDS spread into Europe, America, and Asia, people sought reasons to exclude themselves from worry. It did not threaten heterosexuals— at least not white heterosexuals. And then: Well, let's think about this, dear. It doesn't affect employed married Christians or nonkosher Jews living on Wisteria Lane. Phew. What else is in the paper today?

In 1986, as the pandemic ran rampant, the United Nations chose Mann to set up the Global Program on AIDS (GPA) within the World Health

Organization in Geneva. He assembled a nucleus of energetic experts inspired by his charisma and his disdain for bureaucracy. They traveled widely to assemble local teams in every country at risk.

Mann knew that any cure or vaccine was years away. Meantime, he faced a social problem. People had to see AIDS as a disease like any other, not as God's curse or a badge of shame. Victims needed care from loved ones, not ostracism. If communities understood it better, they would neither fear it nor demonize it.

AIDS was spread first in Africa by traders and travelers who moved freely across borders. Epidemiologists traced it via truckers' rest stops from Congo and Rwanda, through Uganda, and on to Mombasa in Kenya. Prostitutes carried it up the ranks of society. Government people and military officers jetted among African capitals for summits or other conclaves, always occasions to party. Early on, just as one example, Zambia's air force was grounded; most of its pilots were weakened by the virus.

While researchers sought breakthroughs in the lab, Mann's team focused on counseling stricken or vulnerable families, public-awareness education, and prevention. In those early years, a young Parisian physician named Michel Lavollay gave up his practice to specialize in the virus. He saw Mann was on the right track and joined GPA. A close friend, he kept me abreast of the early obstacles.

"The way to fight AIDS is to help people not to get infected in the first place," Lavollay told me back then. Medical science would eventually find answers, perhaps a vaccine or even a cure, he said, but endangered societies could not wait. "People have to understand the causes. They should know the threat but not let it become some bogeyman. There is an incredible amount of fear and ignorance and denial."

Over the years, Lavollay battled the virus from every angle, at U.N. agencies, as a French government specialist, in a private foundation, and at the Global Fund for AIDS. He set up local programs and looked at others in Africa, Asia, Latin America, and Europe. His spirits whipsawed from heights to depths. He was thrilled that Bush focused on AIDS but saddened to see an America-does-it-better approach that duplicated bureaucracy and wasted money.

Two decades after our first conversations, Lavollay says much of the world has yet to catch on. And most reporters still miss the point. HIV/AIDS, beyond disease, is a societal and economic scourge. That doggerel slogan "ABC: abstinence, be faithful, condoms" misses the point. Sex is here to stay. If that crucial "C," condom use, is blocked by moralists, the virus will spread yet faster.

In 1992, I followed Lavollay's leads to the pandemic's epicenters. HIV/AIDS was still mostly a mystery. When people got sick, they developed symptoms of other diseases. Doctors often misreported deaths. Many thought the virus was a myth, a Western invention to mess with their way of life. Others devised their own strategies, such as finding preteen virgin sex partners to limit the risk.

Uganda was hit hard at first. Families were decimated as the death toll soared. Then, with help from Mann's GPA, Uganda turned itself around. The government took firm, early action. Voluntary agencies ran clinics to treat families as well as victims. People began to see the virus as everyone's enemy. And, they saw, it could be contained.

Kenya, next door, ignored the threat. Government officials concealed the true numbers, assuring people that the threat was overblown. Casualties soared. Some countries, such as Botswana, reported low infection rates during the early 1990s, prompting not only a laxness in prevention but also a certain attitude of superiority. That would change dramatically over time.

In Uganda, Noerine Kaleeba took on AIDS as a personal foe after her husband died in 1987 from blood donated by his brother. Her extended family was decimated. By the time I met her, early in 1992, "the virus" had infected 1.5 million Ugandans and was quickly doing worse.

"We have given this thing our effort, our emotion, but still this monster doesn't seem to budge," she said at the immaculate but impoverished Nsambya Hospital in Kampala. Her support group, TASO, had worked hard to learn more about what they were up against. By then, TASO was world famous, and Noerine was on GPA's advisory committee.

"We need to organize the local scene and tell Geneva what we think," she said. "We know what we think will work in Uganda." For Africans, she said, "the virus" had to be demystified, taken as a simple fact of life so that its victims are not stigmatized in their communities.

Kaleeba had little faith in impersonal public health campaigns, which, she said, seldom worked. Africans liked to talk back and ask questions. Instead, she pushed for widespread testing.

If a promiscuous young man—a jumpy-jumpy, among Ugandans—tested negative, he was likely to heave a sigh of relief and watch out in the future. If positive, he could protect his family and alert friends to the danger.

Sister Miriam Duggan, an Irish medical missionary in Uganda for twenty-three years, administered Nsambya. She decided to devote the hospital to HIV/AIDS. "After all this time, we are still making surveys and all of these beautiful reports," she told me, bustling through an overcrowded ward like a white tornado. "Our priority should be people."

In Geneva, Lavollay realized the Ugandans had found a key. "We've learned that you need care and counseling together to establish trusting communication," he told me back then. "It has to be all mixed together if people are to work for prevention."

Countries that took a public head-on approach saw new infection rates slow; in Uganda, they began to drop. Elsewhere, it was different. If Uganda was a best case, India was a worst.

At the Executive Club in Bombay, where whiskey was cheap and cockroaches grew to three inches, I watched young men drink up for an unwitting game of Indian roulette. When I arrived in 1992, one prostitute in three was HIV positive in large cities, yet few of their clients knew that a two-dollar quickie could be fatal.

"You can't see AIDS, so what is it?" Deepak Sharma, a twenty-six-year-old travel agent, asked me. "You can see leprosy, deformity, but not AIDS. You will not make people understand just by telling them about it." He used condoms, he said, but hardly anyone else he knew did.

Tara Bibi, squatting over her cash box in a squalid brothel, laughed off the danger. This was six years after Indians began dying of AIDS. "We heard about it a few months ago," she said with a shrug. "Sometimes, customers use condoms. If they don't want, what to do?" One of the girls, Soni Nepali, twenty-one, had unprotected sex four or five times a night when she was not too weak from coughing away the last of her life.

Rob Oostvogels, a U.N. consultant, told me about a well-schooled truck driver he knew named Sunil. He visited fifteen prostitutes a month and regularly slept with two wives, a girlfriend at the other end of India, and the young boy who cleaned his truck. "I try to persuade him, but he just can't make the connection," Oostvogels said. "He is full of health, and he says his sex drive proves it. He says, 'If you are right, big problem.' "

During the crucial 1990s, India's approach was common. National authorities denied the danger. After all, they insisted, AIDS could not be a problem. Their society shunned unmarried sex and had no prostitutes.

Today, Noerine Kaleeba works in Geneva, fighting for minor successes at UNAIDS, the successor to Mann's GPA. "We have to be optimistic," she told me when I found her again. "If we are not, think of the consequences."

India still struggles with a pandemic it is loath to acknowledge. When the world's sixteenth biennial conclave on HIV/AIDS met in Toronto during 2006, Anand Grover, an activist Indian attorney, delivered the Jonathan Mann Memorial Lecture. Now drugs are available, and 700,000 Indians need them, he said. Yet India's target was to provide free first-line treatment to no more than 188,000 and then only by 2010. Meantime, no provision has been made for second-line drugs, which will be badly needed.

Similar problems bedevil the rest of the world, Grover said, because of governments but also because of drug manufacturers who seek profits beyond what is reasonable. In many countries, he said, American obstacles prevent developing countries from supplying cheap generic drugs, even to the point of denying data about the safe use of the originals.

"It is high time that we tell U.S. pharma companies and the U.S. trade representative with one voice that we shall not succumb to their money power," he said, "and we will fight to see that the rights of our people to affordable drug prices are protected."

People who know the pharmaceutical industry well hear truth in Grover's words. "Look, this is not about AIDS," a well-placed specialist told me. "Companies are scared shitless this will become a precedent and people everywhere will want cheaper drugs for other things, too." They can afford to be more generous, he added. True, he said, drugs cost money to develop. But those numbers are not public. At some point, high prices can offer huge excess profits. "Believe me," my source concluded, "they do all right."

Grover raised human rights issues, unresolved after twenty-five years of debate, over consent for testing and to what extent potentially lethal AIDS victims can be prevented from knowingly infecting others. A great many carriers and sufferers of HIV/AIDS do not know they are infected. He assailed U.S. prisons where many inmates, particularly blacks, contract AIDS for lack of condoms. And he added a broader reproach: "President Bush has to be told again that his ABC policy is killing people in the U.S."

But Grover's main theme was Jonathan Mann. "It was because of him," he said, "that we have an understanding that communities that are marginalized by society are vulnerable to HIV." That is, the people who need the most help are the ones who get the least. As a result, HIV/AIDS spreads upward and outward to every level.

Now HIV/AIDS runs rampant among drug users in Russia, spreading fast to a broader population. After years of denial, China now acknowledges a critical problem it ignored while focusing on other priorities. In 2004, President Hu Jintao appeared on television with AIDS victims, shaking hands and chatting. But authorities can only guess at the true extent of the problem. During the first ten months of 2006, health workers found a one-third increase in HIV-positive Chinese over all of 2005. Figures from UN-AIDS show that infections have grown by 30 percent annually since 1999. Privately, U.N. officials say the actual number may be five times higher, somewhere above a million. Government surveys show that only 39 percent of Chinese prostitutes use condoms. And 51 percent of drug addicts still share their needles.

Like so many scourges that once could be limited to specific parts of the planet, the virus has gone global.

HIV/AIDS gained an early upper hand, at first because too few people understood it and then because too many people wanted to play the leading role against it. In hindsight, it is a distressing example of how human nature and national politics can stymie urgent worldwide action.

As a new medical mystery, the virus fell under the purview of the U.N. World Health Organization (WHO). Halfdan Mahler, a Danish doctor who took over as WHO director in 1973, had infused new energy into a somnambulant agency. In 1985, Mahler cautioned against exaggerating the danger of AIDS. A year later, he told a news conference that he had made a "gross underestimate"; in fact, it was "a health disaster of pandemic proportions."

As many as 10 million people were already infected, Mahler said, and within five years that figure could be 100 million. AIDS was threatening to spiral out of control in Asia. Mahler estimated WHO would need $1.5 billion by the 1990s. Even with that, he said, some member states lacked the "political guts" to confront the virus. "We're running scared," he told the New York Times, adding that he could not imagine a worse health problem in the twentieth century.

"We stand nakedly in front of a very serious pandemic as mortal as any pandemic there ever has been," Mahler said to the Times. "I don't know of any greater killer than AIDS, not to speak of its psychological, social and economic maiming. Everything is getting worse and worse in AIDS and all of us have been underestimating it, and I in particular. . . . Just to speak of sickness and death is not a proper identification of the AIDS problem because you must also take into account the psycho-social dimension that makes it a tremendous problem to parents, religious organizations, schools, political authorities, you name it."[1]

Mahler set up the Global Program on AIDS in Geneva, and he named

Mann to shape it. Shortly after, he retired. Hiroshi Nakajima, a Japanese doctor with another approach entirely, succeeded him. Underlying friction soon worked its way to the surface.

With his flamboyant style and dramatic cause, Mann often outshined his taciturn boss. He made waves by rallying world support. When health ministers underplayed the threat, he pointed fingers. And this was Nakajima's power base. At U.N. agencies, directors are chosen by committees of member states. Political and personal accommodation can outweigh competence.

Nakajima, an old-school medical man, saw AIDS as a disease, not a social or economic issue. He favored research to find a silver bullet to kill the virus. More, WHO insiders told me, he resented GPA for overshadowing the rest of his broad program. As his reelection approached in 1993, U.S. and European governments supported someone else to do the job. Nakajima's supporters fought back.

WHO sources gave me a list of gift-bearing visits the director's aides made to Third World commission members. I wrote the story, but AP editors were cautious. Finally, a cut-down version ran on April 29, only days before ballots were cast. The dispatch began:

"The Japanese head of the U.N. World Health Organization appears likely to be reelected, though his agency has been tainted with bribery allegations under his stewardship. If Hiroshi Nakajima is reelected, some donors may cut back funds to WHO, which leads the world fight against AIDS, infectious diseases, and tropical maladies that endanger millions in developing countries."

Donald Henderson, the new U.S. deputy assistant secretary of health and human services, confirmed that Japanese supporters had given cash, expensive jewelry, or cars to voting members. "There have been payments made," Henderson said. WHO sources said secret payments ranged between $20,000 and $50,000.

Nakajima won the election. Disgusted, Mann left GPA. His successor cut back on counseling and prevention, following Nakajima's emphasis on finding a medical solution. Mann took his team to the Harvard School of Public Health, where he continued work on a multifaceted campaign, but he had limited impact on policy and few funds. In 1998, he died when his plane crashed en route to Geneva. Nakajima, though never charged with anything, was eventually forced out.

Michel Lavollay stayed at GPA. Getting nowhere, he joined a brilliant Australian named Elizabeth Reid at the U.N. Development Program

(UNDP) to find new ways to attack the pandemic. UNDP's AIDS busters ran two-week workshops, with role-playing in a range of scenarios, to train teams from stricken countries. It was a novel U.N. approach, thinking outside of boxes and telling governments hard truths.

Soon the UNDP program came under attack by a new team at GPA. An inevitable U.N. inertia dulled its impact. Frustrated at yet more bureaucratic obstacles from people who should be saving lives, Lavollay joined the Jonas Salk Foundation. The grand old man who defeated polio had turned his attention to HIV/AIDS. As Salk's point man, Lavollay helped assemble a consensus among agencies that had often worked at cross-purposes. But Salk died, and the energy behind him dissipated.

In his next job, as the French embassy science attaché in Washington, Lavollay hammered away. He worked quietly behind the scenes, acting as a bridge between American, French, and other specialists. He worked with Richard Holbrooke to shape an initiative to persuade private business to contribute in the fight. Lavollay helped push HIV/AIDS to the top of Kofi Annan's U.N. agenda. But for all the words member states aimed at a pandemic that threatened them all, they gave little for research, social programs, and prevention campaigns.

Finally, in 2002, world leaders vowed to get serious. A G-8 summit established the Global Fund to Fight AIDS, Tuberculosis, and Malaria to channel billions of dollars into national programs that showed results. Richard Feachem, a British medical professor at the University of California in San Francisco and Berkeley, was chosen to head it. Lavollay signed on as a senior adviser.

Feachem moved quickly and pledges piled in. But those world leaders, with little time for fine print, neglected some basics. The Global Fund mandate did not say how it would fit in with UNAIDS, the operational agency which replaced GPA. UNAIDS had few resources for its broad program. Feachem wanted to fund national programs that followed his own approach. Predictably, a turf war ensued.

Meantime, Nakajima's successor at the World Health Organization devised a program of his own, the "3-by-5" initiative to give antiretroviral drugs to three million people within five years. Without coordination from other agencies, the program fell far short of its goal.

During 2003, I went back to Geneva to look at the new approach to AIDS. The pandemic ran rampant in Africa and India but also threatened China, Russia, and Eastern Europe. It had gone beyond sex. People sold their own untested tainted blood. Drug users passed around needles.

"Coping mechanisms are collapsing," Feachem told me. Speaking epi-
demiologically, he was blunt about the previous decades: "On an effectively
large scale, we have done nothing. We haven't achieved any of the changes
that would have made a difference. If in 1982 when we became aware of
the virus we had decided to do nothing in order to observe its course without intervention, the world would be roughly where it is today."

Down the road, Peter Piot, the Dutch director of UNAIDS, agreed that
denial and inaction allowed the virus to spread out of Africa to an alarming
degree. "In Asia and eastern Europe, the political leadership isn't there," he
said. He added that at a recent meeting in India, "I heard great speeches, but
as for action, zero."

The U.N. General Assembly was about to gather for a special session
on AIDS, buoyed by a promise of $15 billion George W. Bush had made
in his State of the Union address. I interviewed dozens of specialists in
Geneva and phoned others elsewhere. Unanimously, they were happy at
the promised wherewithal, yet skeptical. Many predicted what hindsight
revealed. Much was wasted because of a go-it-alone approach. Condoms
were shunned. After four years, about $4 billion in fresh money reached 14
targeted countries. By our new unit of measure, that equaled two weeks
in Iraq.

Jockeying by other bilateral donors, U.N. agencies, and voluntary
groups blunted a common effort. Some of the neediest nations lost out to
others where authorities knew how to work the system.

"I don't think there is malevolence here but rather genuine confusion,
a sort of land scramble, where everyone is competing for the same small
amount of funding," David Miller told me. He was a senior UNAIDs specialist from New Zealand whom I had come to respect when he ran the GPA
program in India. "You've got every country learning their own lessons.
Nothing is clear. It's like gazing at a plate of spaghetti."

Lavollay was outraged. "You've got the money in one agency and the
operational people in another," he said. "It's a five-minute drive away, but
it's an unbridgeable gap." Meantime, 95 percent of infected people did not
know they had the virus. "We are still not collectively capable of seeing the
kind of world AIDS is going to create."

Even new billions pledged amounted to "peanuts" compared to what
was needed, Feachem said. The Global Fund had sought a "cruising speed"
five-year budget of $7 billion to fight AIDS, tuberculosis, and malaria.
That is, less than one donor alone spent each month on a pointless war. By
then, the G–8 nations that set up the Global Fund had collectively given

$4.7 billion. UNAIDS, with a staff of 250, had a yearly budget of only $95 million.

Before leaving Geneva, I lured Noerine Kaleeba to a lunch table far from her UNAIDS office. Years of battling the monster had done nothing to muffle her belly laugh, but she struggled with frustration. Though encouraged by Bush's interest, she knew the crisis was about more than money. Those first lessons of the early 1980s had yet to sink in.

She dismissed rich-world claims that antiretroviral cocktails were too sophisticated for the Third World because they must be taken regularly and on time. "People still say Africans can't use drugs because they don't have watches," she said, with a mirthful rumble. "We have roosters." If few Africans have access to the drugs, she said, studies show that 85 percent of those who do take them exactly as ordered. In the developed world, the figure is 70 percent.

I remember that lunch when I read fresh stories about HIV/AIDS. Some rave uncritically about new initiatives, cash infusions, and statistical blips suggesting progress. Others are unfairly dismissive. The reality is mixed.

We spent twenty-five years doing far too little—and often the wrong thing. We miss the lessons of our failures. Now, movers like Bill Clinton and Richard Holbrooke beat the bushes to raise billions from private industry. Bill Gates and Warren Buffett reach into their own deep pockets.

"I'm still an optimist," Noerine concluded. "It is never too late to take action. But the question is how much has this already cost us?"

Lavollay was disgusted at the replenishment meetings in London in 2005 where donors came up with Global Fund pledges. According to the plan, the United States and the European Union would each provide a third of the fund's resources. Others would make up the rest. Before the first meeting, as donors had agreed, specialists produced ballpark numbers. An effective fight against HIV/AIDS, it calculated, needed $8 billion in the first year, rising to $10 billion and then $12 billion over three years.

But in the closed meeting, Lavollay said, the U.S. delegate insisted that no numbers be used. Washington, having overspent in Iraq and elsewhere, wanted no invidious comparisons. After days of wasted time, the numbers were adopted. In the end, the Global Fund asked for a minimum $7.1 billion. It got $3.7 billion. The United States gave 15 percent to the European Union's 55 percent.

When internal problems crippled the Global Fund in 2006, Lavollay moved on yet again. By then, the fund's donors—the world's richest nations—had committed a total of $5.5 billion in 132 countries to fight not only AIDS but also tuberculosis and malaria.

T he virus, in the meantime, raged on in the very places it first started a quarter century ago. Look, for one chilling example, at Zimbabwe.

I met Robert Mugabe at his first African summit soon after he led Britain's colony of Rhodesia to independence in 1980. A bitter war could have left deep hatred, but the young prime minister sought reconciliation. The place was an epitome of storybook Africa, rich and beautiful and full of game. White commercial farmers grew cash crops, and black families tilled food that they took to market.

In Salisbury, now Harare, a lovely city where purple jacaranda blooms floated onto lush gardens, the deposed white leader, Ian Smith, had his say in Parliament. With full granaries, good hospitals, and a smoothly run civil service, Zimbabwe defied Africa's detractors.

Late in 2006, Daniel Howden of the London daily *Independent* found how much places can change. Mugabe had evolved into a power obsessed despot with a thin grip on reality. Eighty percent of Zimbabweans have no work, 85 percent live in poverty, and the country faces 2,000 percent inflation.[2]

Among other things, Mugabe ignored the threat of AIDS. As a result, the World Health Organization tracked women's life expectancy from sixty-five a decade ago to the lowest in the world: thirty-four. Privately, WHO officials told Howden the true figure may be no more than thirty. Men live marginally longer. But in the army, the HIV infection rate is 90 percent.

AIDS, along with a food crisis and an economic collapse, kills 3,500 people a week. Destitute families pool their savings into burial societies. One twenty-six-year-old woman told Howden, "In the last three months we've had to bury 14 of the 50 people in our society."

Despite repression from secret police, the activist group Women of Zimbabwe Arise (WOZA) has swelled to perhaps thirty thousand members. Its founder, a businesswoman named Jenni Williams, keeps on despite arrests and death threats. "It's very hard for a policeman to intimidate us when his mum, his sister, or his girlfriend is there as one of us," she told Howden. "I'm very proud to be a Zimbabwean woman right now. Why should a woman carry all these burdens and be silent?"

Why indeed? In such a situation, HIV/AIDS is a verifiable and observable weapon of mass destruction.

During 2006, Michel Lavollay saw new hope. Bill and Melinda Gates made their dramatic announcement: Warren Buffett had doubled the resources of their foundation, so they had $60 billion to spend on selected projects. Much of that would go toward fighting AIDS and malaria. Meantime, Holbrooke's campaign to involve private business began to pay off. By 2006, American corporations were kicking in significantly.

But, as usual, hope bumped hard against reality. Whatever resources can be marshaled, the answer is more than money. New programs tend to push aside hard-fought victories: "not invented here." Donors wrangle over the morality of birth control and the ability of poor people to take pills on schedule.

Late in 2006, UNAIDS published an update. The pandemic was growing in every part of the world, and it seemed to be resurging in countries where success had been declared. Even Uganda was sliding backward. In eight African countries, the virus had declined among young people, showing that prevention helps. Yet 2.9 million people died in 2006, the worst year ever, and another 4.3 million were infected. Peter Piot, at of UNAIDS, said "countries are not moving at the same speed as their epidemics."[3]

As new strategies lagged, I went back to see Lavollay. As both friend and physician, his judgment had proven sound over thirty years. Long and lanky, with brooding eyes under bristling black brows, he has never taken the world lightly. Now a speckled gray beard lends an air of the kindly wise uncle. He is more troubled than ever.

Lavollay had given up on the press, American and European. When he finally got fed up with UNDP, he wrote a twenty-page report that explained why international efforts to curb the pandemic were failing. A French newsweekly wrote about it, but no one else did. The mainstream was not interested in one insider's truth without he-said, she-said "balance" from the usual suspects. AP was typical. Beat reporters covered medicine from headquarters; actual observation from abroad was discouraged. "There was a three-page article in *Le Point,* and that's it," Lavollay said with a bitter laugh. "Next."

During the Global Fund battles, he saw, few reporters paid attention or understood what was at stake. Distortion by smart press spokespeople resulted in self-serving, and misleading, headlines. Thoughtful articles by specialists raised only limited interest among readers.

Lavollay's broader optimism, which he describes as fed by pessimism and growing anger, was beginning to wane. He saw some specialists who had done the most damage writing books and presenting themselves as pioneering heroes. He saw the same mistakes being made while yet more money and time were wasted.

The future is guesswork, but of all the HIV/AIDS experts I have met since those early Jon Mann days, I trust Lavollay the most. Unlike others, he has no job to protect. He prefers the background, and this passage will likely embarrass him. With his close-at-hand knowledge of the epidemiology, he believes that in the coming years, perhaps even a decade, 70 million more people may die of AIDS. Never mind how much damage that could do to national economies. That is seven holocausts.

"We know what works. We don't need any more studies," Lavollay said. "We know the combination of factors: political will, priorities, finance. If a university looked at this as a case study, there would be a solution in two hours. But something about these issues makes them belong to another planet."

Much has been done against HIV/AIDS, he allows. "We are in a better place today than we were five years ago but very far from where we should be. Once a political moment is finished, you have a technical moment in which you have to make things happen. Political attention never remains high for long. We have now sufficient mechanisms in place for what is required to solve the problem. This creates the delusion that we are solving it. This is where I always get in trouble, by asking, 'What about this? What about that?'"

Now, Lavollay concluded, we need to hold public officials accountable so that so more time or resources are squandered. "No one has the right to do these things," he said. "There has to be a place where moral and political dimensions are expressed, and that would make it impossible for these people to behave in this way. We have a Security Council that considers war and peace. How can it be that we are not looking at this in terms of war and peace?"

HIV/AIDS is the pandemic we all talk about most. Tuberculosis is a much older and more familiar killer. TB can be treated with a simple course of four antibiotics at a cost totaling as little as eleven dollars. Yet nearly 2 million people a year still die of it.

The catch is that the antibiotics must be taken daily for six to nine months. Local health clinics need a steady supply. Patients must keep at it even when they stop coughing and in spite of nasty side effects. If they move on, as destitute migrants do, they risk a more virulent TB that is resistant to the basic drugs. Once this happens, treatment takes two years at a prohibitive cost of $10,000. In some places, because of poor adherence to treatment, many cases are now incurable.

Doctors devised a strategy in Tanzania during the 1970s which is now common across the Third World. It is called Directly Observed Treatment, Short-Course, or DOTS. Patients rely on a friend or family member to make sure they stay the course. China, after switching to DOTS, raised its cure rate from 52 percent to 95 percent. With help from the World Bank, China pays village health workers to find patients and shepherd them through full treatment.

Proponents say DOTS brings a return to local societies of sixty dollars for every dollar spent. It costs little because health workers, rather than physicians, do most of the work. However the figures work out, the approach demonstrates that the worst medical challenges can be stopped when someone decides to confront them.

Lesser-known diseases with more syllables than most people want to pronounce keep on killing. Schistosomiasis affects 200 million people, and almost none of them are American. (Only the more common name, bilharzia, appears in my Microsoft spell-check, and it is spelled wrong.) Ask any African living near a lake what happens when the little parasite penetrates human tissue. Trypanosomiasis is African sleeping sickness transmitted by the tsetse fly. Onchocerciasis is river blindness.

As scary as those diseases may sound, they kill far fewer children than the familiar strains of measles that kids in richer places shrug off with a few days home from school. And malaria, which we once seemed to have beaten into submission, continues to plague vast areas.

Malaria ought to be a modern success story. It is carried by the anopheles mosquito, which takes flight only for a few hours at night. Bed nets impregnated with insecticide can protect children, the most vulnerable victims, while they sleep. Mosquitoes carry malaria from an infected human bloodstream to healthy ones. With fewer infections, the number of cases diminishes sharply.

Carlos "Kent" Campbell, head of the Gates Foundation malaria program, has worked out the numbers. Bed nets, he calculates, would drop the child mortality rate from malaria by 80 percent. One day's expenditure in Iraq would buy ten nets for every African child at risk. That would save 800,000 lives a year.

Campbell grew up with a Renaissance intellect and an evolved conscience in eastern Tennessee, the oldest son of an oldest son of an oldest son in an affluent Methodist Baptist family. "We had a very strong sense that if you had the luxury of being well-educated, that came with certain obligations," he said. Fighting pointless wars was not one of them. He sat out Vietnam at Haverford College in Philadelphia and studied medicine at Duke. At Harvard, he specialized in pediatrics and public health. As a young doctor in El Salvador, he watched malaria up close.

After more work at Harvard, Campbell went to the Centers for Disease Control and Prevention in Atlanta, where for fifteen years he ran the malaria program. But after a time as founding dean of the University of Arizona's College of Public Health, he ached to get back to the real world. And he heard that the Gates Foundation wanted a malaria expert.

Campbell bounces peripatetically from Zambian wetlands to wetter Seattle to meetings in Geneva. Though known mostly among health experts, he earned notoriety in a *New Yorker* article for an accurate remark: "I don't think Americans give a rat's ass about the death of millions of African kids each year."

He thought that was off the record, he told me later, but it was true. "How you tell is where people put their money and time," he said. "We give far and away less than anyone to poor people in Africa. It isn't that we're callous, but we just don't grasp what is needed. And that's pretty discouraging when you look at our willingness to spend money to kill people."

But he still faces an uphill fight, not only because of public indifference but also because of entrenched ideas from the past. Some aid people argue that bed nets are a bad idea because they end up as bridal veils and market baskets. Others push for massive spraying, with the return of the DDT that seemed so effective when targeted in malarial zones but was banned as a danger to bird populations.

With long field experience, Campbell dismisses the first objection. "Of course, there is always some slippage in Africa," he said, using a polite term for theft. "You cannot expect a perfect system." To the second, he has a more scientific reaction.

Contrary to common wisdom, mosquito larvae seldom grow in large bodies of standing water. They are mostly in tiny puddles, such as in footprints or the folds of leaves. Aerial spraying, he believes, wastes money and rattles the ecology. The mosquitoes' short life cycle and tenacity are such that malaria is not likely to be eradicated in any particular area, but it can be cut to a minimum and regularly controlled to prevent new outbreaks.

More than kill insects, Campbell believes, health workers must protect people. He expects Gates Foundation bounty to allow specialists to go beyond old development models. "There has always been a quantitative approach to public health," he said. "We've never had this kind of resource. Now we can concentrate on the qualitative aspects to make a much more broadly based commitment. With serious big money, we can do serious things."

Campbell knows from experience that a hundred different million-dollar grants carry far less power than a single $100 million project. Rather than try something in hopes of renewed funding, specialists can design for the long term.

"When we started, we insisted on a ten-year assured funding stream," he said. "We would rather have less money over a larger period of time." The idea is to partner with affected countries and help governments make their own plans. Rather than fund outside contractors, as USAID does, Campbell prefers to build local capacities. The fresh Buffett money allowed him to expand his program fourfold.

"We provide a blend of technical advice with local experience," he said. "A lot of learning goes on from both sides. This gets us away from the project model, with a continual uphill fight for more funding. We can work with governments to figure out how to best program over time."

Campbell is enthusiastic about the Gates approach. "They're coming at this with an agenda, a strong sense of responsibility. I walked through Zambia with Melinda recently and saw her sense of this."

In a larger sense, Campbell added, "I actually believe this is about driving the way nations think about what they do. Bill and Melinda Gates now have the kind of influence that presidents of large countries have. They are in a position to drive the agenda. Their approach is not just about service provision and filling gaps but to really transform how people think about these problems. What kind of arrogance must Bill and Steve Balmer have had to take operating systems and transform the way the world thinks? Yet they have done it."

The challenge now, he concludes, is to show dramatic results within three to five years before people lose heart. Malaria is a not a major world priority. "We've been given an enormous opportunity. We don't have any excuses. It is not that African governments aren't interested. They are. In the absence of viable excuses, we have to perform."

The microbes behind our plagues and pandemics are not the only cause of disease. New studies show the next generation's greatest crippler will be mental disorders. For far too many of us, dealing with life in a fast-changing world has gotten to be beyond our control.

The causes of killer stress are everywhere, as interconnected down deep as they seem disparate on the surface. For some of us, the problem is confusion from the pressure of too many choices. For others, it is the lack of any choice at all.

As the new millennium dawned, the Harvard School of Public Health and the World Health Organization, with a hundred specialists around the world, embarked on a ten-volume study of what will cripple us in 2020 and 2030. Its report, *The Global Burden of Disease and Injury Series*, is harrowing. In much of the world, it concludes, the greatest cause of disability and premature death will be depression. Partly, this reflects better health care. But more, a new sort of world is driving many of us, quite literally, nuts.

In the coming decades, HIV/AIDS is projected to take the greatest worldwide toll: 12.1 percent. But unipolar depressive disorder, or depression, comes second at 5.7 percent. HIV/AIDS is followed by birth complications in the poorest countries, depression is a close third. For rich countries, mental problems head the list at 9.8 percent. Heart disease is next, at 5.9 percent, just above Alzheimer's or other dementia.

According to studies by the International Rivers Networks, for instance, 80 million dam refugees have been uprooted from their lives.[4] Some are doing fine. Many more live on an edge, their souls and spirits as shattered as their livelihoods. In India, desperate farmers for whom globalization is no panacea are killing themselves at alarming rates.

At any one time, 20 million human beings—persons of concern, in U.N. parlance—are on the move in search of help toward a livable life. These are people displaced by war and some other mostly man-made calamity. Many will die of exposure, bad water, or the simplest of diseases. This may not qualify as a pandemic in public health terms. But why quibble? As world crises worsen, the numbers will grow until we cannot ignore them even if we choose to try.

If we cannot agree on a common strategy to confront something that is not as well defined as HIV/AIDS, it will be harder still to address shapeless misery. The first step is for us to better understand what is going wrong—and why. From there, we can look for some solutions.

SIX

THE GENEROSITY SHAM

Someone recently forwarded me one of those moronic e-mails that choke our in-boxes. Eighteen Middle Eastern and South Asian nations that receive U.S. aid, it said, often vote against Washington in the United Nations. "And," it concluded with a nonsentence, "the American workers who are having to skimp and sacrifice to pay the TAXES."

An ironclad article of faith across the United States is that Americans are wildly generous to a less fortunate world. And few things trigger resentment like perceived ingratitude for this selfless largesse. That e-mail, which missed the point on several counts, was a perfect example.

We would be far safer, and likely more prosperous, if we were as open-handed as we believe. Allister Sparks, a wise South African journalist, offers irrefutable logic: Poverty begets hatred; hatred begets terrorism.

In fact, when it comes to official aid, we are the stingiest of the world's wealthy nations. True enough, Americans' private gifts and foundation grants add up to substantial help. But development assistance takes a coordinated, comprehensive approach by donor governments.

Try this exercise: Ask people around you how much the United States gives of its annual gross domestic product (GDP) for emergency relief as well as long-term aid to help countries develop, reduce poverty, and avert calamities. Answers will likely fall in the 10 to 15 percent range.

But look at the numbers. In 1992, rich countries pledged at a poverty summit in Rio de Janeiro to give 0.7 percent of GDP to help distressed societies to catch up. That is not much; more than a billion people live on less than a dollar a day. In 2006, we gave 0.17 percent of GDP, one-half the average of other donors. Only Greece did worse, by 0.01 percent.[1]

Our total development assistance was $22.7 billion, about four dollars a month per American, and that included aid to Iraq. Bill Gates and Warren Buffett alone fund a foundation with three times more. And even at that paltry level, rhetoric on Capitol Hill denounces our profligacy abroad when aid is needed at home.

Sweden gave the most: 1.03 percent. Norway, Denmark, and Luxembourg were close behind. Ireland reached 0.53, just ahead of Britain, Belgium, Austria and France. In all, "ODA"—as aid pros refer to the basic data—came to $103.9 billion, a 5.4 percent drop from 2005. These numbers are calculated by the Organization for Economic Co-operation and Development. Others quibble, but orders of magnitude do not change.

Late in 2006, OECD analysts produced a chart of predicted ODA increases for 2010. Not forecasts, they were based on public announcements by member governments. European Union members were committed to raise aid levels from 0.44 percent of GDP in 2005 to 0.59 in 2010, a 51 percent increase in real terms. Greece was expected to augment contributions by 239 percent. United States ODA was predicted to be 0.18 percent of GDP, the lowest behind Japan's 0.22 percent. That would be a drop of 11 percent. Numbers are only part of it. What really matters is the purpose of aid, the way it is dispensed and monitored, and, in the end, whether donors learn from their mistakes. Nordic nations examine each project in hindsight, with brutal public criticism of whatever goes wrong. The United States and other Western European countries often find excuses for their foul-ups, which are repeated elsewhere.

In terms of intent and past history, America deserves much credit. Legislation on aid to other nations is meant to be noble. It says nothing about buying U.N. votes. Any European who is old enough knows how the Marshall Plan put together the pieces of a shattered continent. We helped to energize a crippled Korea and tried hard to aid emerging Africa. We still have the will to do the right thing. Our trouble today is defining what that is.

In fact, we seldom reach desperate people whose poverty breeds resentment to our wealth. Foreign aid is often designed to help developing states to be trading partners. Much of it goes to U.S. shippers, contractors, and high-salaried experts.

When tragic images draw America's attention to a specific emergency, we rush to help. Up-close disaster reporting triggers fast response, and people care as long as the cameras keep running. But these spurts of momentary charity mask a much larger generosity sham. We neglect development: durable aid to halt land erosion, build roads and infrastructure, train teachers and health workers, along with police who do not abuse the citizenry.

A holocaust recurs every hundred days—10 million people die—mostly because families lack things rich nations could cheaply provide: clean water, basic health care, and a single daily meal. With catchment dams and market roads, many could then take care of themselves. Well-conceived larger projects could kick-start economies.

Helping poor nations was always important, but optional, for simple human reasons. Now we can no longer rely on the whims of public interest or be deterred by politicians who distort the realities of aid. We need to get effective help to the right people. In a changed world, our own prosperity and security are at risk. This is not only about *them*; it is as much about us.

Over the last half century, richer countries have given poorer ones at least $1.4 trillion. That is roughly equivalent to annual world arms sales, and it is near the cost of the Iraq War. Much of this was stolen. And, more, badly conceived, made things worse.

Some recipient states should not need help. Nigeria, Africa's biggest nation with huge oil reserves, is a mess of its own making. Only now Nigerians are trying to trace $400 billion in oil revenues that disappeared in the 1970s and 1980s. Congo, eternally destitute, has mineral wealth beyond description. Leaders simply steal it. Sudan, with a stretch of Nile running from rain forest to desert, could feed all of Africa.

Critics insist this is a reason to stop providing aid. But that would kill millions more people, while swelling the ranks of a bitter underclass.

During 1985, a year after outsiders began to notice African famine, I talked to Tarekegne Taka, an Ethiopian economist who directed African development for the U.N. Food and Agriculture Organization (FAO). No question, he said, some leaders in Africa neglected land and agriculture, hid famine to save embarrassment, kept food from political foes, and condoned theft, corruption, and incompetence. But the victims of this have no control over their fate. "If the donors are not equipped to handle the crisis, the recipients are even less so," Taka told me. "Either you want to save lives or you don't."

The previous year, 1984, everyone had sung "We Are the World." When the cameras moved on, people assumed the crisis was past. In fact, it was just beginning. Africa is like a man dying, Taka said back then. "When vital organs go, the rest follow. Drought hits hard because the body is weak. The West thinks once the rains come, it will be over. That's not true."

Although Africans are the most desperate, most share a resource beyond value: an indescribably positive spirit and an ability to work miracles with whatever they have at hand. Serious money applied sensibly, and sustained over time, could finally set Africa on an upward path. The women alone could probably do it.

Years ago, I came across a Harvard study that rang true: It found a typical 130-pound African woman can carry twenty-six pounds on her head for most of a morning without burning any extra calories. Think what she could do with a market road and a lift on a neighbor's truck.

Latin Americans, Asians, and others need different sorts of help. Sometimes, a fairer shake for commodity prices is enough. More often, local imbalances require careful analysis and long-term assistance to be put right. But all foreign aid has one thing is common. If it is designed to help the donor more than the recipient, it will feed frustration and hard feelings down the road.

Taka at the FAO foresaw growing hostility among Africans who saw their families and fields perish because of Western indifference. Over the next quarter century, his words took on deeper meaning by the year: "Our children will never forgive you. They will never forget."

Foreign aid numbers confuse more than they reveal. Much of that global total was spent on hiring friends during the decades when the United States duked it out with the Soviet Union in a postcolonial world. African dictators played Washington against Moscow, packing away aid fortunes their people never saw. Useless white elephants and stupid schemes ate up billions. Each year, leaders of former French Africa visited the Elysée Palace to pick up a check to cover their deficits.

It is a different world now, but much of the old approach remains. Foreign assistance is tied to political objectives and economic interests. Any impoverished nonpermanent member that joins the Security Council can expect a jolt of fresh U.S. aid. Recipients are not usually the neediest. More often, they are those that attempt, or feign, our way of doing business. Laws still stipulate a role for U.S. contractors and suppliers.

Prevailing social philosophy plays its part. When a Republican president opposes condom use, family planning and AIDS prevention feel the impact.

Funds given through multilateral organizations like the World Bank and U.N. agencies must be factored into the mix. Some is stolen; much is squandered. It is spread among a lot of pockets, legitimately or not. Debt relief as aid can amount to no more than helping kleptocracies survive to oppress their poor yet more.

Military grants take different budget lines. Some bankroll proxy armies. Colombia is getting $4.7 billion over six years so its tough-minded officers can combat drug production. That also helps them quell political dissidence, and Washington looks the other way.

The biggest regular U.S. payments go to Israel, at $3 billion a year, and Egypt, at $2 billion. This was part of a Nobel Prize–winning peace package to help both nations work toward Middle East peace.

That anti-aid e-mail I mentioned at the start of this chapter singled out Egypt for particular abuse. In fact, the money is well spent. Egypt, populous and secular, takes risks to keep a lid on a rough neighborhood. If Cairo sees things differently from Washington at the U.N., it is wise to understand why. It would be better if Hosni Mubarak were less of a tyrant. But that is not our call.

Pakistan, the e-mail said, votes three-quarters of the time against America while receiving $6,721,000. If that tiny number were correct, the price of six Cruise missiles would be a pretty good deal for a country that watches our back in Afghanistan, sort of, while we are busy in Iraq.

During the five years following 9/11, Pakistan actually received billions, but it is not simple largesse. General Pervez Musharraf put his life on the line—separate assassination attempts missed him by seconds—to enable Washington to pursue a Taliban that earlier Pakistani leaders were instrumental in creating. Had Washington helped Pakistan develop its public school system, as real foreign aid, there would likely have been far fewer of the extremist madrasas that feed terrorists' ranks.

Qatar is mentioned as voting against the United States 67 percent of the time. The little emirate did, however, allow U.S. troops to mount an invasion from its soil. And, sitting atop trillions of dollars' worth of burnable energy, it can afford to send foreign aid to us.

To his credit, George W. Bush has tried to push foreign aid levels higher, particularly in Africa. For fiscal year 2007, his administration asked something in the range of $10 billion in overseas assistance. As usual, after protracted haggling, Congress approved less. But the reality is not in whatever facts speechwriters pull out for self-serving summaries. Before arguing foreign aid, take a look at www.whitehouse.gov/omb/budget and at least horrify yourself with a quick overview of the complexities.

Much was made over $3 billion earmarked from Bush's Millennium Challenge Fund. But that aims at making poor nations into useful participants in our sort of globalized economy. Only $1.5 billion—a few days in Iraq—was budgeted for child survival and health.

Andrew Natsios, administrator of USAID, quit his job in disgust at the end of 2005 after budgetary wrangling. When he finally threw in the towel, Natsios had had a long career of pushing rocks up a hill. As director of the U.S. Office of Foreign Disaster Assistance in 1991, he tried to help starving Somalis when the United Nations shunned the place as, in the words of one official, "unfit for humans." The Swiss-based International Committee of the Red Cross, designed to ease conflict, not feed the hungry, ended up saving Somalia.

By the time America sent military convoys to help distribute food, the famine was broken. United States troops did help tens of thousands. Before long, however, Somali women were dumping grain on the ground to keep the more valuable plastic sacks it came in. Then U.S. forces embroiled themselves in disastrous battle with Somali warlords and left in defeat. President Bill Clinton proclaimed that America had saved a million lives. Aid veterans muttered darkly and moved on to the next crisis.

Natsios's frustration has been a common theme among USAID administrators for as long as the job has existed. The position needs political clout from Congress to be effective, but each session some legislator leads a tirade against all that taxpayer money vanishing down a rat hole.

Ironically enough, the more leaders steal aid, the more their impoverished people need help. "Voters" in such states have no more real say in choosing their leaders than Iraqis did in "electing" Saddam Hussein. If our aim is assisting societies in real trouble rather than influencing U.N. votes, we must figure out how best to do that.

Peter McPherson, USAID director in the 1980s, saw the answer back then. "You have to simplify, build irrigation systems that villagers can run, if not repair," he told me. The individual farmer is Africa's real source of strength, he said. Whether it can change depends on him—or her. But, as usual, U.S. aid took the opposite course, toward prestige projects of dubious value.

P erhaps the best thing outsiders can do is to find ways to stop leaders from plundering their own economies. Fairer property laws and less bureaucracy would help. Hernando de Soto, the popular Peruvian economist, decided to challenge common wisdom. He and his team looked at poverty up close in the Philippines, Egypt, Haiti, and Peru. Then they assessed the rest of the developing world.

"Even in the poorest country, the poor save," de Soto wrote in *The Mystery of Capital*. "The value of savings among the poor is, in fact, immense—forty times all the foreign aid received throughout the world since 1945. . . . But they hold these resources in defective forms: houses built on land whose ownership rights are not adequately recorded, unincorporated businesses with undefined liability, industries located where financiers and investors cannot see them." He offered a number: "By our calculations, the total value of the real estate held but not legally owned by the poor of the Third World and former communist nations is at least $9.3 trillion."

That, he adds helpfully, is double the circulating U.S. money supply. It nearly equals the value of all companies on the world's twenty biggest stock exchanges. It is twenty times direct foreign investment in the Third World and former Soviet bloc in the decade after 1989. And it is forty-six times what the World Bank has lent, and ninety-nine times what donor nations have given in aid, over the last thirty years.

In the West, 9 trillion bucks' worth of property amounts to solid collateral. The most common source of capital for a new small business in the United States is a mortgage on the entrepreneur's house. But to secure a loan, you need a sheaf of papers for the banker.

De Soto explains: "They have houses but not titles; crops but not deeds; business but not statutes of incorporation. It is the unavailability of these essential representations that explains why people who have adapted every other Western invention, from the paper clip to the nuclear reactor, have not been able to produce sufficient capital to make their domestic capitalism work. This is the mystery of capital."

In Bali, de Soto tells people, dogs bark the moment you step from one piece of property to another. They know who owns what, but neither the courts nor the banks do.

Unraveling this mess is a little more than we can expect anytime soon. In many countries, leaders like it that way. It maintains an oligarchy's stranglehold and leaves open a thousand channels for artful corruption. Nations where capitalism works are not easily disposed to make room at the trough.

But de Soto provides an insight that anyone familiar with the "Third World" can confirm. The term "developing," refers to structures, not human capacities. To achieve that free-market capitalism we always push, these societies need tangible resources, not economic lessons.

To put his findings into practice, de Soto founded the Institute for Liberty and Democracy in Lima. Peru and El Salvador hired the institute to run registries to simplify proof of ownership. In Peru, a business can be legalized in one day at a single desk—and for $174, nearly a tenth of the former cost. De Soto's disciples expanded across Central America to Mexico and Haiti. They now also work in Egypt, Tanzania, the Philippines, Albania, and beyond.

As always, there is the opposite take on things. Detractors dismiss de Soto as blinded by market ideology. In many cases, they note, far more than a lack of collateral keeps people mired in poverty. On such macro matters, obviously enough, no one is all right or all wrong. It helps if we pay closer attention and draw conclusions that make sense based on our philosophies.

Some aspects of aid should be dead simple, such as fixing outmoded programs and policies that make no sense. During 2006, as much of the world went hungry, Celia Dugger of the *New York Times* nailed a boondoggle that has amazed foreign correspondents for decades: Public Law 480.[2]

"It seemed like a no-brainer," Dugger wrote, "changing the law to allow the federal government to buy food in Africa for Africans facing starvation instead of paying enormous sums to ship it from the American heartland, halfway around the world. Not only would the food get to the hungry in weeks instead of months, the government would save money and help African farmers at the same time."

The Bush administration sponsored the bill in a Republican-flavored Washington. Departing from its go-it-alone policy, it sought to put America, by far the world's biggest food donor, in step with such rich countries as Canada. Congress stomped it to death.

Public Law 480 is a political bargain that has underpinned U.S. aid for half a century. It insists that generosity to the world's hungry must also help

American agriculture. The law says that all official food aid must be grown by American farmers and mostly shipped on U.S.-flag vessels.

Dugger gets to the heart of why the bill died: "The administration's proposal has run into opposition from three interests some critics call the Iron Triangle of food aid: agribusiness, the shipping industry and charitable organizations. Just four companies and their subsidiaries, led by Archer Daniels Midland and Cargill, sold more than half the $700 million in food commodities provided through the United States Agency for International Development's food aid program in 2004, government records show. Just five shipping companies received over half the more than $300 million spent to ship that food, records show."

For all our self-praise, this paralytic system means that aid often arrives long after desperate families have had to abandon their homes, triggering famine. Had PL480 not slowed relief to Ethiopia during 1984 or to other places before and since, far fewer people would have died.

Christopher Barrett, a Cornell University economist, assails PL480 in a book, *Food Aid After Fifty Years: Recasting Its Role.* "It's the middlemen who enjoy most of the gain, not the farmers," he told Dugger.

Barrett's work shows the deep stake that nonprofit aid agencies have in maintaining the status quo. With coauthor Daniel Maxwell, a CARE official, he found that at least seven groups, including Catholic Relief Services, depended on food aid for a quarter to a half of their 2001 budgets.

In fact, PL480 procedures have turned private voluntary agencies into grain traders. They sell large amounts of the donated food on local markets in poor countries to generate tens of millions of dollars for their antipoverty programs. But at least fifty cents of each dollar's worth of aid goes for transport, storage, and administrative costs. If the money were put directly into long-term development, it would go twice as far. And, if well used, it would sharply reduce the need for food aid.

Canada took a different approach in 2006. The leading aid agency, the Canadian Foodgrains Bank, teamed with the Canadian Federation of Agriculture, the country's main farm-group organization, to support a sharp cut in the amount of food bought in Canada. The federation president, Robert Friesen, told the *Times*, "Farmers are not going to say you have to source food in Canada regardless of whether starving people are waiting for it."[3]

In Washington, then-Senator Mike DeWine, an Ohio Republican, tried to add wording that would allow 10 percent of food aid to be bought in poor countries. "It's a question of trying to save lives," he said. But Bob Goodlatte, a Virginia Republican who headed the House Agricultural

Committee at the time, said even that small compromise "would break a coalition that has resulted in one of the most successful food aid programs in world history."

One never knows if a remark like Goodlatte's reflects self-delusion or simply selfishness. Either way, if he ventured out of his cave and beyond the Beltway, he would see a world full of evidence to the contrary. It is not about noble intentions but rather about what saves lives.

When enough corn to save starving Zimbabweans can be trucked in days across the border from Zambia, at minimal cost, does he really want them to wait so that an ADM stockholder can afford yet another lavish meal?

M ost veteran aid professionals, whether official or voluntary, want to blur the line between development aid and emergency relief. It is much easier to raise money for the latter. But if the former were not so neglected, those large urgent infusions would be far less necessary.

When the world focuses on a famine, a natural disaster, or fighting that sets refugees on the road, governments rush to help. Sometimes extra funds are appropriated, but most emergency aid is at the expense of the longer term. As a result, countries are left weaker when the next crisis strikes. It is as Tarekegne Taka, my Ethiopian economist friend, said in Rome: Once the vital organs go, the rest follow.

Disaster response is often arbitrary, depending on the national mood. In 2005, when a tsunami swept away 150,000 people from Indonesia to Sri Lanka, Pfizer's gift of $35 million in cash and drugs was more than double the U.S. government's initial offering. As the need sank in, Washington did much better. U.S. Navy helicopters brought aid to cutoff communities. Other American help poured in, public as well as private, but much was plundered from other budget lines. Then, when survivors had to pick up the pieces and rebuild their lives from nothing, we moved on. A lot of promised aid never arrived. In the end, Australia and Europe were considerably more generous.

The pattern is classic. Cameras arrive and help follows. Then, almost invariably, compassion fatigue sets in before the crisis is past. Even at home with Americans watching, aid to Katrina victims dwindled fast. Families were left in squalor. Huge sums were wasted. Billions were stolen or paid in fraudulent claims after Katrina. In the hills of Kashmir, with few reporters to notice, abuses get much worse.

Sudden storms and volcanoes are the exception. Most major emergencies can be foreseen. Aid experts know that with functioning systems in place and reliable funding, most of these can be averted. Or, if they strike without warning, their impact can be blunted.

If there was ever a deep-reaching example of the old adage "a stitch in time . . ." it is the business of richer nations helping poorer ones.

Jan Egeland, the U.N. emergency aid coordinator, has a useful rule of thumb: It normally costs eighty times more to confront a full-blown famine or a raging epidemic than it would have if effective action had been taken at the first signs. That, of course, refers only to money. No one can quantify the dimensions of human suffering when people begin to die by the scores of thousands.

Fred Cuny, the wonder-working tall Texan reporters used to call the Red Adair of humanitarian disaster, was murdered in Chechnya in 1995 while confronting yet another crisis. As a private consultant with long experience and good friends in Washington, he understood what worked. Cuny knew that just about every desperate refugee situation could have been avoided with early, focused action.

To the end, he wavered between optimism and frustration. "We are still doing things that we have known for decades don't work," he told me. That was fifteen years ago, and little has changed.

But then, Cuny had just helped American officials return desperate Kurds who fled during the first Gulf War. "When change comes, it comes quickly," he said. "We showed that we can solve these problems and put the burden on the country that created them."

More than anything, he believed that swift, smart action can blunt the impact of any emergency. Once, in Somalia, Cuny watched U.S. aircraft burning fuel to push pallets of food toward the wrong people. "Whenever you see those C-130s," he said, "you know somebody fucked up."

North of Goma, as I watched terrified Rwandan refugees run shrieking from off-target U.S. aid pallets they thought were bombs, I remembered Cuny's classic line. It was 1994, just after Hutus fled an advancing Tutsi army that came from Uganda to stop genocide that had taken 800,000 lives.

Desperate, penniless columns crossed the border into the Congo, some dropping dead on the way from malnutrition and disease. Before long, cholera swept through makeshift refugee camps. Deaths rose into the scores of thousands.

"No one who covered those days in Goma, Zaire, will ever forget the smell of that banana patch," I wrote in the AP's in-house log. "When cholera began its awful scythe sweep around the million Rwandans huddled in squalid camps on volcanic rock, the sight was too overwhelming to register. Sensory overload mercifully converted the rows upon rows of corpses into something else, inanimate elements of a story to be reported."

As often happens, an ad hoc cluster of U.N. and voluntary agencies scrambled to meet the challenge. French troops provided security. Congolese Boy Scouts heaved cadavers onto trucks for mass burial. Doctors from a dozen countries rose early and stayed up late to treat the sick.

There was plenty to do, but the delivery of relief supplies was under control. Flights stacked up over the Goma airstrip to deliver food and medicines. Private relief agencies organized convoys to speed them to remote camps.

Under pressure because of heart-sickening coverage on nightly newscasts, U.S. officials decided to get into the act. They ordered C-130s from Germany, with a staging base at Entebbe, to air-drop relief supplies north of Goma.

Relief workers objected. The ridiculously high cost was not the problem; that was up to the Americans. But they argued that it would disrupt a working system, tying up trucks to collect and deliver what was already moving swiftly in far larger amounts.

Washington gave a rough time frame but, for security reasons, was not specific. Aid agencies halted their convoys for days, awaiting word. Finally, a dozen giant transports flew south. Most of the aircraft aborted because of bad visibility. In the end, only five tons of the twenty-seven tons dispatched were released. They missed the airstrip drop site by miles.

One pallet fell over a school. Another missed a convoy of U.N. vehicles by a few feet. Refugees, fearful that Tutsis were attacking in retaliation, ran in panic. I slogged through hip-deep water to where a British volunteer was recovering a pallet. He slashed at nylon chute cords with a long knife, and boxes spilled into the slime.

"Those fucking bastards," he yelled, waving a fist toward the air. "Those stupid fucking bastards!" More calmly, U.N. and European team leaders described how what they called a publicity stunt had set them back for days.

Back in Goma, I wrote the story as I saw it and sent it to New York. Some hours later, I saw the rewritten version. Most of the information came from a U.S. public affairs officer in Germany, but the story, dated from

the scene, carried my byline. The lead was that American aircraft had suc-
cessfully dropped urgent relief supplies to Rwandan refugees, thus saving
the day.

I called my foreign editor and railed. He appeared to be listening. Yet
twelve hours later, the new version on the AP wire for afternoon newspapers had barely changed. Some of my description from the scene was included, but the story, still dated from Frankfurt, described what seemed
clearly to be an American triumph.

To this day I am not sure why. I do not believe my editors tried to mislead on purpose. But American officials had spoken. Surely, their version
must be true.

The lesson is as Fred Cuny often laid it out. Helping people in trouble
is endlessly complex, with fast-changing obstacles to overcome. Above all,
you have to think of the victims and not play to the crowd. Washington,
stung by its role in letting the genocide happen, poured plenty of money
into Goma. But getting it right depends on experts up close who make decisions fast. And a distant public that really cares needs its own eyes and ears:
reporters.

Strongly held opinions vary widely when it comes to aid, particularly in
dramatic circumstances when the world stops to notice. Perhaps the
most popular approach dates back to the 1984 Ethiopian famine when pop
stars raised world consciousness. Bob Geldof kept at it. And then Bono of
U2 fame, another Irish rocker, took center stage. Bono, unlike many
celebrity activists, travels often to see the up-close details and works hard to
see the broader picture.

I clipped an op-ed article from the *Times* of London on Bono, a long
interview under the headline "How Starving Africa Got Under My Skin."[4]
He recounts how he visited Ethiopia and decided to do more than sing
songs. Bono often travels with Jeffrey Sachs, the Columbia University economist who advised post-Soviet Poland and now offers prescriptions for ending poverty. He has appeared at the United Nations and the White House
to plead for a desperate Dark Continent.

But I also found a *New York Times* op-ed piece by Paul Theroux entitled
"The Rock Star's Burden."[5]

"There are probably more annoying things than being hectored about
African development by a wealthy Irish rock star in a cowboy hat, but I
can't think of one at the moment," Theroux wrote. It was nearly Christmas,

he added, and he knew he sounded like Scrooge. But he recalled a different Dickensian character, from *Bleak House*: Mrs. Jellyby. "Harping incessantly on her adopted village of Borrioboola-Gha 'on the left bank of the River Niger,' Mrs. Jellyby tries to save the Africans by financing them in coffee growing and encouraging schemes 'to turn pianoforte legs and establish an export trade,' all the while badgering people for money."

For things like emergency relief, affordable drugs, AIDS education, and small, well-designed projects, Theroux wrote, outside help is essential. But, he continued, "I am speaking of the 'more money' platform: the notion that what Africa needs is more prestige projects, volunteer labor and debt relief. We should know better by now. I would not send private money to a charity, or foreign aid to a government, unless every dollar was accounted for—and this never happens. Dumping more money in the same old way is not only wasteful, but stupid and harmful."

He concluded: "Africa has no real shortage of capable people—or even of money. The patronizing attention of donors has done violence to Africa's belief in itself, but even in the absence of responsible leadership, Africans themselves have proven how resilient they can be—something they never get credit for."

Theroux, who is fond of riling people, often upsets comfortable notions. In this case, he is on firm ground.

We first met in Uganda in 1967. I went to cover peace talks between Nigeria and secessionist Biafra. He had been expelled as a Peace Corps teacher in Malawi—the president accused him of links to a coup plot—and was teaching at Makerere University with V. S. Naipaul.

Both of us have kept close tabs on Africa since then. I am more tolerant of some aid wastage if the basic job gets done. But few outsiders are better placed than Theroux to see reality. A few years ago, he asked my advice for a trip he planned, on foot and in hitched rides, from Cairo to Cape Town. I listed the most dangerous spots I thought he should avoid. He used them to plot his route.

If his *Dark Star Safari* unsettles people far from Africa who want to help, it is a text on avoiding traps.

In Malawi, for instance, he visited his old school, which he had left with a full library, an energized staff, and fresh paint. Malawi had since seen thousands of foreign teachers, doctors, and nurses, along with tens of millions of dollars. It was poorer and more desperate than ever, he said, although a new president had ordered for himself a fleet of wildly expensive Maybach sedans. The fleet never arrived. After word went around that President

Bingu wa Mutharika had made a hefty down payment on three top-of-the-line Maybach 62 limousines for his family—at a cost of about $1.5 million—opposition parties brought corruption charges. The government decided to cancel the purchase. On Sept. 10, 2005, the London *Sunday Times* quoted Finance Minister Goodall Gondwe as saying, "We will instead buy something for around 50,000 pounds." A lush wooded country of 3 million had become "an eroded and deforested land of 12 million; its rivers are clogged with sediment and every year it is subjected to destructive floods."

The school was a stripped-down, weed-choked shadow of itself. Theroux's old headmaster, greeting him warmly, implored him to send his two sons to teach at the school. Louis, by then, had a popular quirky interview show on BBC. Marcel wrote novels and made TV documentaries. The man was shocked when Theroux asked him why his own sons did not teach at the school. They had good jobs in America.

Talking to university students at Cape Town, I was amazed at how many young Africans share this view. Celebrities who fly in to feed their reputations and self-concept on Africa's complex realities are not wildly popular. Students instead want jobs from investment that is not stolen by despotic leaders, fair prices for agricultural products, help with simple basic health care, and access to small loans they are willing to pay back.

Above all, they want a seat at the table, as full-fledged people. Solutions must go beyond handouts.

Routinely, some Western official visits Africa and drags out the old proverb: Give a man a fish, and he eats for one day. Teach him to fish, and so on. Africans have been catching fish expertly with sharp sticks and reed nets since forever. If outsiders want to help them, they need to do something about their drying waterways.

I once talked to a lanky midwesterner in Mopti, Mali, a Peace Corps volunteer, as we watched the Niger River struggle by, half empty from stubborn drought. "I'm going to teach these people how to farm," he said, detailing the hybrid seed, fertilizer, and insecticide they needed. He might as well just bring grain, I remarked. Malians had been growing millet on near-concrete for two millennia. Without water, they knew well enough already, it dies.

Jean-Claude Shanda Tonme, a lawyer and writer from Cameroon, fumed at this mentality in a *New York Times* op-ed piece of his own. He rankled at well-known outsiders for "their willingness to propose solutions on our behalf." Such do-gooders, he said, "still believe us to be like children that they must save."[6]

The White Man's Burden by William Easterly makes much of these last points. A New York University economist who spent decades advising the World Bank on foreign aid, he defines his stand in a subtitle: *Why the West's Efforts to Aid the Rest Have Done So Much Ill and So Little Good.*

Easterly takes aim at drop-in poverty foes he labels "Planners." More effective, he says, are those who find innovative ways to help by asking and involving the recipients. He calls these "Searchers." If sometimes oversimplified and inconsistent, his main argument is on the mark: You cannot just come in and help. Big-money projects designed by grand thinkers while flying in first class tend to miss their goal.

I thought of Easterly's argument when I came across a line in Patrick O'Brian's "Master and Commander" series; it underscored something I had seen over a lifetime of reporting in "underdeveloped" places: "Imagine the collective wisdom of a village being wrong over time," Stephen Maturin, the Irish physician and spy, remarks. "That does not happen."

The most sensible reporting on poverty is by those few correspondents who stay put in the poorest places, swatting at bugs and eating with families when their canned tuna runs out. A few of them make a career specialty of reporting on development.

Nick Kristof of the *New York Times* took his contest winner, Casey Parks, to Equatorial Guinea, which I remember as among the eeriest and evilest places I've ever visited. In a column, he explained why it best underscores what is wrong with the worst parts of the world:[7]

"The founding president of this country was a witch doctor who murdered tens of thousands, put enemies' heads on pikes, denounced education, and spread land mines on the road out of his country to prevent people from fleeing. This was then so vile a place that an American diplomat stabbed another to death here in 1971 and claimed in his trial that he had been driven insane partly by the screams of all the people being tortured.

"When the president was finally ousted in 1979, he ran off into the bush with $60 million packed in suitcases. But he was pursued, and in a shootout, the nation's entire foreign exchange reserves burned up."

Kristof took Parks to Equatorial Guinea because it exemplifies one of the biggest challenges facing Africa today. "That," the column explained, "is the need for better governance, meaning both less corruption and better economic policies. The single greatest need to fight poverty and injustice isn't more aid, although that is needed. What matters most is the local decision makers. The single biggest reason Africa is so poor is that it has had unusually bad leadership—a reflection, in turn, of colonial misrule."

That has a resounding ring of truth. When I first reported from Africa in the 1960s, a fresh colonial past explained away a lot of calamity. We are beyond that now. Africans are not in trouble because they are somehow inferior. They have been exploited by rulers, who were enabled by outside powers with something to gain.

Private voluntary aid is a vital component of the picture. Tax breaks allow corporations and individuals to help where they believe they can do some good. Many citizens give up their lunch money, a dollar at a time.

According to the Foundation Center, 71,000 different foundations gave $40.7 billion in 2006, breaking the previous year's record of $36.4 billion. Much of that went abroad. But the actual overall totals of American private aid are all but impossible to quantify. Some of these nongovernmental organizations spend huge amounts on advertising for fund-raising. A few are off the wall. In Mogadishu, some time ago, a new Toyota Land Cruiser was emblazoned "Vegetable Outreach." But most do a great deal.

Until the 1980s, when African famines demanded massive response, private voluntary agencies were mostly small and flexible, able to act quickly with a minimum of fuss. When USAID found it was too big and hamstrung with regulations for most emergencies, it contracted private agencies. As a result, some of these also grew into large bureaucracies.

These days, at the locus of any world-class disaster, scores of gleaming white air-conditioned Toyota 4×4s crisscross from tent camp to meeting site. Vehicles are easy to fit onto a spreadsheet, and the names on their doors are highly photogenic. Too often, however, budgets do not cover basic simple relief necessities. It is the relief workers' old complaint: Everyone is ready to pay for the jeep. No one wants to put gas in it.

During 2006, the world's two richest men set the aid picture on its ear. Between them, they put to work more than $60 billion. The Bill and Melinda Gates Foundation already had $30 billion to spend on poor countries, as well as American schools. Then Warren Buffett added $31 billion to their pot. Unlike many philanthropists, he did not need to see BUFFETT on Toyota doors. Gates was doing it right; he would help.

As Melinda Gates explains it, the couple looked at the poverty around them on a visit to Africa and decided they could help. Much of their effort is toward fighting AIDS, malaria, tuberculosis, and a half-dozen maladies most people don't even know about that kill young Africans en masse. Another portion helps education in America.

Gates had pledged to spend 90 percent of his Microsoft earnings on charitable work. Buffett, promising no specific figure, followed his lead. They set an example others scurried to follow. Richard Branson of Britain's Virgin empire focuses on the environment. Greedheads who decide to keep all of their monster fortunes will have a harder time looking in the mirror.

Private giving, the Gates way, is changing the paradigms. Most aid agencies, public or private, court reporters energetically. If anyone shows the slightest interest, press officers ship piles of documentation. They are generous with jeep space and space on relief flights. This makes sense. Funding depends on how taxpayers and donors perceive them. They want to show off their work.

Before Gates announced he would step aside to focus on his foundation, and before the Buffett bombshell, I visited Seattle. A senior insider had sent a note explaining my purpose to the director of public affairs; he knew her well. When I reached the woman by telephone, she asked all the questions. After a long screening to pin down who I was, what I was after, and why, meetings were arranged.

Landing in Seattle, I phoned the foundation number to ask for the address. A pleasant woman on the telephone told me that was confidential. Finally, I got the press officer. The nondescript building on Eastlake Drive had no markings other than discreet numerals with the address.

At a hefty steel security gate, a guard found my name on a clipboard. He pointed to an empty parking spot. Inside, I was equipped with a badge and assigned to a seat until my escort took me in hand. It was plain that these guys knew exactly what they wanted to do, and they did not need outsiders poking into the process.

For all my initial misgivings, I saw some hope. Gates goes about aid just like he devises software. Turbocharged people in determined smiles and khakis deconstruct the problems they face. With sensible logic and whatever know-how they can hire, they find answers.

Still, in the end, I left worried. Each time I posed questions based on obstacles I had seen over the years, I was told, politely but clearly, that I was framing things in the wrong way. The key was can-do optimism. Perhaps. But what makes eminent sense in Seattle can look vastly different in translation.

With Buffett's infusion, the foundation emerged from the shadows. Work started on a gleaming headquarters near the Seattle Center, where four hundred people would find ways to disperse philanthropy, and presumably declassify their address. Clearly enough, whatever the drawbacks, much good would be done. Just as clearly, it would not be enough.

Each March, *Forbes* magazine lists America's richest four hundred people. In 2006, for the first time, the poorest of the bunch was a billionaire. Their combined net worth climbed by $120 billion to $1.25 trillion.

And each February, Slate.com posts its Slate 60 list which keeps tabs on individual philanthropy. During 2006, Buffett gave away $44 billion. The other fifty-nine people on the list, whose net worth approached $600 billion, came up with only $7 billion. Only a fraction of that went beyond American borders.

According to Slate lore, the list was started a decade ago after Ted Turner suggested in an interview with Maureen Dowd that generosity ought to be noted somewhere just as pure wealth is celebrated by Forbes. Whether that helped or not, there seems to be room for progress.

How can, say, Larry Ellison spend a net worth that is fast heading north of $16 billion? At a 10 percent return, Christopher Carroll at Johns Hopkins University calculates, he would have to spend $183,000 an hour on things with no resale value before he even started to eat into principal. Surely, someone could use the excess.

Whatever the level, private largesse can do no more than supplement an overall umbrella of official assistance. If grand spirits such as Gates and Buffett choose to share their wealth with people who need it, may glory be upon them. On a smaller scale, other companies are finding it is simple human decency, as well as good public relations, to help stricken victims in time of need. As the Gates Foundation is discovering, however, philanthropy is best focused on specific problems. However noble its intentions, it is influenced by donors' philosophies. Corporate generosity tends to focus on places eager to develop market economies and be like us. Too many people fall through the cracks.

Development aid is something else. It is long term, thankless, and anonymous. What wealthy family would—or should—fund rural schools so Mauritanian kids can learn enough about the world to put their Prophet's teaching into sensible context? Such assistance is often without measurable result. It can help to fortify governments that function. And where governments do not function, it can help build infrastructure and social services. This takes as much diplomacy as money.

This, of course, depends on whether comfortable, complacent citizens are ready to agree. Not long after 2000, the world reached a milestone. The clinically obese are now as numerous as the malnourished; this is not because we feed more hungry people. Perhaps tightening our belts just a fraction might be a pretty good idea.

Keeping up to speed on these issues is not easy. For reporters, development stories are an even harder sell to editors than the environment. Too many of those rock stars and celebrities skew the focus. As travel budgets shrink, reporters seldom go beat bushes to find stories we should know about. Instead, they need an angle, and famous outsiders are the story. When Brad Pitt and Angelina Jolie had their baby in Namibia, the government referred all visa requests to Pitt for approval. One Hollywood birth got more coverage than a decade of news from Namibia.

Heartstrings can be tugged only so hard and so often. Generosity is part of it; if that is why we decide to help, so much the better. But this is really about our own interests. Those U.N. votes are cast by governments, which change as societies evolve.

Americans who want to help can spend some time looking at what really works. Public aid is the backbone. If legislators are held to account, what we do give will be better used. In time, totals may reach the range of real generosity. What matters more than overall amounts of aid, public or private, is the manner in which it is given.

Small credits that are paid back often show a tremendous return. Self-help groups, usually run by women, can turn around villages and small towns, with a ripple effect as others follow their example. The Grameen Bank in Bangladesh won a Nobel Prize in 2006, after Mohammed Yunus spent decades showing what even a little help can do. But even these micro credits have their drawbacks, impacting on fragile structures that underpin societies.

What most poor families need is a fair break on commodity prices, protection from meddling authorities, and simple transportation to markets. They will take care of the rest. Costly prestige projects, those big dams and the like, usually end up as bad ideas.

People in the "Third World" are often poor and, by standards we define, backward, but their intelligence levels are hardly inferior. Opinions form in family circles and village councils. Common views are spread in churches, mosques, or animist gatherings. If a donor does something useful and helpful, they all know it. If they are left to fend for themselves, they know that, too. Never mind that the more people develop, the more they add to our economies. It is more basic than that. Those who believe official aid is charity better used at home might keep Allistair Sparks in mind: Poverty begets hatred.

The thing about hatred is that you have to have somewhere to direct it, someone to blame it on. Reducing poor peoples' desperation is the biggest single thing we can do to deplete terrorist ranks. Any way you look at it, peace is cheaper than war. And it is infinitely better in terms of life, liberty, and pursuit of happiness.

In the end, generosity beyond our borders is less about geopolitics than it is about people. That remark by Eric Schmidt of Google strikes a chord whenever I think of it. The human genome does not apportion intelligence according to nationality. Africans, Schmidt noted, are mostly too busy looking for dinner to develop their potential.

I once lunched with a friend in California who said we should not worry about keeping poor Africans alive. They will only grow up to hate us. But I have another old pal who was my predecessor when I went to cover Nigeria in 1968. A former Peace Corps volunteer, he and his wife had adopted a Nigerian son, Jide. The family settled in Boston, where he did rather well.

Jide played football at Harvard and then earned millions as a senior executive of a leading investment bank. Among other things, he helped white-ruled South Africa turn an important corner. He is brilliant, gentle, and wise, the sort of guy I'd want my daughter to marry. In fact, his type of multicultural hybrid root stock might be just what we need these days.

It should come as no surprise that any one of those desperate kids in refugee-camp pictures could grow up to lead our world in a smarter direction. Still, it is always a treat to see their mere presence demolish the reticence of people who underestimate them. I wish Jide had joined us at that California lunch table. The discussion would have ended with more than uneasy silence.

Today, a differently shaped world poses another challenge for Western donors. Back in the 1960s, rivalry among big powers was strategic and political. These days, it is far more pragmatic and economic. Even if foreign aid is designed to encourage product loyalty or gratitude when the General Assembly votes, the game has changed.

China, with little interest in exporting intangible values, sees Africa and other Third World regions as billions of future consumers who want reliable goods at cheap prices—and who have oil and strategic metals to sell.

India takes a different approach toward a similar goal, building multinational companies without the three-martini-lunch expense accounts.

Each year since freeing its African empire in 1960, France has organized a grand summit, rich in fine food and expressions of friendship. Participants go home with fat checks to balance their budgets; *Le Figaro* editorializes about lingering French glory. In 2006, Africans also went to Beijing, with little of that ceremonial folderol. China coughed up $5 billion in easy loans, promising much more to follow. China's trade with Africa, near $50 billion in 2006, should double by 2010.

Propelled largely by exports to Asia, annual growth in Sub-Saharan Africa went from 3 percent to 5.8 percent in five years. Aid projects are geared to infrastructure that gets mineral wealth to market. In Angola, Chinese engineers are reviving the hundred-year-old railway that links Africa's grand lakes to the Atlantic.

China's interest does not extend to morality lectures. And the president of Botswana, chatting with reporters recently, referred to "those little yellow men." This is not about being buddies; it is business.

The challenge of poverty goes far beyond Africa. It also goes beyond our outworn set of received ideas. This is no longer a matter of geography in an interlinked world where borders are mostly notional lines on a map. These days, development and aid amount to a two-way flow. When a poor society improves itself, richer ones benefit.

When the immigration debate raged in 2006, I heard some guy with a Carolina drawl interviewed on NPR. He wanted to fence off Mexico bigtime. "We should electrify that thing, and if someone jumps up against it and fries, well . . ." His voice trailed off in pleasant musing. I was in Tucson at the time, just back from a rally at Armory Park. I had spent the day talking with people who might have ended up as charred ash in that cracker's fantasy.

A woman named Beatriz had asked me, "Do you think I like cleaning your toilets for three dollars an hour? Tell me the option." About fifty, with a pleasant round face and strong hands, she had sneaked across a border a generation ago. Now, with two smart daughters, one headed for medical school, her family has all the legal papers it needs.

Just then, some white-bread heckler yelled at no one in particular: "Where's your flag?" People at earlier rallies waved Mexican colors, sparking controversy. Beatriz pulled the Stars and Stripes from her bag and flapped it at the guy. "Here," she said. "Want to burn it?"

Beatriz laughs bitterly at the standard remark so many Americans make: "Why don't you just stand in line?" There is no line. No more immigrant visas are given for Mexico than for the Dominican Republic. Without some priority or special skill, the wait is forever.

Had enough of us faced simple facts of life a long time ago, Beatriz would likely be happily ensconced in Mexico with a little income, cleaning her own toilet, and hanging out with family and friends who share a way of life she treasures. Her daughter might have chosen to replace heart valves in Hermosillo. Who knows?

Beatriz and I had a lot in common, but I was luckier. When my grand-mother showed up at Ellis Island with five kids in 1921 after a yearlong odyssey from the Russian-Polish frontier, no one worried about visas and quotas. Now it is different. As uncounted millions of people around the world do each year, Beatriz just picked a place to go and figured things out for herself.

For all the tough talk about immigration controls, international bor-ders across the world are as porous as kitchen sieves. No one really knows the numbers, and the categories are complex. After a working life spent watching other societies up close, two things are clear to me. When people can feed their families at home, they mostly stay put. It is not us or our Western way of life they love; it is the chance to send home a paycheck. But if they decide they must go, they go. Some try America; others, the European Union. With no legal path, they sell what they can and go any-way. This enriches organized mafias, as well as freelance coyotes, snakeheads, and *passeurs.* They die by the dozens off Spain or suffocate in shipping con-tainers someone forgets to open. East Germany's watchtower-studded walls could not keep desperate people in, and no barrier we build will keep them out.

Movement across borders is complicated, and authorities think in terms of categories. Refugees and "internally displaced persons" are chased from their homes by war or mayhem. Their number, usually about 6 million in flux at any particular time, depends on who is fighting whom in the world. The luckier ones find U.N. and voluntary agency support, with eventual settlement elsewhere. Some live in squalid camps for months, if not years. A lot go back home when things calm down. If they are resettled somewhere, they come in as legal immigrants.

Then there is the broader—and much larger—range of "economic refugee." This includes some people fleeing real danger at home who cannot convince authorities that the threat is real. Mostly, though, these are poor people simply looking for a way to feed their families. Since few qualify for visas, they have to find some other way in.

True enough, every nation must control its borders, and none can afford wide-open immigration. But Gestapo at the frontiers is no answer. That deters honest emigrants who would happily file visa applications to explain why they seek entry and when they will go home. And it spurs the most desperate and the criminal-minded, who find a way in no matter what. Instead of temporary workers who pay taxes, we have undocumented hordes we choose to call aliens.

As with the other global crises we face, these human ebbs and flows are part of the larger picture. Smarter foreign aid and fairer trade agreements can create more jobs through development.

Obviously, there are a lot of ifs and buts. Each country's requirements are different, and this is an emotional issue. Whether we want to remember Emma Lazarus's words of welcome now that we are safely in the door is a personal matter. Still, nothing is complicated about the philosophy. When the front doors are opened wider, it is easier to keep track of who comes in and goes out. And the back door, with less traffic, will be easier to bar. However we do it, this is like foreign aid. It may seem to be the generosity that it is meant to be. In fact, more rational movement across borders is in our own interest.

For those who evoke the specter of terrorism, consider the Interpol database in Lyon, France. Several million stolen legal blank passports and other travel documents now float around the world. Since Washington is reluctant to share such information with others, the number of missing virgin U.S. documents is not known, but it is substantial. When terrorists want to cross borders, they find a way.

As the immigration debate droned on, Congress approved yet one more security expenditure, a seven-hundred-mile wall along the Mexican border, estimated at $1.2 billion. History may have to rephrase Ronald Reagan: "Mr. Gorbachev, tear down that wall! We need it in Arizona."

Trafficking people is a chart-busting global growth industry, but most of it eludes journalists. We write about it when authorities break up a major ring. Sometimes intrepid reporters get an inside look, but it is hard to penetrate and all but impossible to quantity. It goes by different terms, depending on whether the traffic is for sex, farm labor, domestic toil, sweatshops, drug running, or mafia grunt work. The simple catch-all "slavery" covers most of it well enough.

According to the International Office of Migration in Geneva and the United Nations, about 4 million people a year are victims of human trafficking.[8] This is probably the fastest-growing criminal enterprise in the world. It requires no start-up capital, and profits are deep in the billions. Unlike drugs, which are a onetime sale, human product keeps on earning. The practice is illegal, but hardly anyone is caught or tried.

Large mafias control major geographic sectors, such as Russia, the former Soviet republics, Eastern Europe, Japan, Hong Kong, and Colombia. They wield political power using corruption, extortion, and vicious violence. Many of them cooperate on logistics. Elsewhere, most trafficking is decentralized. Small networks specialize in recruiting, transporting, or "retailing" the product.

The U.S. State Department draws a careful line between trafficking, which involves coercion with involuntary servitude, and human smuggling, which is an illegal industry to help willing immigrants evade border controls. Smuggling is largely a cottage industry of people who run small boats, forge documents, and act as guides. The total numbers, worldwide, are much greater. Smuggling is more of a condition than an industry.

In practice, the lines are blurred. Both trafficking and smuggling add up to unknown millions who float around undetected in the United States and Europe.

I spent years, off and on, tracking down clandestine people-smuggling. In Morocco, I found a jovial sea captain who ferried jobless young men from the coast near Tangier to an opposite stretch of Spanish beach. Each paid about $1,500, a life's savings, to climb into his open boat at dark. Unlike some others, he did not do a sneaky U-turn at sea and dump his human cargo back in Morocco. But if Spanish gunboats opened fire, he hit reverse. His passengers then had a very long swim.

One afternoon in Manhattan, Ko-lin Chin, a Chinese American sociologist who moves easily in Asia, took me on a brief slavery tour of Chinatown. He pointed out the unmarked brothels, one after another, where a curly-haired reporter with a substantial nose could not get past the door. "Indentured labor" is a better term for most of the workers who, some legal and some not, spent years at hard labor paying off debt to the snakeheads.

The Albanian mafia is especially scary. Fortunately, I had the much safer

Kosovo war to cover, with no time to learn up close how thugs grab young women off the street and smuggle them to Italy and beyond. Keeping control of their property is a piece of cake. Each girl has family back home she does not want to endanger by making any fuss. It is not much different with women from Russia and elsewhere in what was the Soviet Union.

The stories go on and on. Two brothers from Mali made headlines by hiding themselves in the landing gear of a jetliner from Bamako to Brussels. Somehow, they managed to survive. Small Mediterranean islands, like Lampedusa in Italy, swarm with people on their way to some back door to the European mainland.

It is harder to sneak into the United States, but plenty of desperate people still manage. The Mexico border is one obvious place. Cubans on rafts are an old story.

Once people reach their promised land, they are stuck. All they can do is work long hours and send money home. Looking at it cynically, this is good for America. It means someone skillful is there to cook fried noodles with shrimp or cheese enchiladas or to clean up the dishes later. When they send wages to Guatemala or Guinea, fewer people will want to risk the trip themselves.

But looking at it as human beings, we need some larger guidelines that make sense for everyone. We have to step back at national and global levels to reflect on what we can do, and what we ought to do, in a world where so many crises are interlinked.

No nation should impose itself on another. But neither should nations collectively let whole societies suffer. Most likely it was because oil was at stake, but, nonetheless, the world reacted in unison when Iraq invaded Kuwait in 1991. Obsessive megalomaniacs and ethnic strife are as old as creation. These days, we are equipped to blunt their impact and clean up the mess.

These linked issues are as obvious as they are urgent. Whether it is Aceh or New Orleans, sudden disasters can catch us off guard, and we will have to scramble to provide emergency aid. But the greater impact of these disasters, whether they are sudden or endemic, depends on a community's ability to withstand them.

We all sang about Ethiopia in 1984, but the following year you could drive from Timbuktu to the Red Sea and not run out of catastrophe. The worst was an oasis at the dead center of Africa: El Geneina, Sudan. I began a four-part AP series from there with what should have been obvious: "Africa's famine is a largely man-made calamity that could have been avoided." Two years later, I published a book on Africa, *Squandering Eden*. This passage might have been written last week:

"In Arabic, El Geneina means garden; the name is now a bitter joke. Dry, hot air sucks the life out of almost anything that grows in a garden. At the height of the 1985 drought, the flyblown little town suffered badly from the cruelties and insanities of well-intentioned food aid.

"The details of famine relief in Sudan offer little comfort to optimists in Africa. But they are lessons to be learned well, and well remembered."

Eric Witt, a smart USAID officer at the U.S. embassy in Khartoum, saw in February 1984 that Sudan would need urgent food aid. He persuaded the mission to rattle desks in Washington. Despite other experts' contrary advice, American sorghum made its slow way to Port Sudan, where it sat in a warehouse. Months later, as children died for lack of a handful of food, it still sat there.

Ekber Menemcioglu, a youthful Turk with the U.N. refugee agency, met me at the plane in El Geneina. "How can this happen?" he asked, over and over. "My people are dying, more every day. The crazy thing is that the food we need is here in the country."

Ekber was used to screwups. We fishtailed across the dunes to his camp. He was afraid of stalling, and the clutch kept slipping. Geneva had sent him two jeeps, both equipped for the Alps with snow tires and monster heaters. One had already rolled over in the sand.

The plan was for the Sudanese to take the grain on a railway Lord Kitchener had built in 1890. The World Bank had put $180 million into repairing the line, and Americans spent $3 million on urgently needed parts. Nothing moved.

At one point, a bitter U.S. official muttered, "There are more people in Peoria concerned about starving Sudanese then there are in Khartoum." And, of course, that was the crux of it. Darfur, Sudan's westernmost province, was peopled by black Africans, like the south, where Arab governments in Khartoum had waged war for four decades.

When the U.S. aid effort stalled in 1985, Richard Copeland, disaster coordinator for Oxfam, echoed a widely heard criticism: "The Americans should have assumed the railways would not work and used trucks as a backup." But at the U.S. embassy, a diplomat defended the decision. When I pushed him hard, he came close to tears. "You work so hard to get the food . . . and it just sits," he said. "It just kills you. We have passed the point now, and there is no way kids won't die."

Today, it is far worse. Government troops ride alongside the dreaded *jan-jaweed*, guerrillas whose essential purpose is terror by rape and plunder. In 2004, the U.S. Congress formally condemned "genocide" in Darfur. Years later, with death toll mounting fast, the question hangs: If it is genocide, why do we let it go on?

Decades ago, French doctors from *Médecins sans Frontières* championed a concept they called humanitarian intervention. If leaders of a government were prepared to let people within their own borders die, shouldn't aid workers have an option to force their way in behind a multinational armed force? The idea got little traction. Murderous tyrants vote along with everyone else at the United Nations. And nations with military force to spare pick their fights for their own reasons.

Forty years after Biafra, we have yet to learn the most lessons. Food "emergencies" can be foreseen. Tidal waves and earthquakes might catch us off guard, but their impact is blunted when communities are prepared. There will be logistical problems, both real and political. Yet people with at least minimum resources can prepare for the worst. The only long-term answer is durable, sensible development.

SEVEN

SHOCK AND "AW, SHIT"

W ell into 2006, America's new best friend, Iraq, put into action the democracy we gave it. Mahmoud al-Mashhadani, speaker of the freshly picked Parliament, exercised his freedom to say what he thought: "The U.S. occupation is butcher's work under the slogan of democracy and human rights and justice."

His bitterness was echoed on the street whenever reporters ventured out from behind barricades to hear it. Two-thirds of Iraqis approved of attacks on U.S. forces, a University of Maryland poll found, and 80 percent said Americans provoked more violence than they prevented.[1]

After Thanksgiving in 2006, the Iraq Study Group, headed by James Baker, the Bush family consigliere, stated the obvious: We were in way over our heads. The most vociferous of warmongers scrambled for excuses to weasel away from early enthusiasm. But no one knew a way out.

Our vainglorious swagger into Iraq recalls Napoleon Bonaparte's old advice, which he should have heeded before wading into Waterloo. When a general asked him how to get out of a nasty quagmire, he replied that he would not have gotten into it in the first place.

It is easy enough to critique a war in hindsight. Yet nearly every reporter with Middle East experience, American and otherwise, saw the likely
result well before final orders to invade. Those who cover Washington
knew the generals' and diplomats' hesitations. But editors and executives,
not reporters, make the final cut.

Our "media" failed us badly in not challenging the administration's
hell-bent rush into Iraq. A few news organizations did their job well; more
were outright cheerleaders. Overall, they acquiesced to what was perceived
as a national mood, and they fanned the flames.

Not only were reporters on the spot unable to make themselves heard
before the invasion, but they were also shouted down from the field by ide-
ologues at home and neophytes embedded with advancing troops. By the
time we all caught on, the damage was done. We have a fat shelf of journalists' books recounting current history in bone-freezing detail. But it is
too late. And, most likely, when flags wave again for some new purpose, these
will be gathering dust along with those thoughtful tomes on Vietnam.

What we should have known is that initial gratitude over Saddam Hussein's fall dissipated almost immediately as stray weapons fire cut down children and grandmothers. Iraqis saw quickly that we had pushed Humpty
Dumpty off the wall with no intention of cleaning up the mess. That is
when we should have beefed up security, sealed the borders, and handed
over the keys to Iraqis.

Outside the White House briefing room, reality was clear enough. The
Congressional Research Service estimated early on that the war's direct
costs were $2 billion a week and rising fast. An intelligence estimate,
though partly suppressed, reported the predictable: fallout from Iraq creating terrorists worldwide at a rapid rate.

Our $21 billion reconstruction effort was tainted with fraud and cor-
ruption. Private contractors hired by our government stole from us and
killed innocents in our name. A symbolic cornerstone, the Baghdad Police
College, was so shoddily built that urine and feces rained into student bar-
racks. "This is the most essential civil security project in the country—and
it's a failure . . . a disaster," a special inspector told Congress.

"In the real Iraq," a *New York Times* editorial said in September 2006 before it got even worse, "armed Shiite and Kurdish parties have divided up
the eastern two-thirds of the country, leaving Sunni insurgents and American Marines to fight over the rest. . . . The civilian death toll is now running at roughly 100 a day, with many of the victims gruesomely tortured
with power tools and acid." It listed only some of the problems: electricity

is off, oil production is depressed, jobs and basic services are few, religious courts govern family life, women's rights are in retreat, courts are skewed, and street justice fills a vacuum. "Iraq today is a broken, war-torn country."[2]

Was it civil war? It was certainly uncivil free-for-all. And Olivier Roy, perhaps the most respected of world experts on Islamic upheaval, had already declared a winner: Iran. The theocracy in Tehran rid itself of two bitter opponents, Saddam Hussein and the Taliban, without firing a shot. Iraq's Shiite majority, which dominates at the polls, sympathizes with its neighbor, allying Arabs with Persians. Iran is an unchallenged regional power.

On the war's fourth anniversary, a poll by *USA Today*, ABC, BBC, and the German network ARD found six out of ten Iraqis saw their lives going badly. One hundred percent of Baghdadis said they were often afraid to approach U.S. troops or even leave their own homes.

In light of all those uncounted dead in the ruins of an ancient country, over a trillion dollars spent to blacken America's name, and yet more zealots prepared to blow themselves up in frustrated desperation, we would be wise to draw hard lessons from our folly in Iraq.

If war is sometimes necessary, it must be based on a consensus rooted in reality. Yet in America, war is a worst-case result of a newsgathering system based upon "coverage" by distant commentators while reporters who look up close are drowned out in the din. In Vietnam, we had waded in deep before correspondents sounded the alarm. By then, cutting losses would have meant ignominious retreat.

Iraq was different. We could have avoided it all. Whether we should stay or go now that our Mesopotamian Petri dish lies shattered is a judgment call. But we were dead wrong to ignore the world's warnings and invade under our own flag on spurious grounds. America, not some "Coalition," is seen as the enemy. To test this, try taking Old Glory on a stroll through Baghdad or Basra.

We spent more on four years of war than we gave the entire world in foreign aid since the 1950s, and the cost is growing fast. Hardly safer, we face a much greater risk of terrorism.

As we keep no count, we cannot say whether Iraqi deaths are closer to official estimates that surpass 100,000 or to more than six times that according to credible calculations. The low figure equates proportionately to 1 million Americans.

As the preinvasion story developed, history had little place. Young editors saw comparisons to Vietnam as facile cliché. Few reporters who covered Southeast Asia in the 1960s were still chasing news. Generals who tried to warn us were muzzled. They knew armies are blunt instruments, not suited to reshaping societies. When proud peoples are brutalized and humiliated, even if not by intention, they will resist in unforeseeable ways.

On August 15, 2002, as the war virus infected Washington, Brent Scowcroft signed an op-ed piece in the *Wall Street Journal*, hardly the liberal loonies' paper of choice, under the title "Don't Attack Saddam."[3] As national security adviser to the elder Bush and to Gerald Ford, the wily old warrior-philosopher knows his reality. Saddam must be defanged in concert with other nations, in the context of larger goals, Scowcroft said. He concluded, "If we reject a comprehensive perspective, however, we put at risk our campaign against terrorism as well as stability and security in a vital region of the world."

Not nearly enough of us were listening.

Before the invasion, American strategists studied the classic film *The Battle of Algiers* for pointers on seizing densely packed Arab casbahs. Had they watched to the end, they would have seen that France's military victory, with its torture and civilian suffering, pushed bitter Algerians to drive them out. The French lost, and they are still paying, forty years later.

When war came to Iraq, Americans missed what is by far the most important element: the human impact. Because news executives did not challenge the Pentagon, the "media" had only a selective look. There was much astute, courageous reporting. But not enough reached newsprint or airwaves.

And from a distance, our "media" failed to remind us, and our hubris-blinded leaders, of the clearest lesson learned in Vietnam: If you plan something akin to open heart surgery, you need scalpels and not machetes.

Among the mountain of Iraq books rising by my desk, a favorite is a grimy little paperback published in 1993, after the first Iraq war: Malcolm W. Browne's *Muddy Boots and Red Socks*. It is a generous and humble account of war reporting by an old pro of natural generosity with no reason to be humble. By the time he took charge of AP's Saigon bureau in 1961, he had been an army tank grunt in Korea, a laboratory chemist, an obsessive reporter on a daily paper, and a domestic AP wire animal. His socks were red because of a personal quirk; his boots were muddy because he slogged nonstop through paddies and deltas.

Browne stayed with AP until ABC made him an offer he decided not to refuse. After he was told to cover a Miss Saigon contest rather than some significant action, he moved on. Off and on until the war ended in 1975, he reported for the *New York Times*. We covered the violent birth of Bangladesh together, in 1972, and I am still putting to use Brownecraft he passed on.

"No secondhand news can touch the real thing," Browne notes in his introduction, which explains why he kept going back to the field in Vietnam after falling out of the sky three times, patching up gunshot grazes, and running for his life from guerrillas. But that is only backdrop to the real business of telling a complex story. "If we sneer at the hyperbole and mawkish sentiments that permeate most forms of communication, it is because journalists, more than many other people, spend their lives boiling in the caustic bleach of reality."

Vietnam reporters were free to see all the reality they could stomach. Whether they got it across to distant Americans was another matter. As now, noisy pundits in Washington commanded attention with guesswork. Such war tourists as John Wayne fulminated in Da Nang against "the panty-waisted liberal sensationalists" of the American press. Official pressure was heavy. At a press conference in 1963, Browne asked the commander in chief of U.S. forces in the Pacific why the military tried to hide their "gray war" from the American public. The star-strewn admiral retorted: "Why can't you get on the team?"

Browne's main problem, as the AP man, was arch-conservative publishers who howled to his boss in New York. But the cooperative was then run by a newsman of deep principle and wide experience who had covered World War II.

"One of the real heroes of the Vietnam War was Wes Gallagher, who, as general manager of the Associated Press, had sent me to Saigon," Browne wrote. "In my view, Wes did more to keep a free and critical press alive during a key period than any of the other top news executives of the era." Or since, many of us who knew Gallagher might add.

When Gallagher visited Vietnam, he put on his own muddy boots, with normal-colored socks, and saw things for himself. He took some converting since Vietnam was so different from any war he had seen. "But," Browne wrote, "Gallagher's instinct was to trust his people in the field implicitly until and unless the trust was betrayed."

Browne shows in detail how Vietnamese hearts and minds quickly hardened against foreign troops, with their wholesale death and cultural distance. If Southeast Asia is too far afield, we might have looked at Iraq itself only ninety years ago: Britain was routed, bled white by a people with a deep aversion to invaders. But Mal Browne's echoes from the more recent past could hardly have been fresher.

As Dick Cheney issued specific public threats to Iraq in the shadows of George W. Bush's generic war-on-terror speeches, we heard a background media chorus.[4] Charles Krauthammer jeered in the *Washington Post* at anyone who questioned the invasion. After Baghdad fell, he told the American Enterprise Institute that the United States was the first nation in history "to destroy a totalitarian regime without destroying the country." This he attributed not only to military power and solid intelligence but also to a deep understanding of the nature of the enemy.

"We have the capacity to wage this kind of war with relatively few casualties, both among combatants on the allied side and among civilians on the other side. And that I think has had a deep impression in the region and around the world," Krauthammer said. "The only people in the world who still think that—who question whether or not we won in Iraq are Upper West Side liberals who aren't quite sure that we won the Cold War either."

Krauthammer, who went from Harvard medical studies to punditry, is a professional opinionator. But his *Post* colleague Jim Hoagland was for decades one of America's finest reporters abroad. I worked with Jim often; he has a gift for seizing on detail that reveals a larger picture. He earned his first Pulitzer in 1971 for a penetrating series on South African apartheid. Had he gone to Iraq for a look, we might have seen that same sharp eye.

From within a Washington cave, however, he wrote: "Colin Powell did more than present the world with a convincing and detailed X-ray of Iraq's secret weapons and terrorism programs yesterday. He also exposed the enduring bad faith of several key members of the U.N. Security Council when it comes to Iraq and its 'web of lies,' in Powell's phrase."

Hoagland concluded, "To continue to say that the Bush administration has not made its case, you must now believe that Colin Powell lied in the most serious statement he will ever make, or was taken in by manufactured evidence. I don't believe that. Today, neither should you."

In that same edition, dovish Mary McGrory pronounced herself persuaded. "The cumulative effect was stunning," she wrote. "I'm not ready for war yet. But Colin Powell has convinced me that it might be the only way to stop a fiend, and that if we do go, there is reason."

Then Richard Cohen added his all-seeing wisdom: "The evidence he presented to the United Nations—some of it circumstantial, some of it absolutely bone-chilling in its detail—had to prove to anyone that Iraq not only hasn't accounted for its weapons of mass destruction but without a doubt still retains them. Only a fool—or possibly a Frenchman—could conclude otherwise."

It was a convincing performance. The *Post*'s editorial that morning, under a headline reading "Irrefutable," said, "After Secretary of State Colin L. Powell's presentation to the United Nations Security Council yesterday, it is hard to imagine how anyone could doubt that Iraq possesses weapons of mass destruction."

Meanwhile, the *New York Times* editorial allowed that Powell "presented the United Nations and a global television audience yesterday with the most powerful case to date that Saddam Hussein stands in defiance of Security Council resolutions and has no intention of revealing or surrendering whatever unconventional weapons he may have." It said the "presentation was all the more convincing because he dispensed with apocalyptic invocations of a struggle of good and evil and focused on shaping a sober, factual case against Mr. Hussein's regime."

We know better today, but against this real-time background Charles Hanley of AP went through Powell's testimony, line by line, and compared it to what he had seen on the ground while accompanying U.N. weapons inspectors. He checked back with inspectors who had firsthand knowledge. His point-by-point analysis would have gone to every paper and broadcast outlet in America had it had gotten past AP's editors in New York.

The *New York Times*, as close as we have to a newspaper of record, ran repeated stories by Judith Miller quoting unnamed sources about Iraq's threat. The morning after one, Condoleezza Rice borrowed a phrase to buttress her point in a TV interview: "We don't want the smoking gun to be a mushroom-shaped cloud." When Miller was finally exposed in her own paper—Maureen Dowd's column was entitled "Woman of Mass Destruction"—she explained there is nothing one can do when a source lies to a reporter.

After a halfhearted mea culpa, and too long a wait, the *Times* finally purged Miller from its ranks. And the lesson here ought to be obvious. Journalists fit no more easily into generalities than any other group of humans. Some old hands ought to be shot. Too much experience can bring laziness, blind spots, or overweening smugness. Fresh eyes and high energy are vital to good journalism. Yet some young ones ought to be spanked. Blind ambition is deadly to solid journalism.

Wise editors weed out self-serving veterans but make good use of trusted people who add historical continuum and help keep young colleagues alive. This is true for just about any important story. In war, it is vital.

Long after it was too late to pull back, investigative journalists detailed the history. In June 2006, a PBS *Frontline* documentary wrapped up any loose ends with damning testimony from principal players. After impressive successes in Afghanistan, the CIA's cautions on Iraq were ignored. Generals were silenced. Then, pushed by Tenet, who joined the winning side, Colin Powell was forced to "reveal" to the world evidence he suspected was spurious. In 2007, Bill Moyers assailed "the media" copout.

Bush took a world to war over two empty accusations. Saddam had junked his unconventional arsenal, as U.N. inspectors knew. And as a sworn foe of Osama bin Laden, he had little to do with Al Qaeda.

When no weapons were found, Washington shifted its stance. Saddam was a bad man. That was true, but he was hardly unique in his evil. Kim Jung II was a real threat to America, but even the blindest of hawks knew invading North Korea was too big a job. Pushovers like Robert Mugabe in Zimbabwe were also bad men, but they had no oil or geopolitical significance.

A disgusted world might well have been right to topple the Iraqi tyrant on general principles. But even if he had poison-tipped Scuds ready to ship to Al Qaeda, America's invasion under its own flag was doomed from the start.

Bush dragged along reluctant British forces and token troops from Europeans who needed friends in Washington. The numbers were enough to knife into Baghdad, but the non-coalition's forces were nowhere near enough to seal borders against infiltrators or to quell resistance.

In the end, the irony was bitter. With a military top-heavy with brass and tied to a long chain of command, we reversed the roles of the Revolutionary War that won America its freedom from Britain. Never mind that we were the good guys. Tactically, we were Redcoats, muscle-bound with modern weaponry and tight formations. Iraqi diehards made Minutemen-type hits and runs. They had an edge because their way of life was at stake. After a certain period, we would be desperate to go home.

Reporters' books are often the best way to look back on a war. Since they must invariably lag behind events by many months, if not decades, they are hardly useful for looking ahead. In many cases, hindsight is nonetheless revealing. Michael Herr's *Dispatches* from Vietnam shows clearly enough what happens to perfectly normal young men when armed and pitted against an enemy who kills their buddies. Neil Sheehan's *A Bright Shining Lie* explains how reckless politicians can be with someone else's blood and money.

Mal Browne shows readers the inevitable sidelight stupidities of war. In 1964, he notes, the Pentagon sold 7,562 surplus 750-pound bombs to a German dealer. Two years later, it bought them back at ten times the price. Even back then, statisticians calculated it cost $100,000 to kill a single guerrilla.

In Nha Trang, Americans found a tasty fringe benefit to war duty: a particular sort of South China Sea lobster, prized by international gourmets for a century. With high demand, Vietnamese fisherman harvested it with grenades, blowing the succulent crustacean out of existence.

But, from the Ho Chi Minh Trail, Browne discovered something of broader substance:

"From the time of World War II, Americans have been brought up to believe that bombers can crack the toughest nut and bring any nation to its knees. Disney wartime cartoons portrayed air power as well-nigh invincible. . . . Although laser guidance and other innovations have improved bombing accuracy, an army of guerrillas is hard to hurt."

Already we have some superb books by great reporters about Iraq, and we will have more. Among many others, there is *Cobra II*, by Michael Gordon of the *New York Times* and Gen. Bernard Trainor. It is a meticulous account of how we got ourselves into Iraq and what went wrong.

Three books by *Washington Post* reporters delve into the details, with colorful, and alarming, example.

Thomas Ricks's *Fiasco* traces the lies, stupidities, and outright crimes that justified an invasion. It details how Donald Rumsfeld and Paul Wolfowitz undercut their generals, sending far too few troops to do impossible jobs. Solid intelligence was ignored or fixed to suit the circumstance.

Rajiv Chandrasekaran's *Imperial Life in the Emerald City* reveals how amateurs selected for neo-conservative loyalties tried to remake an ancient society behind fortified blast walls in between bacon breakfasts, ham-sandwich lunches, and pork-chop dinners. Alex Dehgan, the man sent by the State Department to win over destitute Iraqi scientists capable of making chemical and biological weapons, was sabotaged by a Pentagon majority. American colleagues threatened his life. One American guard helped him, Chandrasekaran wrote, "but on the condition that Dehgan procure a full-length mirror from outside the Green Zone so the guard could look at his Iraqi girlfriend's backside when they had sex in his trailer."

Among the most telling is Anthony Shadid's *Night Draws Near.* Unhindered by translators, Shadid teaches us some useful Arabic. *Ihtilal,* for instance, the word for occupation, is heavily charged with connotations of humiliation and defeat that go back a very long way.

At one point, while Ricks accompanied an American patrol, Shadid followed fifty yards behind to interview Iraqis in his fluent Arabic. "Everybody likes us," one young specialist told Ricks. Asked if he thought Iraqis wanted Americans to stay, the soldier said, "Oh, yeah. I'd say ninety-five percent friendly." But a man named Mohammed Ibrahim, representative of the bystanders, spoke for himself: "We're against the occupation—not one hundred percent, but one thousand percent. They're walking over my heart. I feel like they're crushing my heart."

The greatest lesson we can draw from Iraq is summed up in that brief remark by an old soldier who meant it with no irony: War is hell. This applies to just about any instance when explosives, napalm, or automatic-weapon fire turns humans to red jelly and charred bits. For anyone who sees this firsthand, it is very hard to convey just how much hell war can be.

Beyond the problems of access, censorship, and false battle reports, journalists can seldom reflect the reality of war. Words are not enough. Even when cameras get in close, as they often do, they seldom show the worst of it. Reflecting reality takes skill, not only the photographer's but also editors' down the line. Good taste and decorum are often wise to avoid shocking readers. But war ought to be portrayed as it is.

Three AP photos tell us all we need to know about Vietnam. Mal Browne followed his instinct to stay with Buddhist monks protesting the war when other reporters wandered away. He was there when the monks splashed gasoline on Thich Quang Duc and set him aflame. Eddie Adams knew of Nguyen Ngoc Loan's hatred of Viet Cong guerrillas who terrorized Saigon. His Leica was ready when the general suddenly whipped his revolver to a prisoner's temple and fired. We saw Nick Ut's photo of Kim Phuc fleeing napalm in Vietnam because Horst Faas had the sense to lobby for it, and AP editors agreed. The thirteen-year-old victim was naked as she ran toward the lens, but her face showed all the anguish of a stupid, needless war.

Reporters, like photographers, know that the heart of the story is in the close-up. Consensus holds that our rapid advance into Afghanistan late in 2001 was a grand success, lauded by the people we delivered from the Taliban. Mostly, it was. But I found a father in Kabul standing in tears at the edge of a gaping crater. His daughter had been playing hopscotch in the street one morning. A smart bomb guided by a less-smart human obliterated her.

Armed conflict, however necessary, is always ugly. Whatever it may resolve, it leaves human wreckage—individual and societal—that no one can ever foresee. Kosovo is our best example yet of a "surgical" air war. Yet thousands of Albanian Kosovars, as well as Serbs who had nothing to do with Slobodan Milosevic's depredations, died during surgery.

Even for those able to shrug off other people's calamities, victors pay a high price. A Charles Krauthammer column in 2006 smirked at the idea that our war on Iraq swelled the ranks of terrorists who hate us. (Later in the year, that White House intelligence report confirmed the obvious: Of course it did.) This is not to pick on one thumbsucker. There are plenty of others who regard reality as a word game played at a distance.

From a distance, it looked so easy even to those Americans who should know better. Before the invasion, I talked with a man I admire, a sportswriter who routinely travels the world. The war, he said, would be a walkover. American high-tech military might was no match for medieval rabble. And then it would be over.

I said he was analyzing it like a game between the Boston Red Sox and the Grinderswitch Hamsters. Of course, he was right if this were baseball. But real hostilities never go so smoothly, or end so decisively. Nonsense, he replied; I was a defeatist. Our conversation troubled me for weeks. If a guy like him could miss this point, with all of his world experience, we were in deep shit.

War is the extreme, but our system of reporting today can be seen in a metaphor Plato might recognize. If you compare the horde of second-guessing editors, commentators, and assorted kibitzers to the handful of seasoned reporters out there seeing things firsthand, you might imagine a giant Minotaur balanced atop an olive pit.

We cannot hope to understand a war without experienced eyes able to see things from the standpoint of people at the wrong end of the guns. I saw this, yet again, when I got to Iraq.

By the time I reached Basra, soon after British troops had secured the city center, the war had already taken an ugly turn in Baghdad and much of Iraq. But the British forces, after weeks of fighting their way into town, had blown off most of the fog. Each morning, soldiers in soft-skinned trucks delivered barrels of water. They wore berets, with no body armor. If they did not act as if they expected people to shoot them, they figured, no one would.

Basra settled precariously into its prewar order. Once, driving by the central market on a road choked with traffic, I saw the oncoming lane was empty. I downshifted my rented monster GMC and made a U-turn, bumping slightly over a low concrete divider. My Baghdadi translator and our local guide were horrified. I had broken the law. Go figure. Here was a country in ruins, pounded by aircraft and artillery, with violent death in every direction. Girls were terrified of abduction. Armed gangs smashed into houses full of people. And these guys, good citizens, worried about a traffic misdemeanor.

Each night, we returned to our rented house just past a British roadblock. We were stopped, each time, a safe distance back. The British were cool but not foolhardy. Papers were examined, and we continued on. I was never uneasy. These troops asked questions before firing.

In those early days, Iraq was still shocked and even a little awed. Saddam was gone, and they had a blank page on which to draw new plans. The British had more practice at handling civilians, but Americans learn quickly. Diehards made trouble, yet Iraq was ready for the next step. During this window, the situation might have gone either way.

Ordinary Iraqis had paid heavily for their liberation from Saddam, but many seemed to take things as Kosovars did when U.S. warplanes drove out the Serbs. Once things returned to normal, they could mourn and start over. Healing would depend on their ability to get back to work, interacting constructively with their liberators. Nothing new could be built until the wreckage of the old, physical and psychological, was swept away.

Soon enough, from my vantage point in Basra, I saw the early window of opportunity begin to close. Initial relief shifted to an awkward wait for something else. As religious fanatics, political opportunists, and criminals poked at the edges of incipient anarchy, they found that no one pushed back.

I spent days with a family of Iraq's surprisingly numerous middle class. The father, an engineer at the state oil company, stayed home with his frightened wife, two teenage daughters, and an older son. The daughters skipped school, terrified at friends' reports that young men invaded classrooms and carried off attractive girls. Day after day, they watched old videos and speculated.

The parents soon lost their optimism and then even their gratitude. Under Saddam, they explained, if you were "clean" you could have a decent life. They hated Saddam. But by staying clear of politics, they ate well, watched videos, and took family outings in a new SUV. In a police state, crime belongs to authorities, and citizens have less to fear from run-of-the-mill evildoers.

Basra's police had all but evaporated away. Politicos quibbled endlessly over tea to divide up spoils. Coalition forces, barricaded in their compounds, dutifully took notes of a mounting tide of robberies, rapes, and mysterious disappearances, but they were not cops. Meanwhile, freelance fundamentalists demanded that women cover themselves and men grow beards to prove their faith.

After Basra fell, I drove north toward the confluence of the Tigris and Euphrates. Since forever, marsh Arabs had poled their little reed craft through the lush marshes that might have fringed the Garden of Eden. After 1991, furious that Shia clans living there supported the foreign coalition that retook Kuwait, Saddam drained the marshes. He diverted rivers, bulldozed dikes, and left an ancient way of life to wither away.

American officials announced in Baghdad that they had restored civilian order in the area. At the crumbling town hall in the district seat, I found the new government: two young U.S. soldiers, who were locked in a noisy argument with six Iraqis—neither side spoke the other's language. They were known as ORHA, an acronym that was even less comprehensible in Arabic than it was in English. (It stood for Office of Reconstruction and Humanitarian Assistance.)

Hundreds of villagers milled around for a chance to join in the fruitless shouting match. Each had an urgent problem to be solved. None had work, and few had money. Many were afraid for their wives and daughters. People mysteriously disappeared. With no one keeping even token order, old scores were settled.

That, as it turned out, was typical. United States forces had their own problems to settle. Former officials were gone. After the American proconsul cashiered the Iraqi army, groups of angry, hungry men roamed around ready to use their specific skills for their own purposes.

By now, we all already know the rest.

From the war's opening moments, it was evident to seasoned witnesses where things were headed. How long it might take invading troops to reach Baghdad was open to question. Whatever, they would get there. No one knew if hardcore Iraqis had the stomach for house-to-house street fighting. Yes or no, it was only a matter of time.

But the faces of American recruits hyped on adrenaline and fear told the story. The race to Baghdad would not win us many Iraqi hearts or minds. Rumsfeld had insisted on a minimal number of troops. That would keep costs low enough for a sympathetic Republican Congress to swallow. It would lessen invidious comparisons to Vietnam. And when slim columns of American tankers rolled into Baghdad, think of the bragging rights: We kicked their ass in street shoes.

Rumsfeld's strategy demanded a prior "softening" by relentless pounding from the air, with the sort of "collateral damage" evident in those photos from Lebanon. A blitzkrieg on the ground required what the military politely calls reconnaissance by fire. Translated, that means blasting the shit out of anything that moves.

Gary Knight, a courageous *Newsweek* photographer whose judgment I had learned to trust in a lot of ugly places, was an accredited "unilateral." He drove his GMC wagon behind invading forces. Unlike embeds, unilaterals went wherever their guts and gasoline supply would take them. They paid for it. If they got hit, or taken by Iraqis, they were on their own. Instead of watching from behind the guns, they saw what happened when shells landed. Embeds were kept clear of civilians. Unilaterals interviewed whomever they wanted.

Knight's conclusion was backed up by others, without exception: Troops advanced under fear of fire, and people died in droves. Carloads of women, old men, and children were blown away, by accident or sheer exuberance. A few young crazies seemed to enjoy legalized mass murder. Mostly, however, it was simple circumstance.

Before British troops moved out from Kuwait, officers lectured them at length on the challenges. They were going after Saddam, not Iraqis; how they treated civilians along the way would reflect on Britain afterward. American officers delivered pregame hellfire. Al Jazeera reporters documented this in a distressing film, *Control Room*. American troops went to war with rousing pep talks and thumping rock music. Lyrics like "Burn, motherfuckers!" pulsed through headphones as they crossed the desert.

Mike Cerre, a marine veteran of Vietnam whose ABC reports won an Emmy, rode with a U.S. tank column. At times, he said, he had to assess potential targets and urgently warn jittery gunners to prevent them from firing at clusters of civilians. That sort of thing happens in war, and there is seldom a seasoned observer to help out.

Cerre, like the others, found plenty of intelligent restraint, bravery, and ingenuity that also characterize American armed forces. Officers overcame planning failures and lack of supply. Their lightning dash to Baghdad was,

in some ways, as brilliant as its proponents say it was. But war, as that old
soldier said, is hell.

As I assembled postmortem accounts, I thought about CNN footage I
had watched, day after day, of the advance toward Baghdad. Walter
Rodgers, a graying old hand, seemed happy as a Cub Scout on a camping
trip. He told us of his touching attachment to Betsy, his Hum-Vee. He said
little of shattered family sedans full of grandmothers and kids.

Keith Richburg, now foreign editor of the *Washington Post*, followed
British troops into Basra. He found commanders astonished at how fiercely
Iraqis fought back, united by a shared aversion to foreign invasion, whatever
they might think of Saddam. At one point, he said, the radio carried a
speech by Tony Blair, who announced complete British control of a peace-
able Basra.

"We were pinned down in the outskirts, and stuff was blasting all
around us," Richburg told me. "I asked the British officer next to me
whether they were in control. 'Does it look like it?' he asked. It took them
another couple of weeks to finally take Basra."

One after the other, those heartwarming scenes of liberation faded in
the light of reality. We all watched that statue of Saddam fall to the ground
to the dancing of joyful Iraqis. It was, in fact, hauled down by a U.S. Army
tank recovery vehicle and a handful of determined young men. Filmed up
close, it recalled the Berlin Wall.

The American patrols that brought Saddam-less freedom to the streets
of Baghdad were quickly termed, "the Jews," in common parlance. One
Iraqi would warn another: "Don't go down there; the Jews have a check-
point." For many Arabs, in Iraq and beyond, the invasion was seen simple
U.S. support for Israel.

Then there was Jessica Lynch. Private Lynch was injured in an accident,
and Iraqis took her to a hospital. Hard-pressed doctors treated her and made
her comfortable, finding her privacy in wards overflowing with wounded
soldiers. When U.S. commandos stormed in to rescue her, relieved doctors
welcomed them. They were shoved aside.

Richburg got to the hospital not long after U.S. forces took Lynch away.
Doctors and other witnesses explained what happened. But that account of
generosity by simple Iraqis ran counter to the nation's prevailing mood. The
Post had already splashed the official version of a daring rescue against fierce
opposition. Richburg's story was buried deep inside the paper, and hardly
anyone took notice. Only later did the *Post* set the record straight.

By the time Bush put on a military costume and landed on an aircraft carrier to declare, "Mission accomplished," irreparable damage had been done not only in Iraq but across the Middle East and the Islamic world.

Iraqi civilian deaths mounted fast, and no one knew the numbers. General Tommy Franks brushed off a reporter's question with stunning callousness: "We don't do body counts." Before long, people who believed human life in Iraq to be worth no less than in America began to make serious efforts to assess the damage.

The Web site www.iraqbodycount.com has done a Herculean task of keeping track of confirmed deaths. On April 11, 2007, for instance, it listed a minimum of 61,202 civilian victims, with a high-range total of 67,146. A click on its database gave names, locations, causes, and sources of information. Other links gave news, background information, and graphics. Franks' words, spoken in our name, are emblazoned atop the home page.

In wartime Iraq, however, only a fraction of bodies are counted. Authorities, like reporters, are limited in their movements. Records are in turmoil. Families bury their dead quickly, according to Islamic custom. Late in 2004, the British medical journal *The Lancet* published a study by Leslie Roberts, an epidemiologist at Johns Hopkins Bloomberg School of Public Health in Baltimore. After nine wars to practice on, he applied the type of random sampling used for opinion polls. With census figures and past mortality rates, Roberts selected a thousand households to represent the whole of Iraq. Since Americans were so hated by then, he said, he equipped Iraqi pollsters with global positioning system devices to find selected clusters.

The study concluded that 100,000 civilians—half of them women and children—were killed in the first year of war. Roberts called this a solid statistical median based on complex mathematics. There may have been fewer deaths. Or there may have been 300,000.

Roberts's numbers came close to extrapolations reported earlier in the *New England Journal of Medicine*. Doctors studying posttraumatic stress disorder interviewed soldiers back from Iraq. They found 14 percent of U.S. army troops, and 28 percent of marines, had killed a noncombatant.

In October 2006, *The Lancet* reported the results of an updated Bloomberg School survey: Because of the war, 654,965 Iraqis had died. Of those deaths, 91 percent were caused by gunshots or explosives. Brown, along with Gilbert Burnham, based the estimate on a nationwide sampling, comparing mortality rates over three years. They concluded they were 95 percent certain that the actual number fell between 392,979 and 942,636.

At first, the British government publicly rejected the findings. In March 2007, however, the BBC reported that documents obtained under freedom of information laws showed that official advisers found the study used sound methods. Roy Anderson, chief scientific adviser to Britain's Ministry of Defense, described the methodology as "robust" and "close to best practice." *The Independent* quoted an unnamed official as saying the study was "a tried and tested way of measuring mortality in conflict zones."

In February 2007, a six-page article in *Johns Hopkins Magazine* examined not only the epidemiology but also the politics that swirled around the study. Brown had insisted the numbers be published before U.S. elections to feed the debate. Burnham, co-director of the Johns Hopkins Center for Refugee and Disaster Response, said he tried to keep public reaction focused. "I have one central message," he told the magazine. "That central message is that local populations, people caught up in conflict, do badly. This is not a study that says, *Ain't it awful.* This is a study that says, *We need to do something about this.*"

As always happens when information is scarce, people went with what they had. For those who wanted to believe the worst, 650,000 dead civilians by mid-2006 was a solid floor for further speculation.

From the beginning, fresh hatreds smoldered and flared in pockets from North Africa to the Far East within a religion that is also a way of life for more than a billion people. Suicide bombers proliferated. Angry young fighters and Al Qaeda operatives headed for those unguarded Iraqi borders.

Global political balances were tilted precariously, perhaps permanently. By forcing a yes-or-no choice, Washington divided its European allies at a time when they needed unity to build a grand new European Union.

Once the invasion was launched, options were limited. Prowar factions reminded Americans that it was their duty to protect our boys. There is no arguing with that. Even then, the Bush administration still had a chance to look at reality and cut its losses. Some effective and courageous reporting within the mainstream and at the edges equipped anyone paying close attention to realize this. But the bulk of that amorphous "media" drowned them out.

Had Bush waited for U.N. inspectors to report, and had he discussed options with other world leaders as his father did in 1991, the resultant mess would not be America's to clean up alone. Nor would an increasingly hostile Arab and Islamic world focus its resentment on the United States.

Afterward, Dominique de Villepin, foreign minister at the time, told me France would have joined a U.N. -backed coalition as it did in 1991 once inspectors reported. Jacques Chirac (Chiraq, to some) once had warm ties to Saddam, but so did Rumsfeld. Who knows? Polls said 75 percent of the French opposed invasion, even with a U.N. resolution. They know a lot about war.

Perhaps France would have vetoed Security Council action, no matter what. Maybe the world's only superpower should have stepped up when others would not. Yet such a decision changes the world. It was made based on spurious evidence by a clique of political zealots in an administration that squeaked into the White House by a disputed vote. We the people were not paying attention.

Whatever else Pentagon planners learned in the first Gulf War, they honed their skills at deploying what they termed "media personnel." Enterprising journalists could avoid the pool system in 1991. With an actual coalition, we used the Egyptians or the French Foreign Legion for access. Or we simply eluded roadblocks and struck out on our own. Twelve years later, the U.S. High Command had it down. Some stunning exceptions aside, overall coverage of Gulf War II was, in a word, pathetic.

News executives back home knuckled under to the military. Some, with little sense of journalism's tenet of objectivity, felt patriotic. But more than that, they needed images, the appearance of access. In exchange for a steady supply of escorted action footage and formal briefings, they gave away the reporter's classic role in wartime. Brave souls who struck out on their own were at great risk of that oxymoron: friendly fire.

In Gulf War II, media muzzles and blinders that once would have been angrily rejected were hailed as unprecedented new access. If the damage were not so calamitous, you could almost admire that sort of blatant official manipulation.

The bulk of reporters were embedded. It is hard to think of a more degrading term, even aside from the "in bed with" double entendre. The implication is to be an integral part of something. In a postmortem, Rick Atkinson of the *Washington Post* described the scorn that sergeants heaped on journalists who struggled through basic training. In any sensible system, the press is not the military.[5]

Embedding offers a vantage point for watching action up close. Yet its soda-straw view cannot begin to replace broad coverage by reporters who are independent from the army they cover. Embedded, even some reporters who sought balance found themselves in the role of cheerleaders.

In any war, reporters face agonizing decisions about what they ought to say. In Kuwait, in 1991, I decided on my own not to dwell on how miserably unprepared Gen. Barry McCaffrey's 24th Mechanized Division seemed to be, with weapons that would not work. I wrote about why soldiers were grousing, however, and I was banned from his area of operations. (It is amusing to see McCaffrey advising on TV how reporters should cover war. After forty years as a correspondent, the only time I spent as a prisoner of war was at his MP guard post. When a U.S. officer then asked the Saudi press liaison to revoke my visa, the man replied, "But, sir, haven't you read your First Amendment?")

Any reporter's abilities go only so far. If you don't see it, you can't describe it. Even seeing it is often not enough. Covering a war requires interpretive skills that are only learned the hard way. Sometimes, the best work is done by young reporters on their first job abroad. But the smart ones stick close to experienced correspondents, not only for safety but also to help draw educated conclusions.

As we geared up for Iraq, I cringed when a colleague, fresh out of the box, observed, "I'm really going to learn a lot about myself." Too much depended on thoughtful, seasoned coverage. He was not the story at hand.

War reporting breaks down into three broad categories.

Up-close dispatches of the sort Ernie Pyle wrote in World War II are indispensable. People back home need to know what is happening with their boys and, now, their girls. Reporters love them, with their potential for color, pathos, and flashes of pithy wisdom. For this, embedding is perfect. But the price is high. Reporters stick with one unit, and access is limited to their line of sight. Good ones might maneuver into decent vantage points. Mostly, it is like covering a ball game from one team's dugout, with no view of the scoreboard or the field and only a reflected sound of the crowd. Kind of like being in a cave.

Official briefings, the second category, are good for seeking comment on what reporters see on their own. But far-back shoutfests in Washington offer little except an idea of how far commanders are ready to stray from reality. Soft-edged jargon conceals ugly human truths. Edited footage of successes passes untested. Reporters far from action can be palmed off with generality and evasion. The Pentagon adores them; they make great television which helps mislead a worried public that is praying for the best. If reporters push too hard to demand real information, an outraged nation sees them as rude and unpatriotic.

The third category is what counts. With real access, journalists frequent military officers to find the inevitable few who understand that truth is important. They can see what a broad range of soldiers feel, up front and far back, and how they react among people they came to defend. In war, correspondents need to start with a wide angle and then zero in on what they see as the details that matter. Rising above bang-bang and hi-mom stories, they can focus on the questions that matter: How is the war really going? What is wrong that needs to be fixed?

Only large news organizations can do this last sort of reporting. Magazine writers such as Jon Lee Anderson or George Packer of the *New Yorker* excel at this multifocus reporting. But, working alone, they can only sample. With its inevitable fog and predictable propaganda, war is most efficiently covered by a well-deployed, well-directed team that moves at will. This needs coordination. Overall dispatches are written by seasoned writers close to the action. Washington reporters follow up on leads from the field. Executives demand access from a Pentagon and a White House that discourages unfiltered observation.

The *New York Times* did this for much of the Iraq War despite fierce battles among its own correspondents that spilled into public showdowns. The *Washington Post* and *Los Angeles Times* often did well. But this sort of broad coverage is a logical role for news agencies. Remember the new-look AP? The Iraq invasion was not AP's finest hour.

In any reporting, what does not get said is as important as, often much more important than, what is. All of us—the U.S. "media" in general—missed much from Iraq. Mostly, the problem in Iraq was overweening control by distant, often unskilled, editors who thought they knew better than seasoned people on the ground.

AP supervised its reporters from the rearguard military headquarters at Doha, where desk people worked long hours to take dictation from the field. Its roundups were often written from New York and Washington, with joint bylines including writers half a world away from the war. After Ravi Nessman braved the early charge in Baghdad, he had to share a byline with a writer on the desk at home who mostly rearranged words on a computer screen.

At one point, exasperated by all the second-guessing up the line, I cracked to an editor in Doha that AP had two war desks, and neither was near the action.

"We're not that far away," he said.

"Oh, right," I replied. "We've got three war desks."

Later on, several of AP's most seasoned reporters told me they turned down temporary Baghdad assignments. They saw no point in risking their lives and their reputations to provide chunks of raw reportage for editors in New York to shape according to their own secondhand perceptions.

While American reporters kept track of U.S. losses, for instance, few had any idea how many Iraqi combatants or civilians died. In May and June 2003, AP made an attempt to count civilian victims. Reporters canvassed hospitals and morgues, presenting their findings in a long dispatch. Anxious not to overstate, it left out casualties that authorities could not verify. It skipped inaccessible rural sectors and the Basra area. AP supplied a credible minimum of 3,240 deaths, noting the real toll "is sure to be significantly higher." That was useful. But with no true measure of overall magnitude, it distorted reality.

In the heat of war, media-military friction grew deadly. United States forces fired on Baghdad's Palestine Hotel, killing several of the hundreds of journalists lodged there. Reuters made a formal complaint. Meantime, an executive of the British agency suggested that accredited journalists should carry transmitters so troops could distinguish them from fair-game battlefield rabble. "Great," photographer Gary Knight cracked at the time, "that gives them something to aim at. And they can track you to see exactly who you interview and where you go."

With muted resistance from news organizations, official policy shaped the public mindset. The Vietnam War ended, in large part, because of all the caskets coming home. After the first Gulf War, the military prohibited such images. The official reason is respect for families. But the caskets are not identified. Surveys show most families would prefer to have their boys come home in public, as heroes, under the nation's flag.

Instead of fighting this ban, or ignoring it by taking pictures when opportunities arise, news executives go along with it. Pentagon officials could deny them access to other images they might need for a competitive product.

In Iraq, via satellite and the Internet, Americans had broad access to foreign coverage of the war. The BBC often seemed to show a different universe than CNN. But the most impact came from Al Jazeera, the new network funded by the sultan of Qatar with the stated purpose of trying hard to be objective.

Many Americans trashed Al Jazeera as Al Qaeda's propaganda machine. This was predictable enough. When Harrison Salisbury went to Hanoi for the *New York Times* during the Vietnam War, countrymen called him a traitor. Peter Arnett, who stayed in Baghdad for CNN in 1991, was widely denounced as a spokesman for Saddam. Al Jazeera, run by Arabs and often the conduit for Osama bin Laden's pronouncements, was a fairly obvious target.

Yet Al Jazeera staked its reputation on proving its credibility. Its staff, mostly trained at the BBC, used the same news agencies shared by others. As humans, its reporters faced the same cultural and emotional pressures as all journalists. The network seemed steadily more hostile toward U.S. forces, but that might be because of an unexplained attack that killed a star reporter.

A reasonable observer might not call Al Jazeera objective. But neither does Fox News meet that standard. In a talk with Tina Brown on CNBC, Christiane Amanpour included CNN in a blunt analysis.

"I think the press was muzzled, and I think the press self-muzzled," Amanpour said. "I'm sorry to say, but certainly television and, perhaps, to a certain extent, my station was intimidated by the administration and its foot soldiers at Fox News. And it did, in fact, put a climate of fear and self-censorship, in my view, in terms of the kind of broadcast work we did."

Asked if there were stories that she could not report, Amanpour replied: "It's not a question of couldn't do it, it's a question of tone. It's a question of being rigorous. It's really a question of really asking the questions. All of the entire body politic in my view, whether it's the administration, the intelligence, the journalists, whoever, did not ask enough questions, for instance, about weapons of mass destruction. I mean, it looks like this was disinformation at the highest levels."

Afterward, Irena Briganti, spokeswoman for Fox News, reinforced Amanpour's dig with a rebuttal that said: "Given the choice, it's better to be viewed as a foot soldier for Bush than a spokeswoman for al-Qaeda."[6]

As a source to be tested with suspended belief, like all news sources, Al Jazeera is a valuable tool. It fills in much of what American reporters miss. And it offers a heavy dose of verifiable reality not available elsewhere.

As I watched one interview with soldiers who explained how they sprayed lethal fire in an out-of-body high, I heard in my head a variant of that memorable line from Vietnam: "We had to destroy the country to save it, sir." Cameras can lie, but they can also show the truth. I saw on Al Jazeera one tearful tirade by an Iraqi mother who spewed a hateful invective of curses at everything that had to do with America. Anyone who believes that was somehow staged, or out of context, is denying reality. I have seen too many of those mothers with my own eyes.

Al Jazeera aside, insightful reporting comes from Arabic-speaking reporters, like Anthony Shadid, for mainstream American media. Their physiognomies blend in, and people tend to trust them. They understand emotional triggers and cultural context that outsiders might not fathom. In a better world, they would report directly to their audiences, fatigue-induced typos and all. A dispatch dictated into a faltering phone under gunfire might not be pretty, but it tells the story.

In reality, a lot of reporters are not particularly articulate. Others are sloppy. Most work as part of a team; finished dispatches include facts and background added by others. For better or worse, correspondents have editors. And editors have editors. By the time someone's firsthand war account finds its way to the eventual consumer, it is likely to have passed through at least a dozen sets of hands.

Editors have guidelines—orders—passed down from on high. These include filters and safety barriers meant to protect management from criticism or embarrassment. Often they get squarely in the way of reality.

During the siege of Fallujah, for instance, AP wires were thick with stories from one side. Embedded reporters told of U.S. soldiers' determination against the odds. Daily roundups spoke of insurgents via secondhand sources. Washington-dated stories gave official U.S. points of view.

In a mood of growing tension, an Arabic-speaking AP correspondent managed to connect with Iraqi resisters defending Fallujah. They spoke their minds, at first reluctantly, then with eagerness to get across their thoughts to a man they believed would present their side to the world. It was a courageous piece of work; some insurgents took hostages. And it was badly needed balance for a worldwide news organization that insisted it was not the America-slanted agency many people took it to be.

The reporter could not name his sources. They were clandestine rebels vigorously sought by Iraqi and U.S. intelligence. AP editors accept anonymous sources in some circumstances. Not this time. The story was killed.

Sometimes the public gets a whiff of this. In September 2004, Farnaz Fassihi, a thirty-one-year-old Iranian-born *Wall Street Journal* reporter with a Columbia University journalism master's degree, e-mailed a private dispatch to her friends. It was remarkably straight, simply reporting things as they were. Reporters lived under virtual house arrest, she said, unable to shop for groceries, eat at restaurants, or talk with strangers. Many Iraqis speak of "the situation," which she said "means a raging barbaric guerilla war."

She said Iraqi police were infiltrated—and murdered by the dozens. Reconstruction was all but paralyzed, and oil was routinely disrupted. "Iraqis say that thanks to America they got freedom in exchange for insecurity," she noted. "Guess what? They say they'd take security over freedom any day, even if it means having a dictator ruler. I heard an educated Iraqi say today that if Saddam Hussein were allowed to run for elections he would get the majority of the vote."

Fassihi's editors were miffed. But the e-mail quickly got to be a cause célèbre, bounced widely around the Internet. Their options were limited. They announced that she had chosen to take a long vacation, although Iraq's crucial election campaign was just getting under way. In speeches later, she said the break had nothing to do with the e-mail. What the editors did not explain was why this clear-eyed view of reality did not show up regularly in their newspaper.

As the Iraq War drags on, it reveals disturbing facets we never stopped to worry about. One is how thin the line can be between conquering legion and ragtag rabble. In his war diary, *The Last True Story I'll Ever Tell,* John Crawford describes what America's formidable fighting machine looked like from the inside.

"Without a supply chain, the equipment we needed to perform our mission fell into disarray," Crawford wrote. "Our night-vision devices were useless without the swing arm to mount them. Our retooled Vietnam-era rifles began to show their age, falling apart with the slightest usage. We became shadows of the shock-and-awe troops that Americans saw on television. My uniforms were torn beyond repair and my boots had no soles on them. Still we walked on, day and night, sloshing the sewage-filled streets."

During 2006, on a trip to Tucson, I saw how war played out on the home front. At Davis-Monthan Air Force Base, where pilots can fly in dry desert air all year long, jet exhaust rattles windows. But that is only noise.

One afternoon, I found a battle being fought on East Speedway in front of the army recruiting center. On one side of the six-lane boulevard, a crowd chanted support. Two men in the group had lost sons in Iraq; they felt that waffling over the war dishonored their sacrifice. Across Speedway, the other side shouted just as loud.

For hours I crossed back and forth to query the protesters, taking each one's arguments to the others. Some were grateful that a reporter was interested. A few brushed me off rudely, presuming I was either a liberal or a conservative, whichever they did not happen to be. No one was ready to give an inch to anyone else's arguments. And no one, on either side, had much of a grasp of what was really happening in Iraq.

War is no time to slip into the senseless generalities we accept as fact in so many instances. Some soldiers are still there by choice, committed despite all the obstacles to finish the job. More were caught by accident, realizing too late they did not read the fine print when signing up for cushy National Guard duty. There is everything else in between. We have both heroes and psychopathic killers over there. Human nature works that way.

The fault is not with troops who go where they are told and put up with conditions as best as their individual mental circuitry allows. Families of the fallen each respond in different ways. Cindy Sheehan's son was among the first to fall when Iraqi insurgents fought back. She chose to memorialize him by mounting a broad-based protest. Roy Velez of Lubbock, Texas, lost a son at Fallujah in 2004 and suffered quietly. Two years later, his other son was killed in Afghanistan, the war we forget. "I can't be angry," he told reporters. "I feel like my heart's been pulled out. We've done what the Lord allowed us to do for our country."[7]

In the fifth year, the war began coming home in other ways. Our folly had displaced 1.9 million people within Iraq but also sent another two million to safety beyond its borders, the U.N. Refugee Agency reported. Some spent year after year camped in sandy limbo outside Jordan's borders. Though we made the mess, America accepted only hundreds on the theory that larger numbers would be an admission of defeat. Iraqis would go home when we won. By 2007, when we began to accept reality, we were faced with another limit. A presidential determination limits the inflow of refugees to 70,000 a year—from everywhere.

When a democracy goes to war, it is the decision of leaders who are supposed to reflect the will of citizens who elect them. A more energetic and less jingoistic media should have told us clearly what we were up against before it was too late. By the 2004 elections, we all ought to have seen enough reality for ourselves, and we could have held those leaders to account.

Plato had much to say on senseless warfare. But Walt Kelly's much-cited cartoon possum, Pogo, probably said it best: We have met the enemy, and he is us.

EIGHT

CORPORATE COLONIALISM—AND WORSE

The Iraq War brings to an absurd peak a paradox I have watched worsen over decades. We Americans so love our flag that many are more fearful of its being scorched than of a global fuse blowing. It obstructs car windows and flies o'er Dunkin' Donuts. Each morning, kids pledge their allegiance to it, hands on hearts. We serenade it solemnly off-key at every public occasion. Sung on foreign soil, it moistens hardened eyes. Yet we let all manner of modern-day privateers and pirates dishonor it in our name.

Far too often, American executives abroad ought to be flying the Jolly Roger. Corporate excesses are bad enough at home where we can keep an eye on them. Outside our cave, U.S. companies quite literally get away with murder. They are protected, when not abetted, by the government. Our elected and hired officials often have much to gain. And we all pay the price.

No blanket generalities apply, since each enterprise has its own purposes and policies. Obviously enough, many companies trade fairly, treating employees, shareholders, and customers with ample respect. In some cases, good people commit unwitting outrage in a system they did not create. But in others, executives willfully endanger lives for their own profit. Taken together, private business supported by public policy results, in places, to what amounts to corporate colonialism.

Debate within our cave over whether this state of affairs is good or bad for a wider world is beside the point. What matters is how other societies perceive American business abroad—and how they react to it.

The economic, social, and political implications of globalization on other countries are an important factor. We will get to this in chapter 9. But what concerns us most directly is how U.S. private activity impacts America. This includes not only American-based multinationals and other legitimate companies but also criminal organizations that operate across borders with near impunity.

"Outsourcing," that ubiquitous nonword of multiple meanings, is a useful place to start. The concept often refers to exporting jobs. Although troubling, this has its advantages; it can shave costs, raise productivity, and pump salaries into a foreign economy that needs them. But outsourcing can take on grave consequences at official levels. There are limits for a government that is of, for, and by the people.

In Iraq and Afghanistan, we franchise life-and-death authority to privateers under our flag. With more than 100,000 in Iraq alone, contractors are almost as numerous as troops. At inflated rates, they do much of what grunts in uniform used to do. They run military supply lines. When they shoot people, accidentally or not, they are essentially beyond the law. They interrogate, manhandle suspects, run prisons, patrol perimeters, and spy on civilians. War, especially war meant to establish moral principle, is not supposed to work that way.

At home, we see a similar trend to hire out authority. Quasi-official contactors with U.S. flags on their sleeves and flexicuffs on their belts provide "security." Private companies collect federal taxes for a cut of the take, and they traffic in intimate details of our daily lives.

Our free-market ideology holds that outsourcing allows private enterprise to provide services at less cost and greater efficiency than the government could. Sometimes this works well. Yet abuses are legion. Companies bilk us for many millions at a pop. Then they are given yet more contracts so they can do it again. Political leaders who confer this power gain so much from it that we can hardly expect anything different unless taxpayers—voters—demand it.

The practice is woven deeply into our system. Old-boy networks tie politicians to companies they once ran or whose stock they own in large quantities. Campaign contributors, lobbyists, and other institutionalized influence peddlers underpin the workings of Washington.

Reporters dig up plenty of hard evidence of outrageous cost overruns, price gouging, and no-bid contracts worth billions to companies that fail spectacularly to deliver. Some facts point to unpunished murders. Yet here again is that lack of resonance. Travesty is exposed on the front page of the *Washington Post*, and tongues are clucked. Inquiries are ordered, and fines may be paid. For the most part, we pay little attention and do nothing about the structure that allows these abuses to recur.

The good news is that systems are in place to keep track of abuse—provided enough citizens pay enough attention to help them to bite with all of their teeth.

As the stench of scandal grew in Iraq, a Texas Republican lawyer with a conscience dug into corporate abuse. Stuart Bowen directed SIGIR, the Office of the Special Inspector General for Iraq Reconstruction. He revealed missing billions, with details of spectacular overcharging, nonperformance, and the absence of oversight in Baghdad or Washington. Many of Bowen's findings went to the Justice Department for likely criminal charges. His mandate ran well into 2008 unless Congress declared its work was done.

Late one night in 2006, Rep. Duncan Hunter, chairman of the House Armed Services Committee, had a staffer insert a line into the Defense Department funding bill: He shut down SIGIR. This was after both parties had spent weeks reaching a compromise on the mammoth document. Virtually no one saw the insert before it went to the White House. Hunter, a Republican from San Diego, had announced he would run for president, with major funding from California defense contractors.

After elections gave Democrats a congressional majority, however, Bowen was back to work. Susan Collins, the Republican senator from Maine, joined with Democrat Russ Feingold of Wisconsin to save SIGIR. "The important work of this watchdog must continue as long as American funds are being used for Iraqi reconstruction," she said.

Since January 2002, Bowen's team had nailed companies such as Halliburton for systematically defrauding taxpayers for services rendered, or not, in Iraq. In a C-SPAN interview shortly before his office was to be closed, Bowen said his agency had ninety-two open investigations of alleged taxpayer fraud, which could total billions of dollars. Five were with the Department of Justice. The majority of corporations under scrutiny, he added, were U.S.-based.

One report, released two weeks before the midterm elections, claimed Halliburton billed the U.S. Army $52 million over ten months for overhead costs on an oil construction project before it was even begun. A separate report, also issued in October, accused Halliburton of wasting $75 million on a failed pipeline project.

Bowen said government officials ignored serious errors and took only "limited action" to reduce costs when projects were stalled. Later, Bowen told the *Guardian* of London that squandered funds might surpass $4 billion, largely because of widespread Iraqi smuggling and black marketeering, which often had American complicity. "Corruption is the second insurgency, and I use that metaphor to underline the seriousness of the issue," Bowen told the paper.[1]

Even with the official auditor back on the job, this was still Washington, where evidence of wrongdoing does not necessarily result in punishment. Bowen said on C-SPAN that as a result of the seventy-two reports his office had issued, mostly on apparent profiteering, four people had been convicted.

Perhaps it just takes a little time. Late in November 2006, the Halliburton subsidiary KBR agreed to pay $8 million to settle charges of overbilling in Kosovo during 1999 and 2000. "The Department of Justice remains committed to vigorously pursuing allegations of procurement abuses affecting the military," Assistant Attorney General Peter D. Keisler declared. But another view came from Patrick Burns of the nonprofit Taxpayers Against Fraud, which supports the federal False Claims Act that dates back to the Civil War. "At a certain point, justice delayed is justice denied," he told the *Washington Post*. "People are going to say, 'When were we in the Balkans?'"

Several False Claims Acts cases were brought from Iraq. In one, whistleblowers accused Custer Battles of cheating the government. A federal jury ordered the company to pay $10 million in March 2006. In August, a judge threw out the decision. He said the Coalition Provisional Authority, in charge of Iraq at the time, was not a U.S. government entity.

Worse than fraud are accounts of torture and even murder by employees of private companies. Given the legal restraints, the mainline media are cautious about reporting on allegations. But occasionally they reach print. In November 2006, I clipped an intriguing *New York Times* piece headlined "Contractor's Boss in Iraq Shot at Civilians, Workers' Suit Says."

An ex–Marine Corps sniper and an ex–Army Ranger sued their former employer, Triple Canopy. The company, among the largest security contractors in Iraq, was set up in 2003 by former Delta Force commandos. The plaintiffs said they were sent to pick up a man from KBR, the Halliburton subsidiary, at Baghdad airport. The suit alleged that their shift leader, due to leave Iraq the next day, told them he was "going to kill someone today." Then, they said, he walked to a stopped white truck and blasted the occupants through the windshield with his M-4 assault rifle.

"That didn't happen, understand," the men said he told them. Later that day, according to the suit, the shift leader said, "I've never shot anyone with my pistol before," and he fired seven or eight shots into a passing taxi. In both cases, the plaintiffs said, they had to speed away without assessing the damage. When they reported the incidents to Triple Canopy's senior supervisors, they said, they were suspended and then blacklisted for future employment. A judge would decide.

In the 1960s, I got to know a trio of legendary "white mercenaries," African leaders hired for their dirty work: Jean "Black Jack" Schramme, a Belgian ex-planter, who claimed a chunk of the Congo as his own; "Mad Mike" Hoare, a South African who laughed about heating coins to bright orange before tossing them to kids; and France's serial coup-maker, Col. Bob Denard. Europeans and Africans alike called them *les affreux*. The term means "frightful" in normal French, but for people on their own wrong side, it translates more practically to bad-ass motherfuckers.

Even then, generalities meant little. Mercenary commanders often imposed strict discipline and a curious sort of Galahad code of honor. They fought their way into violent mayhem to rescue planters and missionaries from horrible fates. Yet their ranks included twisted maniacs who regarded rape and plunder as fringe benefits of the job. A few were little better than modern-day slavers. In tight situations, I was thrilled to see a column of "mercs" arriving to scare off crazed Congolese rebels. But I was also happy to see they were not flying my flag.

Today's hired guns package themselves better. As before, some are noble souls doing dangerous work for an honest wage. The job is thankless; nearly nine hundred privateers killed in Iraq by 2007 evoke less emotion than three thousand uniformed GIs. Yet the basic principle is the same. Mercenary ranks include Serb killers on the run, assorted escapees from justice, and rebels with no particular cause. Their employers are not only African bandit-kings but also the U.S. government. That is, you and me.

G overnments have always hired businesses; that is a fundamental way of doing things. Yet limits must apply. Raytheon and McDonnell-Douglas may build our warplanes. When that U.S. Air Force star gets painted on the tail, however, they do their job in America's name.

Ever since Francis Scott Key scribbled lyrics on the back of an envelope, America has gone to war under its own colors. Mercenaries have been around as long as prostitutes and journalists. In the 1960s and 1970s, they fought most of the battles for African despots. But real nations run by people who want to inspire others ought to do things the right way.

Other countries manage. Those skirling bagpipes and regimental standards that Britain takes to war serve little military purpose. Still, friend and foe alike get the message: The queen is making a point. The vaunted French Foreign Legion is made up of misfits and malcontents, many fleeing another country's justice. But once whipped into shape by French officers, they march under the *tricolore*.

Far beyond symbolism, the point is accountability. War, we know, is hell. When the fog settles in and obscures vision, anyone with a weapon has a license to kill. Flawed as it is, a system of military justice governs troops and their commanders. Private contractors can get away with just about anything.

In Iraq, we have built ourselves a Frankenstein's monster upon which many of us heap praise. Though most obvious in war, it applies often enough to where there is peace. We are outsourcing not only sectors of our economy but also our national integrity.

In *Mission to Civilize,* a book I wrote about the French decades ago, I noted an essential difference between France and the United States: "If you want a dog to look at something and you point at it, the dog will look at your finger. So will the French. France can be led by a logically moving finger to all but the most egregious objectives. Others might forego their objective if they cannot find the way there among their repertoire of principles. Or they might ignore their self-inflicted restraints, which, to the French, would be hypocrisy."

Nations borrow from one another. We have given France the McDonald's *royale cheese* and the half-caff latte. They have given us the concept of flexible morality. But we have missed the essential factor. The French expect their leaders to lie and double-deal, to apply what statesmen call *raison d'état* when the need arises. A recent poll in Paris found that 60 percent of Frenchmen assume public officials steal and cheat. Few are shocked when their leaders take a low road. Books describe elaborate scandals: how French companies run sizable chunks of Africa as private fiefdoms; how France's equivalent of a Supreme Court chief justice allegedly channeled illicit wherewithal to his mistress; how a past president accepted diamonds from a despot.

Americans want their leaders to take a higher road. This is why so many Frenchmen once admired us. We believe that our intended approach is more useful in creating a better world able to define good and evil. Perhaps we once lived up to this. These days, we inspire even less than the cynical French for a simple reason: we are hypocritical about our hypocrisy.

What is good for Halliburton is not necessarily good for America. Find a spare hour and poke into Halliburton's role in Iraq. As always, be wary of sources. Citizen critics can get wild with unsubstantiated assertions. But there is plenty out there. For starters: After late 2002, when Washington began rattling sabers at Iraq, the company's stock spiked from below 10 to above 40.

Halliburton is hardly the only example, but it is a good one. An edge given to a company so intimately linked to a sitting vice president illustrates how we have blurred the line between functional expediency and a national purpose that defines who we are. In England, possibly even in France, a deputy chief executive would have resigned at even a fraction of the obvious questions of impropriety.

Where this can lead was evident when the ITT Corporation pleaded guilty in March 2007 to sending classified military data to other countries—China, among others. The company agreed to pay a $100 million penalty.

ITT was contracted to supply night-vision goggles. To save money, government attorneys said, it outsourced part of the job. In one instance, two Chinese optical engineers worked on company designs at a plant in Singapore with local engineers who trained with ITT night-vision specialists in Virginia. In another, sensitive data was sent to Singapore, from where it was forwarded to other companies in England and China.

In a statement, U.S. attorney John Brownlee said the obvious. "ITT has put in jeopardy our military's nighttime tactical advantage and America's national security."[2]

In February 2007, the *New York Times* published a two-part series that captured the enormity, and the absurdity, of the problem. When the General Services Administration ran short of people to probe a case of incompetence and fraud by federal contractors, it found the usual solution: It hired another contractor. The *Times* noted:

> *It did not matter that the company they chose, CACI International, had itself recently avoided a suspension from federal contracting; or that the work, delving into investigative files on other contractors, appeared to pose a conflict of interest; or that each person supplied would cost taxpayers $104 an hour. Six CACI workers soon joined hundreds of other private-sector workers at the G.S.A., the government's management agency.*

During the Bush administration, the *Times* said, spending on this fourth branch of government rose from $207 billion in 2000 to about $400 billion in 2006. Work extended to intelligence collection and budget preparation. An analysis of the figures showed that only 48 percent of "contract actions" were subject to competitive bid, down from 79 percent in 2001. Successful contractors were not necessarily the most qualified but rather the most adept at selling themselves.

"The United States is quickly becoming," a *Times* editorial observed, "a government of the contractors, by the contractors, and for the contractors."

The rationale for placing government responsibility into private hands should go deeper than economy or convenience. Appearances, as well as the substance that should follow behind them, count for a great deal.

During 2006, Bush provoked public wrath by attempting to let a Dubai-based company run American ports. The debate focused on potential terrorism. After all, Dubai was full of Arabs, Muslims, and we knew all about them. But that, I believe, missed the larger point. Why should any private company, whether Middle Eastern, British, or American, administer U.S. ports of entry?

Few objected when a London-based company ran the ports. To our generality-type thinking, Brits are the good guys. Sandy-haired gentlemen with silk ties and umbrellas sail through our security spot checks. Bearded, turbaned Sikhs have a harder time of it. That is a separate issue, though. The government, God knows, is involved in far too many things and yet some things are basic. Authorities who answer directly to the public should be at the door when people and goods arrive from elsewhere.

How far this goes depends on one's philosophy. Private courier services are a godsend. But some people want to fully privatize the U.S. Post Office. Surely, a postal system must be entrusted to a government whose most basic laws forbid tampering or snooping. Or have we lost that one? Prisons are how a society punishes and rehabilitates those who break its laws, but private-enterprise guards have enormous power over inmates. Despots used to send mercenaries out to collect back taxes in exchange for a cut. Now we are attempting the same thing.

Much of this conflict is out of sight. Security rent–a–cops are visible enough. Yet we have only limited leaked knowledge of how much the Bush administration uses private contractors to gather and analyze sensitive intelligence. It is hard enough, these days, to trust our elected officials. Do we really want to contract out functions of the IRS and the CIA?

The principle here is clear. In public service, people we pay to uphold our laws and our shared values are bound by swear-to-God oaths. This goes from mail carriers to presidents. It ought to have some meaning.

The phrase "corporate colonialism" has come to mean the way big business—principally American business—dominates small countries unable to resist the economic forces. Their familiar logos represent us to the outside world as much as our Stars and Stripes. It is more than that. In important ways, corporations are also colonizing America. They shape how we work and live at home.

World leaders understand this new shift in who gets to call the shots. When Chinese leader Hu Jintao visited America in 2006, he stopped first where it mattered: in Seattle. After calls on Boeing and Microsoft, China's modern mandarin went on to the ceremonial part in Washington. One can argue that Washington state is a logical stopover en route to Washington, D.C. But China puts a lot of stock into subtle symbols; that itinerary delivered a message.

There was never much truth in that old saw "What's good for General Motors is good for America." When the automobile market boomed during the 1930s, GM and others bought up public transportation systems and dismantled them. In league with oil companies with as much to gain, automakers condemned us all to a future of ever wider roads and an ever growing thirst for polluting fossil fuel.

Back then, however, much of the Henry Ford mentality infused America. Just as Milton Hershey mass-produced chocolate bars, Ford figured out the value of smooth production lines operated by loyal people. His cars were reliable, easily repaired, and, above all, cheap. Anyone with a decent job could afford one. Low-cost sameness was part of the deal. If you wanted red, you had to buy a paintbrush. If you were rich, you could drive a Maybach.

The philosophy was clear. People who worked hard and learned their jobs well settled down for the long haul. If their kids were raised in a solid community and given good schooling, they would grow up to take their parents' place. Obviously enough, things no longer work that way.

The basic structures of an economy, a society, and a body politic are matters for collective decision. However each of us makes these subjective judgments, we have to get our facts straight. This is difficult in a nation colonized by a corporate mentality where facts, like principles, are flexible.

Business practice has eroded the notion that words mean anything. Just as an example, take Balsamic vinegar, which relatively few people beyond the hills near Modena have ever tasted. Balsamico, like Champagne, is a specific label with centuries of loving labor behind it. The real stuff, thick and sweet enough to enliven strawberries, costs marginally less than Chanel No. 5. That supermarket glop is bogus. This may matter only to committed foodies. But consider the implications.

Executives can now conjure up any reality that suits them. "Corporate communications" people find the essential flimflam to equip busy reporters and consumers with evidence of that reality. A fig leaf of legality for minimal cover is enough. Right and wrong are not in the vocabulary of our new lingua franca, Corporate Sleaze.

Occasionally, Corporate Sleaze is bluntly descriptive. "Personnel" is now "Human Resources," a department that might be just down the hall from "Animal Waste." This suggests, accurately, that the blood and energy that give life to any company amount to yet another input like steel sheets or soybeans.

But words that have no truth behind them blur reality beyond any recognition. One company swallows another and then boasts of attributes that it transforms into something else or kills outright. Take the staff of life, chocolate. The head of Campbell Soup, on holiday, dropped in at Godiva, Joseph Draps's little shop in Brussels. Before long, grim industrial candy was being sold at ludicrous prices as if it was a gifted craftsman's personal handiwork.

As happened with the primitive trading language of Swahili, Corporate Sleaze rapidly spread beyond borders. During all that hate-France business over Iraq, I was amused to hear Motel 6 commercials on the radio. That wonderful Tom Bodett voice still evokes the pleasures of a simple family inn, always ending: "We'll keep a light on for you." Then a quiet tagline notes the company belongs to Accor, the Paris-based group that owns all those cheesy Ibis and Mercure properties. While patriotic parents shunned Beaujolais, their kids' school lunches were served up by Sodexho, a French multinational octopus.

At the marketing level, this might be a simple case of caveat emptor. We can read labels, such as they exist, and the stuff we buy is not likely to kill us in any immediate time frame. The crisis here is how Corporate Sleaze and the practices it masks endanger not only the American middle class but also an informed, motivated electorate.

Not being partial to conspiracy theories, I am uneasy with the term "corporate media." Nonetheless, there is something to it. And the problem goes far beyond that. In previous administrations, but essentially under George W. Bush, American society has been reshaped for businesses' convenience. "No child left behind" is a jobs program that produces low-skilled drones instead of helping children to be the best that they can be. And so on, at every level.

Somehow, the doublespeak of Corporate Sleaze has convinced many of us that our lives improve as company earnings grow. In plain English, horseshit.

The *New York Times* has been good on this issue. Paul Krugman hits this hard regularly in his columns. Louis Uchitelle, who was AP Buenos Aires bureau chief before me, moved to the *Times* in 1980 and developed a specialty of business reporting. His book *The Disposable American* examines the impact of the mass firings managers use to pump up short-run financial numbers. Uchitelle punctures three myths behind the layoffs of at least 30 million full-time workers since the 1980s.

For one, a revitalized corporate America is supposed to emerge, with job security, full employment, and rising incomes. We only have to be patient. As we all know, this is not happening. The second myth is that workers have to save themselves. If they lost their jobs, it was because their value to their employers did not match wages and benefits. They should have retooled themselves.

The third myth defines our new economics-obsessed thinking, that the pros and cons can be measured in money. Uchitelle wrote, "I found this myth hard to challenge until I encountered and documented a layer of human damage that is difficult to quantify, but is alarmingly destructive, so much so that it sets back companies that are supposed to thrive the free-wheeling use of layoffs."

The book looks hard at this human damage, which undermines not only companies but also much of what underpins our society. Do your own reporting on this. Interview people who have lost jobs and then look at what has become of employers and industries that were supposed to benefit as a result. Be sure to go beyond quarterly numbers and stock price charts. Your subjects will be easy enough to find. Start with your family and friends.

O ur simple old construct, "rich versus poor," is hopelessly outdated. The gap between well-off and ex-middle class widens monthly. Worse, the abyss between hyper-rich and destitute has veered into the immoral. So far, the trusty Roman approach of bread-and-circus is calming the masses. How long can this last?

For years, I have depended on a reliable compass for charting my way through a baffling America, a Columbia University sociologist and close pal, Jeffrey Fagan. As a criminologist, he travels the world to speak at academic conferences and testify at trials as an expert witness. He studies the growing tensions of poverty and race, not only in the United States but also in Western Europe.

Jeffrey has always insisted that people in America tend not to resent the rich. "A guy at the bottom figures, hey, that could be me," he says. "That is totally unrealistic, but that doesn't stop people from believing it." These days, he is not so sure. Now, he says, we are breaking down into a class system.

The numbers are plain. For these, the most reliable come from Emmanuel Saez of the University of California at Berkeley and Thomas Piketty of the Ecole Normale Superieure in Paris. In March 2007, they reported on an analysis of U.S. Internal Revenue Service data for 2005.

The top 1 percent, with yearly incomes above $348,000, pocketed their largest share of national income since 1928; their average income was $1.1 million, a 14 percent gain, or $139,000, over 2005. Meantime, the bottom 90 percent averaged a dip of $172, or minus 0.06 percent. The top 10 percent, who average above $100,000, also saw their highest share of income since the Great Depression.

An elite layer of 300,000 Americans earned as much as the bottom 150 million, half the U.S. population. Per person, these happy few averaged 440 times as much as the typical working stiff. This nearly doubled the gap since 1980. The top one-hundredth of 1 percent had an average income of $25.7 million, up nearly $4.4 million in a year.

In fact, these numbers are understated. Wealthy taxpayers find ways to shield much of their incomes. Wage earners are stuck with W-2s. The IRS estimates that it accurately taxes 99 percent of wages but only 70 percent of business and investment earnings. Since the rich tend to file later, much of their data was not included in the study. Senate investigators who probe offshore tax havens say that 70 percent figure is likely far too optimistic.

Meantime, the Commerce Department reported that in 2006 Americans spent more than they earned, for a negative savings rate of 1 percent. That is the lowest level since 1928. For 2005, it was already minus 0.4 percent.

Saez said he expected 2006 inequalities to be at least the same, if not larger. While wages hardly moved, the rich had substantial stock market and business profits.

David Cay Johnston of the *New York Times,* one of the few American journalists to specialize in tax matters, noted the significance in terms of social stability.

"If the economy is growing but only a few are enjoying the benefits, it goes to our sense of fairness," Saez told Johnston. "It can have important political consequences."[3]

Credit cards max out, and unpaid mortgage companies eventually foreclose. When it really hurts, people finally begin to ask why.

In earlier studies, Saez and Piketty showed how government policy once helped to translate rising productivity into higher income for Americans at all levels, with minimum wage increases and a social safety net. Full employment was a priority, and unions gave workers bargaining power. From the mid-1970s, the gap widened fast. Legislators balked at raising the minimum wage or shaping taxes to help the working poor. Ronald Reagan's supply-side economics slashed progressive taxes. After a respite, Bush took up the knife, with tax breaks that were heavily weighted toward the top.

On paper, these are all a bunch of numbers. It gets clearer when you add up unconnected fragments. These are a couple from my miscellaneous pile: In Los Angeles, one hospital left a paraplegic man on the street in a gown and a colostomy bag; he pulled himself through the streets, gripping in his teeth a plastic bag with his belongings. In Philadelphia, a small investor who believed a firm cheated him shot three brokers and then himself.

Poverty is spreading from its usual places into once-flush suburbs where people moved on up to a better life.

The obvious question looms: Why can't a suffering majority replace the politicians who make these decisions? Every voter gets to say those words that terrify so many wage slaves when a porked-up bully with suspicious hair delivers them on TV: "You're fired."

The oil business is particularly galling. When the ExxonMobil CEO retired, Bill O'Reilly finally wrote something to agree with: "In the time of the French Revolution, Lee Raymond and his $400 million pension would be running one step ahead of the guillotine."

Just the name ExxonMobil sounds like an Orwellian spoof. A few companies control a vital industry that merely extracts a natural product of the planet's geological past. When the price per barrel rises, companies declare themselves helpless in a world market. So they jack up the price at the pump. The industry netted almost $140 billion in 2005, according to the Congressional Research Service; ExxonMobil alone made more than $36 billion.

It is not only oil. In 2006, *Fortune* magazine looked at U.S. executive salaries. Charlie Munger stated the ideal: "The CEO has an absolute duty to be an exemplar for the civilization." His partner, Warren Buffett, added: "The only cure for better corporate governance is if the small number of very large institutional investors start acting like true owners and pressure managers and boards to do the same." At the other extreme, *Fortune* looked at Bob Nardelli of Home Depot, who had just accepted a $250 million pay package although his company's stock declined.

"We have an enterprise here that stands tall among corporations in America," he told the magazine. "The last thing you want to do is withdraw into a fetal position on some of this stuff."

In January 2007, under pressure, Nardelli resigned. He took along a $210 million severance package that was agreed upon in 2000 when the company was anxious to hire him. His successor, Frank Blake, accepted a mere $8.9 million a year in salary. And he cancelled the traditional executive suite free lunch.[4]

Suddenly, CEO pay was a hot issue not only in board rooms but also in Washington and state capitals. The Securities Exchange Commission required more data from companies. Even George W. Bush made the obligatory noises. People starting notice things like Barry Diller's 2005 pay of $469 million even though his company's stock lagged badly behind the S&P. Writers trotted out John Kenneth Galbraith's remark: A chief executive's salary "is frequently in the nature of a warm personal gesture by the individual to himself."

Soon, however, hard reality blunted the object lesson. These days in America, greed pays. Nardelli was offered a huge salary by a private equity firm, one of those shadowy companies with uncounted billions it can use to pluck low-hanging, or rotten, corporate fruit.

A new trend is clear. "Five or ten years ago, it used to be that private company CEOs wanted to return to the public markets because they wanted to run their own ship, not have private equity managers second-guessing their decisions," Jeffrey Sonnenfield of the Yale School of Management told the *New York Times* early in 2007. It is different now. "You regularly hear public company CEOs talk about how they can make two or three times the money in what they feel is half the effort because they don't have the same degree of scrutiny."

This includes the big fish. John Browne, CEO of British Petroleum, announced in January 2007 he would move beyond petroleum. As chairman of the advisory board of Apax Partners, he would be free of public shareholder meetings.

Some private equity firms can be a force for good. Some are a scourge. The problem is that we have to guess which is which. As a general rule, by slashing jobs and rewarding a small pack of executives, they widen a growing gulf.

All in all, Voltaire put it succinctly enough: "The comfort of the rich rests upon an abundance of the poor." No one is storming the Bastille yet, but it seems like some sort of reckoning will have to come.

As 2007 approached, with America flailing in Iraqi quicksand, China decided to stop playing humble. With four times the population of the United States and a double-digit economy that could go anywhere their leaders want to take it, the Chinese mused aloud about what it takes to be a superpower. Empires have risen and fallen since ancient times. Maybe it was time for a change.

China's Communist Party has a slicker exterior than the 1960s Mao model. But if it decides to take any great leap forward in any direction, it does not need to bother with a referendum. Engineers pushed ahead with the Three Gorges Dam, despite warnings across the world that it may end up as the greatest man-made calamity ever built. With blogs in the millions, closets full of Christian Lacroix, and honeymoons to Venice, these are not your father's Chinese. Yet no one forgets Tiananmen Square.

When Chinese multinationals go abroad, to trade or to acquire essential

natural resources, the lines are thin between private and public. Free markets
in China are a convenience, not doctrine. If authorities decide to favor development over the environment, then rivers dry and gases choke the cities.
If local leaders fear rabies or even fleas, all family dogs are whacked. When
it comes to competition on a global scale, China's way may not be noble,
but it is expedient.

Underlying an all-business top layer is a deep-seated cultural foundation. China—the concept, not the country—has never stopped seeing itself
as the Middle Kingdom. I remember early on in Singapore when an aide
reminded Lee Kuan Yew that a British cabinet minister was waiting to see
him. Let him wait, Lee replied. His visitor had only a scant few centuries of
civilization behind him; Lee's culture was rooted in five thousand years of
recorded history.

I took it seriously, therefore, when the New York Times ran a long piece
on December 9, 2006, headlined "China, Shy Giant, Shows Signs of Shed-
ding Its False Modesty." A twelve-part series on China Central Television
examined the reasons why nine nations rose to world power.

Spain had a devoutly religious queen who sent explorers into unknown
reaches. Britain's navy locked up sea lanes to commercial entrepôts that cir-
cled the globe. The United States organized markets and forged national
unity. With a fast-growing military, a diplomatic corps that ranged the
Third World, and $1 trillion in foreign exchange reserves, why shouldn't
China take its shot?

Up until now, American and European companies have been falling
over each other for pieces of the action as China booms. With all of its
growth, most workers still pedal to pittance-paying jobs on bicycles. An energetic auto industry has yet to make cars that Western drivers want. Then
again, we all laughed at the first syllable in Toyota when those first odd
sedans showed up on American streets.

It is not only China. It may seem unlikely when one watches the show
in Brussels, but the European Union is for real. It amounts to a sort-of nation with half again as many people as the United States and a larger economy. Already, its twenty-seven member states are dissolving internal
borders, standardizing laws and customs regulations, and opening the way
for ever larger conglomerates with executives who learn to cut throats at
Harvard and Wharton.

Russia, India, and Brazil are full players in a new great game. If you
think Korea is anything like what we see on M*A*S*H, take another look.
Even Kazakhstan, Borat notwithstanding, throbs with modern industrial

growth. We will get to these places shortly. But, in thinking about America's role in the world—certainly in the world of business—they bear keeping in mind.

For now, American industry and business models still dominate the world. Some U.S.-based companies have gotten so big that they manage to entrench a reality that they themselves define. Wal-Mart, perhaps the best example, shows what we ought to be worried about.

Sam Walton's original idea made a great deal of sense. By buying carefully, keeping scrupulous track of inventory, and not squandering a cent on frippery, his company could ask unheard-of low prices for reasonable quality. The idea caught on fast, and Wal-Mart flourished across America. Then it decided to conquer the world.

That good idea went bad when Wal-Mart directors, pushed by shareholders, decided that employees were one of those fripperies on which not a cent should be squandered. Instead of living wages, they were given titles. Many of those "associates" worked killer hours with no health insurance and the flimsiest of benefits.

Public pressure has made an impact on Wal-Mart, which has made some concessions. But there is a long way to go.

Maryland passed a Fair Share Health Care Law that required large employers such as Wal-Mart to spend at least 8 percent of their payroll on employee health care or pay into a state fund. The idea was to protect workers while preventing rich companies from saddling taxpayers with bills of workers forced to rely on public care. In July 2006, a federal judge struck it down.

Meantime, Chicago's aldermen, reflecting concern over big-box exploitation, passed a "living wage" ordinance. It affected ten thousand employees of stores with surface areas above ninety thousand square feet and annual sales over $1 billion. The hourly minimum wage would jump to $9.25 in 2007 and $10.00 in 2010. Companies would provide health insurance worth at least $3.00 an hour by 2010. But the close vote caused a storm in Chicago.

Joe Moore, the sponsor, told Amy Goodman: "It is absolutely unconscionable that you can work a full day at a job, try to play by the rules, and yet still be in poverty. This ordinance is designed to . . . lift these employees out of poverty." He said Wal-Mart spent millions to lobby against the bill. Wal-Mart declined an invitation to the microphone but sent a statement:

"This vote sends a message that Chicago is closed for business, closed for development, and closed for job creation."[5]

When the measure passed, Wal-Mart, among others, threatened to move just outside the city limits. Moore insisted this was an empty threat; the suburbs were saturated, and big-box stores needed the Chicago markets. Similar measures worked in San Francisco and Washington, D.C., they said, because families had more money to spend.

But Mayor Richard M. Daley used his first veto in seventeen years to overturn the ordinance. "We have to create jobs," he told NPR. "Basically, they said we'll go right across the street into two suburban areas."

One alderman who switched sides to support Daley summed up the problem: "I felt that seven dollars an hour was better than no dollars."

Beyond America, Wal-Mart has had its problems. It had to slink out of Germany and South Korea for varied reasons. In part, large locally based competitors can do the same thing with products and styles that appeal more to their own cultures. But it is more than that.

For older European societies, life is about more than the price of a cellophane package of nylons. Even many people who struggle by on pensions prefer to shop where they can poke at real tomatoes and discuss streaky fat with a third-generation butcher. That costs more, but it is part of their richness. Governments worry that huge stores with cheap, and often inferior, goods are depopulating the villages and family farms that still define national character. Blacksmiths went a long time ago, but now shoemakers, fishmongers, hardware shops, and even bakeries are threatened.

The change is inevitable. A quarter century ago, I visited Monsieur Turpin, an extravagantly mustachioed vegetable man and pheasant plucker on the Ile Saint-Louis in Paris. Each morning, he rose at 4:00 A.M. to cruise the monster market at Rungis. He knew each one of his eggplants personally. That morning, he looked as if he had seen a circle of Dante's hell. "These people," he said, referring to tourists strolling past, "they are walking while they are eating."

Back then, I watched an elegant Frenchman order his first Big Mac. "Not too well done, please," he told the counter person. Now, one-tenth of all new McDonald's opened around the world are in France. José Bové got a lot of attention when he busted up a McDonald's about to open in Millau back in 1999. He was protesting U.S. duties on Roquefort cheese. Today at lunchtime, five separate lines of clamoring French people jam Millau's "McDo" to order *un beeg mac avec frites.*

The problem is not so much size, or even standardized taste, but rather the notion of power that bigness gives to corporate executives who, in the end, rely on customers and shareholders for their personal survival. This shifts political heft from people we elect to people who put themselves in the driver's seat.

Large companies with little commitment to moral concepts beyond what a compliance officer cannot sidestep, are not candidates for good governance. That is neither in their nature nor in their interest. The English praised themselves for shouldering the White's Man Burden. The French took pride in a "mission to civilize." Corporate managers need worry only about manufacturing and selling.

Jack Welch of General Electric excelled at both. When he made his long, emotional exit in the 1990s, news reports depicted a beloved monarch. He was called tough-minded yet human, the sort of man we need to put a thumping heart into corporate America if not America itself.

At about the same time, a story inside the *Washington Post* reproduced a thank-you note from GE Investments to Harty Press, a contractor that had polled shareholders. "The hard part," it said, "came with our request to be able to 'secretly' identify each respondent in the most discreet way." With hidden coding, the anonymous survey showed which investors, mostly GE employees, rated service as unacceptable, average, or outstanding. Betsy Potter, president of a union local with members at GE, told the *Post:* "I'm appalled, although I'm not surprised."

Juxtaposed against sentiment for Welch, that was a revealing piece of duplicity. The boss of a conglomerate cannot keep track of all its intricacies. But he, or she, defines its character. For most, deceit in the defense of profit is no sin. And such venial transgressions as hoodwinking poll respondents are the least of it.

These days, that subterfuge is so small-bore as to be laughable. Once, an energetic press helped keep companies in line. Spokespeople courted reporters and answered questions; a damning "no comment" suggested they were hiding something. Now many once helpful PR flacks merely stonewall behind e-mail addresses or voice mail. In a new atmosphere, corporate executives can abuse trust in the manner of Third World dictators.

When inside news leaked from Hewlett-Packard, the company's own security force and Boston detectives used possibly illegal impersonations to track down reporters' telephone records. Smokinggun.com, an investigative Web site, broke the story in 2006, and Patricia Dunn resigned as chairman of the board. That, of course, did not stop HP stock from rising.

A disturbing book by Canadian journalist Wade Rowland makes its point in the title: *Greed, Inc.* "It is not capitalism, or market capitalism, that is the real problem," he writes. "It is corporate capitalism." Rowland argues persuasively that far too many companies deceive the public to the point of endangering lives in order to pile up profits. His long list begins with Merck for keeping Vioxx on the market long after it was called into question. It is easy to be bitter in such cases—unless your retirement account is long on Merck.

For an extreme example, spend an evening with the documentary film *Enron: The Smartest Guys in the Room.* It details how Enron's worker bees were lucky to get away with a few thousand dollars in severance; their stock, pensions, and medical plans vanished. Investors were fleeced while the top guys got millions. Yet beyond the depredations by executives, I was stunned at the taped chatter among young traders as they turned out the lights in California.

For a time, Enron cornered a market on power in a state that amounts to the world's fifth-largest economy. Unhindered by regulation, it played on the principles of supply and demand with dizzying complexity. Grids designed to keep the lights on were worked in reverse. Key power plants were shut down, and consumers paid up to five times the normal rate for electricity. As traders worked the levers, microphones recorded their patter. No docudrama, this had the unmistakable ring of truth, so callous and corny that no screenwriter would have gotten away with it.

"Burn, baby, burn," one wit offered, as Enron's team ordered turbines stopped, and blackouts began to bite. Another chortled at all the suffering grandmothers; he must have had a bad childhood. "What we need is a fucking earthquake," one trader said, eager to ramp up the desperation for electricity, even at killer rates. To which another replied, "Now I know I'm going to be able to retire at thirty." As the pain increased, someone wondered aloud if what they were doing was right. Then he added, with a laugh: "It's what we do."

It is bad enough watching Kenny-boy Lay (as Bush called Enron's CEO while directing favors his way) dither over the color scheme of a new executive jet as the ship began to sink. One gets the measure of Jeff Skilling when he dismisses someone on a conference call—"asshole," he mutters—who wanted to know how Enron stayed afloat. The scary part is how everyone played the game to the end and attacked the few people with the courage to speak out.

Watching *The Smartest Guys in the Room,* you get a sense of what a troubled society regards as smart. You also see that without effective regulators, overseen by legislators whose personal values outweigh their greed, it can happen again. I thought about Enron the other day when I came across a *New Yorker* cartoon. Two happy-looking snakes faced each other, flicking tongues and dripping venom. "Hey," the caption had one of them say, "it's what I do."

Remember that line from Mr. Bernstein in *Citizen Kane* who reflects on the fortune amassed by Orson Welles's dramatized version of William Randolph Hearst: "It's no trick to make an awful lot of money if all you want to do is make money."

The lines between acceptable corporate practice and criminal enterprise are finer than most of us realize. Generality here tars blameless companies while minimizing the damage done by dirty ones. Yet if the criterion is only what can be called legal, we ought to be incensed.

The annual budgets of some sovereign states fall far short of what large corporations earn. Their leaders need wherewithal to fortify a tenuous hold on power. Many are eager to salt away fortunes before they relinquish their offices. In such circumstances, laws are easily proposed and passed.

These phenomena are exaggerated in small places where no one can vote the rascals out of office. Fresh income flowing into a small state's treasury can be a great benefit if it is put to good use. A broader tax base builds infrastructure without foreign aid, just as the champions of globalization argue. But corporations are not in the development business. If money they bring in stops only long enough to bounce onward to a European bank account, the effect is the opposite. Corruption grows more entrenched. The gap widens between the haves and the don't-haves. And resentment stews at higher temperatures.

Wages in workers' pockets find their way to local economies. But the few dollars a factory hand takes home after a twelve-hour day of hard labor is not the stuff of economic revolution. Often, conditions of work hark back to preunion days in the coal mines, with company stores and a constant threat of layoff. That, after all, is why companies outsource. Not only is labor elsewhere cheaper, but also local authorities tend to stay out of their way.

If these processes are true for companies that operate under the cover of law, they are amplified with criminal enterprise, where no one bothers with legal niceties. Globalized crime now flourishes with an ease that would have given a Godfather of yore heart palpitations of envy.

On any good day, trillions of dollars are exchanged openly across borders among the world's banks; much of that moves in or out of the United States. That covers business transactions, securities trades, and the other countless reasons for sloshing wealth around the world.

The same tools that allow executives to watch their assets on five continents from a Montana hunting lodge enable a space-age consigliere to scrub dirt off of ill-gotten gains. Bank controls, although amped up to draconian levels because of terrorism, cannot cope. Sloppy amateurs get on watch lists for legal transactions that ring bells. Professionals who work the system have it better than ever. And many of our controls are subjective scattershot that can make a normal person's life miserable.

As bankers are held responsible for dubious customers, the simple business of managing a life can be the stuff of Kafka. Because I travel often to remote places, I keep a personal-service account with a large New York–based international bank. The woman I have dealt with for fifteen years, charming and amusing, works hard to handle her customers' problems. Sometimes, she tears her hair out.

I went in once to add my wife's name. A three-by-five signature card should do it, I thought. My banker sighed. She hauled out a form long enough to deal with an organ transplant and the purchase of a large island. She asked if I was a prominent person. Before I could reply, she clarified: "You're not." If I were, she said, she would have to throw me out of her office. A signature change would take up her afternoon, with no end of compliance forms and stupid questions from higher-ups. That was for someone known to the bank. A stranger might be denied an account if an officer thought his suit was too flashy.

If these measures somehow made us safer, or worked against cross-border crime, there might be a purpose. But we are way too far past that point. International crooks, whether Eastern European mafias that kill without pause, or more housebroken bandits content with mere massive fraud, are changing how all of us live our lives.

In Washington, I went to see Louise Shelley, a professor at American University, where she directs the Terrorism, Transnational Crime, and Corruption Center. With fluent Russian and a quiet under-the-radar approach, she moves in closed circles like a female Zelig. On some days she testifies in Congress or the Russian Duma. On others, she hangs out with crime lords who happily spill the beans on activities to make your hair stand up straight.

Shelley was my prime source for stories I never got onto the AP wire. She told me how Russian mafias parked their money in Israel and along the French Riviera. Early on, she saw how criminal organizations trafficked in young women as sex slaves and domestic servants. For obvious reasons, such stories had to be short on named sources and hard numbers. Editors hate that.

By late 2006, Shelley was more worried than ever. Thriving mafias in Europe and Asia were building links to terrorist groups. It is a natural alliance. Terrorists need weapons, the less conventional the better, and crime lords can supply them. Tightly sealed cells of Islamist and nationalist extremists offer useful logistics for infiltrating people or moving illegal money that is harder to hide in heavily monitored banking systems.

"Most of these people are not all criminal or all terrorist," she said. "Many of them have overlapping sympathies." They have overlapping purposes as well. The Afghan poppy boom increases Russia's drug problem; addicts working at nuclear facilities are recruited by organized crime. Bribes allow smugglers to load cargos on Moscow-bound trains, from illegal caviar to components for a dirty bomb. More bribes produce cell phones and modems so jailed mafia leaders can run their businesses as usual.

Late in 2006, Shelley warned in the *Bulletin of Atomic Scientists* of smuggled nuclear components to Turkey, the Middle East, and Western Europe in spite of technical safeguards. She wrote: "Such measures fail to take into account the more elusive 'human element'—the criminals and terrorists who, because of endemic corruption in the former republics of the Soviet Union, may increasingly have access to nuclear materials." In Georgia, she reported, authorities found highly enriched Russian uranium on its way to the separatist region of South Ossetia.

That is a corner of the rug. Since organized crime breaks laws out of sight, little public pressure keeps busy lawmen focused on bringing cases to overburdened courts. Eastern European neo-mafiosi preen in plain sight; their impact on the price of upscale real estate and luxury goods is obvious enough. The other day in Miami's South Beach I noticed the unmistakable swagger of gold-draped Russian "businessmen." They are one reason—but just one—why a single claw at Joe's Stone Crab now costs ten bucks.

In the end, to discuss high crimes, corporate misdeeds, and just about everything else going wrong outside the cave, I went to the comfortably padded and lovably cynical Washington lawyer named Jack Blum, whom we met earlier. Journalists dream of a guy like Blum; he is a favorite source for big-name investigative reporters who have earned his trust over the years. He was my main source for the Central American Contra-drugs story. At the time, Blum was chief investigator for Sen. John Kerry.

Now in private practice, Blum investigates corruption, money launder-ing, tax havens, mafias, and drug trafficking. His specialty is crime that crosses borders, not only international frontiers but within the fine skein that delineates pockets of power in Washington.

Blum always reminds me of that I. F. Stone line: All you can do is lie in your bathtub and not want anything from the bastards. He lives simply and pursues wrongdoing with deep outrage upholstered in amused resignation. His Columbo-like approach confounds the inattentive, but long contact re-veals his depths. His lifelong friends include such luminaries as Hannah Arendt. He travels almost nonstop in the former Soviet Union, the Middle East, Asia, Europe, and parts beyond. He knows, essentially, everybody. No one I have encountered better understands how things work in the real world.

During Iran-Contra, I asked him why Congress never seemed to un-derstand foreign affairs. He explained the facts of life: "Some people in Congress are better than others, but if you add up the total of their under-standing of the world it would equal the weight of interplanetary dust. Most have, at best, comic-book knowledge of foreign affairs and how other people see things."

At one stage, Blum got frustrated enough to run for a seat in Congress from Maryland. His platform was simple: honest good government. He sat through long briefings by a Democratic Party politburo boss about what he stood for, how money should be raised, and what logs had to be rolled in various political deals. "Finally, I told him, 'Why do you think I'm running, you stupid son of a bitch?'" he said. They got another candidate.

I reconnected with Blum in 2005 and, over a year, spent full days in conversation. He was still hard at it, but even the redoubtable Jack Blum was beginning to despair. Saying "I told you so" gave him no pleasure. His biggest disappointment was how newspapers and television, for the most part, had sunk to such a low common denominator.

Few editors saw their role as holding public officials to the basic princi-ples they are sworn to respect, he said. If one newspaper makes a splash, few others follow it up. People decide what they want to believe, and nothing changes their minds. Television mostly entertains and comforts prejudices. Washington professionals understand this, he concluded, and they play it for whatever purpose suits them best. Reality is irrelevant.

Once we met for a seminar at Tufts University. At our Medford hotel, a crossroads for businesspeople and academics, we never managed to find a *New York Times* or even a *Boston Globe*. No one asked; none were ordered.

I could usually scare up a *USA Today*. People took the sports section and left the rest on the counter.

If people are so badly informed, I asked, what can an electorate do to fix the world? He rolled his eyes. For once, my prime witness, the world-class optimistic pessimist, had nothing to say. Then he started rattling off ideas. Jack Blum the lawyer, no less than Izzy Stone the journalist, was not about to stop seeking answers. As he said in one of our talks, "What is the choice?"

International crime was among Blum's biggest worries for a basic reason: Unlike other crises we face, it is impossible to gauge. Lawmen and journalists demand figures, but few have any meaning. Money laundering spins on beyond any control. Estimates of smuggled drugs and contraband emigrants are based on a flawed theory that police stop a certain percentage of the traffic. In fact, dramatic seizures often suggest whole new areas of hidden rot. Cash-flow guesswork is even farther off the mark.

"You don't know what you don't know," Blum said. "There is no way to quantify. Criminals do not check in and fill out forms: this is how much money I stole and got away with. Official numbers mean nothing. If you throw a lot of cops into a neighborhood, the crime rate goes up. This is total seat of pants. The truth of the matter is that nobody has a fucking clue."

Patriot Act banking controls aimed at terrorists have made it harder to move around dubious money, but criminals find obscure back alleys in which to wash dirty cash. Cross-border police cooperation still relies on personal relationships among officials who trust each other. "Think of international crime as zooming down an autoroute at a hundred miles an hour," Blum put it. "Law enforcement pedals behind on a bicycle, hoping for a crash."

But now he has a new worry. Financial fraud is growing beyond all measure as small-time freelancers and sophisticated mafias find new ways to pluck their victims clean. Computerized accounts offer new potential. And, mostly, crooks can operate with impunity.

As Blum sees it, American law and order is rooted in seventeenth-century Britain, resting on a premise that 60 percent of citizens obey the rules. Because of upbringing and moral codes, it is not in them to do otherwise. Another 30 to 35 percent will transgress if they think they can get away with it. That leaves 5 to 10 percent, sociopaths who flout the law no matter what. Cops hammer away at that bottom tier in hopes of scaring the middle group into line.

"The system is designed for a guy who walks into a Seven-Eleven waving a pistol and smiles up at the camera, hopefully in color," Blum said.

"When it gets complicated, it does not work. The more people realize that police enforcement is mostly only a shadow, the faster the system goes to hell."

For starters, fear of the feds is overrated; 95 percent of law enforcement is at state and local levels. Occasionally local prosecutors push to uncover crimes that reach far beyond their purview, but few have the resources, or the will, to do it.

Blum spent months on a case for Robert Morgenthau, the Manhattan district attorney, to unravel a fraudulent Florida mutual fund based in the Bahamas. On top of the original crimes, a series of crooks had conned one another.

"It was a circus of criminality," he said. "We had crimes stacked from here to hell and gone . . . SEC crimes, tax evasion by victims. There were questions about who had which jurisdiction over what. It was hopeless. Think of how the legal system is organized. Each incident is a count. Every transaction is a count. You had five hundred guys selling bullshit to ten thousand guys. Paper piled up in hallways, and twelve poor schmucks were hauled off on a bus to sit there for six months while lawyers say, 'Oh, this is just a standard business deal. It isn't a crime to be stupid.' The jury glazes over. When you involve three or four national borders, a thousand people, a million pieces of paper, and a hundred thousand separate incidents, you've brought the entire system to its knees."

The Web has added new dimensions to financial fraud, and the Russian mob, among others, has weighed in for high profit at low risk. "The cost of prosecuting is prohibitive, and all the crooks know it," Blum concluded. "If you don't run up and down the street and put red paint on your nose, nobody will bother you."

As criminal organizations amass fortunes, they find countries where they can operate with impunity. During the Clinton years, I had talked to Jonathan Winer, Blum's former Senate deputy. Winer was deputy assistant secretary of state in charge of watching narcotics, international crime, and human trafficking. He named thirteen countries he said were essentially run by criminals. When I asked Blum about how this had evolved over a decade, he threw up his hands.

"If we're looking at countries where corruption is pervasive and outrageous, dear God, where do we start?" he replied, with a rueful laugh. "Georgia and Kirghizistan are beyond laughable. All the former Soviet republics are fearfully corrupt, godlessly corrupt, and nobody knows how to deal with it. In China, there is enormous corruption at low levels, mid

levels, and high levels. China could very well disintegrate the way the Soviet Union did. It is all built on a sandpile. Panama. Suriname. Holy shit,
where do you want to begin?"

In the Caribbean tax haven of Anguilla, Blum said, U.S. investigators
decided to run a sting operation and went to the British for help in setting
up a charter bank. "It had so much business the feds didn't know what to
do," he said. "Twenty percent was drug money. The rest was Americans
trying to evade taxes. The Brits were so embarrassed they closed it down."
That was just one island, he added. Under Prime Minister Lester Bird, An-
tigua was essentially for sale to the highest bidder.

In the Cayman Islands, people still remember Blum as "the TV star." In
1994, he wore a hidden BBC camera into a dubious bank. He had been
tipped off by a born-again Christian minister who did business with the
bank. "The island is so small that everyone has relatives in every bank, like
a sister who runs the Xerox machine." The bank manager told Blum on
camera how to launder money. "After this aired, I was famous," Blum said.
"Locals were so pissed they threw the guy off the island."

The bank manager moved on, and Blum tipped off a Bahamian editor
who ran a front-page story on his subsequent activities. The man linked up
with a Caribbean mob. Eventually, he was arrested and gave up the Cay-
mans bank. The sting produced two thousand criminal tax cases, but Blum
said the U.S. Internal Revenue Service was not interested. Its resources
were stretched too thin.

That was a microcosm of the problem. You can imagine the bigger picture. "Now," Blum said, "we're into something much better: structured finance." That is, grand theft in plain view, within American borders. With
that, he launched into Enron-type depredations. Whether the problem is
corporate colonizers, private contractors out of control, or mafiosi shunting
money around the world, the structures in place cannot cope.

Yet Blum is still at it. Giving up is no real option. Our systems could
work if voters insisted they be reshaped and reinforced. Eventually, he figures, enough Americans will resist being fleeced like mindless sheep.

NINE

THE WORLD, IN FACT, IS ROUND

Beyond the familiar U.S. and European multinationals that plant their logo-flags in far-flung outposts, a new class of players is evolving in a block known as BRIC: Brazil, Russia, India, and China. These countries supply not only energy and raw materials but also capital and brainpower to make our globe spin faster.

This is a central idea behind Thomas Friedman's best-selling disclosure: *The World Is Flat.* Yet as Tom surely recalls from his foreign correspondent days, the world is actually round.

Consider a brief essay by Alison Smale, an AP star until she joined the *New York Times* foreign desk. British, married to a Russian composer, and living in Paris, she takes a wide view. Her French, German, and Russian are flawless. Now, as managing editor of the *International Herald Tribune,* she observes the globe from the front row.

"It is these lands," she wrote, reflecting on BRIC while at her vacation dacha in Tarusa, south of Moscow, "that will be new titans of our planet, and any self-respecting Westerner not ensuring their child learns Mandarin is suffering from serious myopia.

"And yet. What seems to make sense from behind the computer at a hedge fund or investment bank rings somehow hollow in Tarusa.... Along with all the conspicuous consumption go the more enduring aspects of Russia. There are the conversations, moving at 19th-century speed rather than the digital nanoseconds of the present day. There are the pastimes—picking mushrooms, reading at the river bank, watching an Orthodox priest bless each corner of a new home—and there are rich characters, ones Gogol might recognize."[1]

Smale wrote that her thoughts were echoed in conversations in Beijing with Yu Hua, whose novels look through the eyes of simple people who live real lives at human pace within hearing of a megaboom.

"In both India and China, for all the financiers' flashy faith in inexorable progress, not just novelists, but politicians are now wrestling with the collision between breakneck change and the quieter, traditional life of the millions of Chinese and Indian Tarusas."

Western Europe, after all, evolved over centuries to its careful balance between old and new. Down the road from my own spirit-restoring dacha in Provence, superscientists are building the West's most advanced center for nuclear something or other. Yet my neighbor Jeannot, who takes his potatoes and chickpeas to market each Saturday in a rattling Citroën, could spend comfortable hours feeling at home in Tarusa without knowing a word of Russian.

From where Friedman writes that he began his musing on a flat world, a business-class seat on a Lufthansa flight to Frankfurt, something called "globalization" makes some sense. If you close your eyes on taxi rides in between, you can circumnavigate the world without losing sight of such familiar icons as those big yellow plastic arches. A Bengali in Calcutta with a dark suit and power tie can look pretty much like a Back Bay attorney in Boston.

On closer examination, globalization is another one of those misleading collective nouns that shortcut thought and trigger discord. Neo-globalists see vast new territory where Western multinationals can outsource jobs and expand their markets. But that is only a small part of it.

Manjeet Kripalani, who took time off as *Business Week*'s perspicacious correspondent in India to be a fellow at the Council on Foreign Relations, sees a wider picture. "I'm a globalist," she told me, but she added a dismissive eye roll for pundits who claim to have just discovered the concept. Globalization is as old as the world. Rather than leveling out the globe, she believes, it adds richness to its lumpy texture. Her own country is a prime example.

"India has always been 'globalized,'" Kripalani said. "It has always faced foreign invaders since Alexander the Great." True enough, Indians have mastered business administration from the time ancient chief executives based decisions on the stars and chief financial officers pioneered accounting. With each set of rulers, from the twelfth-century Moguls to the British Raj that ended in 1947, India absorbed occupiers into its capacious midst.

For centuries, Indians settled across Africa, the South Pacific, and just about everywhere else. After the economy was liberalized in 1991, Indian entrepreneurs expanded abroad, starting small and then building their own large multinationals. "They are perceived as kind to their workers and as understanding that they can't force people to do their best," Kripalani said. With high productivity and hard-headed management, India is evolving as a major competitive force.

Young workers excel in call centers and data processing operations. "Indians are quite used to adapting," Kripalani said. "If they have to speak with an American accent, that's not a problem." But these outsourced jobs employ only a few million people in a workforce of 450 million. Much more important are Indian companies that employ engineers, scientists, and other specialists that graduate at a fast-growing clip.

A new sort of India is giving the world fresh ideas, from innovative films and fashion to high technology and industry. Kripalani sees similar phenomena across much of the world. "People are now more equal than ever, and that's a good thing," she said. "America has been basking in sunshine for two hundred years, and now others are seeing the dawn," she said. "We should let them."

Globalists like Kripalani see hope in expanded commerce. Beyond general philosophy, what counts is how many people have access to those free-market forces that so many social engineers champion.

But what also counts, in seeking a better balance, is how many people do not have this access. Since 1997, Indian authorities have reported that more than twenty-five thousand peasants have taken their own lives, often by swallowing pesticides, because of simple desperation.

Dr. Vandana Shiva, of the research group Navdanya, blames debt brought on by a globalized, liberalized market that drives down prices.[2] She noted that in 1998 World Bank structural adjustment policies forced India to open its seed sector to such multinationals as Cargill and Monsanto.

"The global corporations changed the input economy overnight," Shiva wrote. "Farm-saved seeds were replaced by corporate seeds, which needed fertilizers and pesticides and could not be saved. As seed saving is prevented by patents as well as by the engineering of seed with non-renewable traits, seed has to be bought for every planting season by poor peasants. A free resource available on the farm becomes a commodity which farmers are forced to buy every year. . . . As debts increase and become unpayable, farmers are compelled to sell kidneys or even commit suicide. . . . Seed monopolies rob farmers of life."

This has larger overtones. Corporate farming narrows agricultural diversity to monocultures that damage the land as much as they do the families—two-thirds of India's population—that live from it. High subsidies paid to growers in America and Europe impact heavily on poor Indian farmers who struggle on their own.

"The rigged prices of globally traded agriculture commodities are stealing incomes from poor peasants of the south," Shiva wrote. "Analysis carried out by the Research Foundation for Science, Technology and Ecology shows that due to falling farm prices, Indian peasants are losing $26 billion . . . annually. This is a burden their poverty does not allow them to bear. Hence the epidemic of farmers suicide."

It is hardly only India. Once again, spin a globe and point. In Ghana, for instance, impoverished market women are left with rotting tomatoes because subsidized canned tomatoes from Italy are cheaper.

Much must be added to this complex picture before attributing right or wrong. This is yet one more example of why global issues are far too complex to be seen in vague shadows on a cave wall. Such grand concepts as globalization are neither good nor bad. They must be broken down and applied with more in mind than a faceless "free market" lacking a human dimension. We've got to leave the cave and look around.

The fatal error in our new information technology is that the space between "virtual" and "reality" can only be covered on foot, by leaving the keyboard and taking a firsthand look. Five-letter words like "India" and "China," in fact, are no more useful than "media" and "press." Two short collective nouns cannot sum up half of humanity. It gets more complex still when you consider what all those engineers are doing in the decidedly unflat mountainsides that separate a big India from a bigger China.

The two nations, which for sixty years viewed each other with distrust if not hostility, plan to link up via the old Burma Road. This was General Joseph Stilwell's highway over the hump, an eight-hundred-mile sort of Ho Chi Minh Trail that allowed Allied forces to confront the Japanese in World

War II. Politics and potholes condemned it to oblivion. By 1945, the jungle had already reclaimed parts of it. When it is reopened as a broad, black highway, it will cut 2,200 miles off a circuitous land route between China and India.

In the late 1900s, the countries' trade was measured in the low hundreds of millions. By 2005, it was $13.6 billion. China is India's second-largest trading partner.

At ground level, the I and the C in BRIC have far more in common than either has with Europe or America. I just noted a news item: Families in a Chinese town stormed a hospital to protest high costs they could not pay. The trigger was a bill for eighty-two dollars. Modern comfort in much of India can amount to no more than tin for a roof and a well within an hour's walk. This is changing, but certainly not uniformly, or steadily.

Along with economic theory, we need deep understanding of human dimensions. If you look at people rather than names on a map, popular catchphrases lose much of their meaning. For individuals who end up as losers in this new sort of world, whether in poor countries or rich ones, life is bitter. And, increasingly, they react.

From the time I first reported from France in 1977, I poked carefully into *les banlieues,* those deceptively dreary settlements at the edge of French cities. Although the word translates to "suburbs," there is nothing like Scarsdale about them. Most are the result of what might have been a good idea had planners thought beyond urban development toward human behavior.

Shoddy blocks of apartments were erected in military-barrack ranks. Most were high enough to require cheap elevators that would quickly break, forcing residents to clomp up eight floors at the end of each bad day. They were separated by dark parking lots, a convenient resource for kids needing a quick stolen radio to pay for a fix.

Though the communities are publicly supported, most properties are privately owned. When families cannot pay rent, the buildings deteriorate. Landlords refuse to repair the common areas, which vandals routinely trash.

Over time, I explored different versions in other countries. In most European cities, immigrant communities implanted themselves ad hoc into city centers. Berlin's Kreuzberg had begun to speak Turkish. In Brussels, along streets heading one way from the Porte de Namur metro, the language was Moroccan Arabic; the other way, people spoke Congolese Lingala. Around London's Notting Hill Gate and the canals of Amsterdam, polyglot mingled with mainstream. A *banlieue* was something else. Separated by high if invisible walls from a fearful bourgeoisie, it was a crucible for watching the colors of Europe change. The language was French spoken in countless accents.

One Friday in the 1980s, I went to Montfermeil, a seedy and often seething *banlieue* east of Paris, with a tough-looking Breton photographer who handled himself well. We had a contact whose first name, Mahmoud, was, to no surprise, a rendition of Mohammed. About twenty-three, he was a Beur. That slang term is a backward play on the French *Arabe*. It usually means a kid born in France to North African parents. Mahmoud's Algerian grandfather fought for France in World War I. His father was born in Algiers when it was as French as Hawaii is American. A third-generation citizen, he hates it when some naturalized white guy born in Eastern Europe calls him an immigrant.

Mahmoud was helpful yet strangely reserved, answering questions with single words and steering us away from his friends. After a while, some Elmer Fudd pronunciation gaffe exposed my hardly native French.

"*Mais, tu es Americain?*" Mahmoud asked. I said that I was. "*Bé, il fallait le dire,*" he replied. I should have said so. His reserve vanished. I was not some nosy French guy on a trip to the zoo; I was from a very cool place, the land of rap and Reeboks.

Thus admitted, I spent hours listening. Again and again, kids told me how it was impossible to find work. If their names or accents did not betray them, their faces did. When they showed up for advertised jobs, they found them miraculously filled only minutes before. After a while, many stopped looking; there were other ways to survive in a rich society with flimsy locks. But many others kept at it, determined to find a way out.

Then we went for Friday prayers. With no mosque at the time, the faithful and the curious made do with a large open space, a basketball court for most of the week. A part-time imam spoke of the Prophet's idea of justice. Standing off to the side, I mentally recorded an image I remembered as Islam moved steadily forward toward the world's front pages.

Worshippers had left their shoes in an enormous pile, a colorful montage of yellow Senegalese slippers, high-top black basketball sneakers, fancy black loafers, and battered down-at-the-heel work brogues. For every set of soles, there was a different story. For most of Montfermeil and similar banlieue all across France, Islam was less of a religion than a sense of belonging. This was not so much a spiritual phenomenon as that good old familiar underclass frustration we knew so well in the real America.

In 1996, I went to the beautifully named *banlieue* of Chanteloup-les-

Vignes. By then I was used to the irony. The ugliest streets lined with the grimmest slums were often named for the luminaries who recalled French glory: Molière, Renoir, Cézanne, the lot. I zeroed in on Noe, the setting of a popular film of the day, *La Haine*. Hatred.

My dispatch began:

"In the bleak housing projects ringing Paris, so tense that police fear to patrol, young Arabs, Africans and poor whites are fast slipping into a desperate underclass. A 17-year-old Portuguese named Tonio is one of them. 'Look, I steal, I deal drugs,' he said, with a casual shrug. 'There's no choice around here but to take the train to Paris and beat up a few Frenchmen for money to live.'

"Tonio loitered in a concrete ghetto near this lovely old village set in lush countryside just beyond the glow of Paris. His pal, Mamadou Sissoko, a Mauritanian rapper in a Yankees cap, spat toward the mean streets named for poets and painters he could not place. 'Here there is nothing,' Mamadou added. 'Nothing. Nothing. You understand nothing? I mean nothing.'"

I found Patrice Bonhomme, police chief for the area, who offered some context: "We are headed for a downward spiral, American-style." On that trip, I had no Mahmoud. A few times angry young men nearly ruined my day. Bonhomme's men, hanging back in their cars where there was safety in numbers, were nowhere to be seen.

Here is where it gets hard to level general criticism at that non-monolith we call the media. AP, the media, had trained me and let me spend time digging into the subject. A lot of newspapers displayed the words and photos across a full page; they were media. Some print and broadcast editors who had no space at the time kept the story on file as background for media coverage later. Newspaper correspondents did their own reporting. A thumping majority of Americans missed seeing what we wrote. That is not "the media's" fault.

Readers who merely scan headlines usually miss the point of complex background dispatches. To find my original text, I googled (that is a verb now) and came across a version from the *Houston Chronicle*. The headline said: "Murderers, Thieves, Dopers Ring Paris in Substandard Housing." Though accurate in the sense that I had mentioned "the occasional murder," it missed the point. I had said, "Deaths . . . are more often by overdose or suicide than gunshots, and there are no drive-by shootings." The real message was reflected by the Chanteloup mayor, Pierre Cardo: "If we don't create jobs, give people some dignity and hope, we'll see mounting violence, a takeover by mafias, unpredictable explosions and a revolt by the middle class."

That middle-class revolt is still in the making, but Cardo was right on the money. In 2005, *les banlieues* exploded around Paris and across France. In Arizona at the time, I watched carefully how the riots were covered.

Fox played its usual role, but others struck similar chords. Islamic radicals, America was told, had stirred up the slums. Young jihadis, perhaps dispatched by Osama bin Laden, worked up young Muslims to a fever pitch. The implication was that our terror alerts should flash blood orange, and our border guards should turn away any European with a suntan or passport stamp from Marrakech.

I remembered that piled-up footwear in Montfermeil. This was not about Osama, or Saddam, or the Prophet Mohammed. It was about frustration and nonidentity. The same riots might have happened ten or even twenty years ago if kids had cell phones to flash SMS messages to each other. There were instigators and planners. Mostly, however, it was the irrational exuberance of pissed-off people whose limited means of self-expression was torching cars.

But the guesswork pundits and parachute reporters were right about one thing. The raw anger those riots reflected suggested rich terrain for radical incitement. Recruiters worked the crowds, in mosques and on street corners, linking local misery to injustices in Palestine and beyond. By then, fallout from the Iraq War had settled over not only the *banlieues* but also all of those other underclass neighborhoods across Europe. This time, had I gone back to do more reporting, I would try damned hard to keep American inflection out of any language I used.

Much is true in what the flat-worlders say, but not, I would submit, the essence of their argument. Corporations outsourcing to the suburbs of Paris would hire a lot of people. Mickey Mouse certainly did when he came to Marne la Vallee. But Disney's human-resources people have a battery of tests and criteria. They want kids who smile a lot. Other companies have their specific requirements. For many of them, their denials aside, a Mamadou Sissoko has little more than a snowball's chance in hell.

Our spherical world is made up of contours so pronounced that they are visible even in that distorted reflection on the wall of our cave. Much divides disparate societies, from simple dinnertime preferences to the most basic of belief systems. If we are to get along, none of us can arrogate to ourselves the ability to decide what motivates others. Intentions do not matter, however good they may be. They are not enough.

But here is a paradox, the human condition that explains why so much of a round world can, indeed, be flattened. At basic levels where it matters, people are much more alike than they are different. Even at its best, the media is only a tool for keeping track of developments in a world each of us must follow via our own intellects and philosophies. There is no right way or wrong way.

My friend Richard is a very smart man, a well-heeled entrepreneur who once published children's books. His new company developed a process that not only clears bacteria from hospital air but can also neutralize pathogens at places like the Pentagon. His interests, more than I can follow, range from saving African wildlife to a mysterious project in Eastern Europe he thinks could save a lot of people. He reads incessantly, from newspapers to costly private intelligence reports. After reviewing my manuscript, he agreed with much of it. But still.

I am, Richard says with only half a smile, a prissy liberal populist. He is, I reply, a well-intentioned elitist who does not get it. One scheme he proposed enthusiastically was that American companies should privatize Mexico—that is, they should own it outright—thus assuring full employment and no corruption. I don't even know where to start with that one, but the Emiliano Zapata poster on my wall should offer a clue.

Benevolence does not loom large in U.S. corporate planning. Still, the main point I believe Richard misses is something else. As much as jobless Mexicans might be ready to take drug tests and company oaths for a steady paycheck, most have at least as much attachment to their own flag and culture as we gringos have to ours.

Across what we call the Third World, few people want to be like us. They might envy our stuff. They might eat it or wear it on their feet. But most simply want a fairer shake so they can stay home with their own stuff and be like themselves. Every country has different needs that require sustained attention from donor countries committed to finding solutions that work.

Where governments exploit their people, quiet but firm diplomacy is needed to bring what international policy wonks call "good governance." In the surprising number of developing countries where leadership is getting better, people need to be spared from subsidies that allow rich farmers elsewhere to undercut their basic commodity prices.

Wherever we live, we are all affected by a planetary shift toward standardization, corporate convenience, and dictatorship by sweeping economic principle. Our world is now so complex, and so many of us are overwhelmed by it, that we choose the path of least resistance.

If you look hard at the worst examples of rural poverty, you will find a main theme familiar to any rich country. Parents want enough to feed their families and find a roof that approaches local standards. But in poor countries, only a few dollars more a day can do it.

Enterprising mothers ready to work need a bare amount of schooling and start-up capital. A little U.S. aid could do wonders in this direction. Polls say 80 percent of Americans favor educating the poor. But we budget only $3.7 billion to fight poverty abroad, everywhere.

Desperately poor Bangladesh, for one, shows what happens when enlightened volunteers and entrepreneurs place faith in the human spirit. BRAC, the Bangladesh Rural Advancement Committee, educates girls at thirty thousand schools, mostly in remote places. Teachers are women, often BRAC graduates trained by BRAC. They make sure girls get home safely and can take off for harvest and peak chore times.

BRAC provides even more "micro credits" to Bangladeshi women than the Nobel-winning Grameen Bank. But Grameen's founder, economist Muhammad Yunus, has taken his idea of tiny loans to enterprising women across the developing world. Thirty years ago, Yunus found a group of forty-two artisans who worked all day to make such things as woven chair seats. With no cash to buy raw materials, they had to borrow money from their buyer at usurious rates. Yunus lent each of them an average of sixty-two cents. That was enough to set them free.

Besides loans, Grameen offers savings, insurance, mortgages, pension funds, scholarships, and credit for fertilizer. Beggars can draw no-interest loans to buy candy and dried chilies to sell door to door.

The philosophy is simple. Commercial banks seldom make small loans to the poor because of administrative costs and lack of collateral. They deal mostly with men; women are a far better risk. Social pressure secures the loans. Women borrow in groups of five, and each must stay current before others can draw fresh capital. A multiplier effect spreads wealth throughout entire villages.

With $600 million in capital, Grameen no longer needs outside help. It has reached a balance to thrill any modern-day philanthropist: It fights the most desperate and dangerous sort of poverty, yet it still makes money.

That is only one example, but it is a good one. Today, micro credits reach 100 million clients in a hundred countries. Tina Rosenberg, who wrote at length in 2006 on the *New York Times* Web site about successful ways to fight poverty, also looked at roads to markets. She focused on Shenggen Fan, now a fellow at the International Food Policy Research Institute in Washington.[3]

Fan grew up in a village that was two days from Shanghai by motorboat and bus. His school was an hour's walk away. Farmers grew only what they could eat or sell to neighbors. Now, his family home is three hours from Shanghai, and that school is a ten-minute bike ride away.

"With roads, people travel out and bring in new knowledge," Fan said. "They change their behavior. Roads are a window to the outside world. In extreme cases, roads are life-saving—in the Ethiopian famine of 1984 and 1985, thousands of people died because they could not be reached by food aid."

People in trouble almost always know why. The old saw tells us that if we give a man a fish we feed him for a day, but we feed him forever if we teach him to catch his own. Poor fishermen do not need lessons. They need a hook. And they need water in their river or lake. Those of us who want to help need more than a checkbook. We have to understand how to help. And that takes our attention.

The easy way out is to tell ourselves that we have no time to pay attention to the world's human topography. But if this is true, what explains those wild riots in American shopping malls whenever Sony or Nintendo introduces a new computer play station? We can make time to go outside, look around, and sniff the air of our real world.

In the end, just paying attention—taking note of what other people need and how those people can help us meet our own needs—is our first essential step toward survival. If we do not, we default our lives to bad government, corporate boards eager for docile "human resources," and the range of destructive processes that now threaten us.

The real world out there only seems flat if it is looked at in distorted reflection, in a single dimension.

This is where we start seeking practical ways to find our way out of the cave—and stay there. No one who is not blinded by some vested economic interest or political myopia can dispute the urgent need for sustained action. But what action? Specifics follow in chapter 10. First we need a broad framework. In 2006, a stalwart old Harvard don sketched the context we need in the *New York Review of Books*.

Stanley Hoffmann was born in Vienna a year before the Wall Street crash of 1929. He lived through World War II in Paris and taught at France's grand schools. Now he teaches American foreign policy, international politics, ethics, and a range of approaches to sensible life on Earth. An academic to the bone, Hoffmann's solemn delivery in Franco-Teutonic inflections can smack of God on a mountaintop. But his article "The Foreign Policy the US Needs" lays groundwork for bringing security, ecological sanity, and a broader prosperity to a round world.

Hoffmann scorns the notion that globalization should come only in the orthodox form of American free-market and probusiness policies. "Many Europeans see this as a denial of the state's responsibility to provide social justice, public services, and safety nets for the poor, the unemployed, and workers," he wrote.

Hoffmann's themes are clear: We think about corporate entities, not people. Our actions belie our words. We support dictators and fail to protect victims of genocide, as in Rwanda and Darfur. Foreigners watch us cut taxes, protect excessive company profits, and weaken our public services. We see a destructive power with little in development or nation-building.

To put things right, Hoffmann says, we must first improve our moral and economic condition by returning to the rule of law, protecting civil liberties, and not trying to evade international law in fighting terrorism. We have to support the Kyoto Protocol and an International Criminal Court. We must reduce deficit and debt to free ourselves from foreign entanglements. We need to tax carbon emissions and slash our use of oil. Beyond obvious other advantages, these steps are crucial to earning respect.

A second prerequisite is a readiness to junk the foreign policies of both Republicans and Democrats. Since World War II and especially the fall of Communism, Hoffmann wrote, "these policies have oscillated from multilateralism to imperialism, but they have assumed . . . that the world could only benefit from American primacy, seen as both a fact of power and a condition of world security and prosperity." Our raw military power is undeniable; the rest is not so clear. What Hoffmann calls "soft power" and "building power" can win friends and influence people.

Other basics include finding a fair solution that allows Israelis and Palestinians to share disputed land. Iraq requires a carefully planned withdrawal, with no "imperial residue" so Iraqis are forced to confront a civil war and societal collapse. True, we started it. But we can't finish it.

Exiting Iraq and avoiding such stupidities in the future would allow for Hoffmann's pièce de résistance, "a drastic long-term policy of demilitarization carried out in collaboration with foreign partners." America's defense costs, more than $550 billion a year, eat up 20 percent of our budget. Rather than deterring rivalry with China, our only potential threat, this is more likely to provoke it.

By reducing military expenditure by half, Hoffmann argues, America can take better care of its poor, set up a decent health care system, improve education, and develop more efficient fuels. It could strengthen societies in Asia, Africa, and Latin America. Conflict would ease with such states as North Korea and Iran, which harbor legitimate fears of American assault.

That all makes sense. In fact, there may be no other way. Of course, as Hoffmann admits, his proposals appear utopian. Yet they are perfectly possible, requiring only an informed electorate that chooses wisely and holds its leaders to account.

We have seen clearly enough the limits of "superpower" on a flat patch of desert. America may well be Number One, but it is time to stop chanting it like beer-besotted soccer hooligans. Before it is too late, we would be better advised to go out into the real world and prove it.

TEN

ESCAPING THE CAVE

A great escape is easy enough. We need only turn around and focus on reality, with all of its complexities, rather than on distorted reflections. Doing something to change things is harder—but not by much. With a little clarity of purpose, it is astounding how effective determined people can be.

If we grasp the issues, we can vote for leaders who will act on them. We can put to good use a democracy most of us only complain about. Each of us can speak up to enlighten others. George W. Bush may not strike many as a great president, but we elected him twice. And if we did not really elect him, how did one party allow another to steal a national election with the whole world watching?

We should not oversimplify. Yet why overcomplicate? We are killing our planet, but we can do things differently to restore its health. We have the resources; how else do we bankroll war in Iraq? We can lessen poverty that breeds hatred and despair. We can demand accountability from our leaders. We can pursue corporate scoundrels and criminals who exploit us. And if not, we can only blame ourselves.

This smacks of a deluded dreamer thundering toward windmills with a blunted lance. But I have seen human nature at its worst and its best in a lot of places over forty years. Nations are no more than individuals writ large. All have dominant character traits, good and bad. And each is capable of change.

Optimism is our only chance. What is the choice? If you believe the cynics, you might as well find some high ground, buy a wide-brimmed hat, and build a solid wall.

On my old olive farm in Provence, which is not yet walled, I keep a battered yellow newspaper delivery box for the Santa Fe *New Mexican* outside the door next to a monster agave plant. I like to have some southwestern roots close at hand. At the moment, it is full of wasps.

To deal with these wasps, I could apply the method currently favored in the White House. That is, I can find a sharp stick and jam it into the mailbox. This is not too smart. While I'm inside gulping down antihistamines, the wasps will be taking over the place.

I might try a can of poison with a huge horn on it like the firemen use, a tactical weapon of mass destruction. But there are other nests. Eventually, ecology shifts would wreak havoc on the lavender, the fruit trees, and all the rest. Besides, God knows what that would do to my karma when I finally find out which of the many religious zealots is right about afterlife.

Instead, I'm moving the spare key out of the delivery box and learning more about wasps. They don't really hate me. They just have basic software implanted by nature that pisses them off if I get in their face. Meantime, the lavender is deep purple, and the mulberries are terrific.

Wild pigs, called *sangliers* down here, are more of a challenge. They tromp all over new plantings, knock down stone walls, and sunbathe by the hot tub. But they have been part of the universe for a very long time, like those lightning storms that burn out the well pump. I could find a way to eliminate them. But it works better just to stay out of their way. Besides, a *sanglier* chop grilled over olive wood sure beats a Big Mac.

And so on; you get the point. We Americans may believe that for some reason we live on our own exalted plane, and we can remake whatever might discomfit us. But the other 95 percent of the world's population, not to speak of the wasps and wild pigs, takes a different view. The sooner we get past this, the better for everyone.

Some psychopathic crazies would hate us even if we made Islam the state religion and put Ann Coulter in a burqa. They do not represent Muslims any more than fanatical Bible thumpers typify Christians. If we stick to values that we articulate so much better than we put into practice, we will build back the respect a strong nation needs to lead.

To be effective, we must join forces with others to confront problems that threaten an entire planet. At this advanced stage of our collective peril, no country can have a national interest that outweighs this. Crises can only worsen if we do not understand at a human level the peoples who share this world with us.

Something more is dead evident down in the olives. On Christmas Day, with 2007 approaching, my trees thought it was Easter. Emiliano, the gnarled old olive by the terrace, grew bright green shoots just as it has, over centuries, each time it senses winter is over. But any day—who can guess when with our new weather?—the thermometer could plummet. It did, of course. Caught off guard, trees that have survived since the Sun King ruled France risked freezing to death.

Forget the polemic. Talk to a farmer, or a sailor, or anyone else who depends on knowing what nature has in mind from day to day. The seasons and rains and currents are off. Whatever the reason, our environmental balances are going dreadfully wrong. Ecology, hardly only the realm of fresh-air freaks and assorted weirdos, is a primal science.

Look anywhere. Across the Pyrenees, bears in Spain are too confused by the new weather to take their winter naps. This is an amusing sidelight until you consider what it really means. For all our talk about global warming, we mostly ignore what may prove to be the biggest climate news of all. Changes in ocean pH, because of carbon emissions, threaten anything with a shell, from tiny mollusks at the bottom of the food chain to monster Maine lobsters. That could mean, eventually, dead seas.

Lurking terrorists but also dying trees and vanishing krill and insomniac bears are all now part of our new sort of world. We need to understand this.

To start off, we must realize that a steady flow of trustworthy information can only come at a tangible cost. Our fancy new technology is useless if we do not have real reporters watching, and listening, as events take shape.

Some argue that whatever reaches the Web belongs to everyone. That might work for people who like seeing their wisdom in pixels, even though it discourages many whose professional output feeds their families. That is each writer's call. Journalism is different. Someone must spend $250,000 a year to keep a seasoned correspondent out where it counts, with contacts and sources. Parachute reporters, untested stringers, or modem-equipped citizens are no substitute. Foreign desks back home capable of solid judgment cost money that must come from somewhere.

When Saddam invaded Kuwait in August 1990, hordes of us rushed to Amman. Each morning before dawn, a skilled if slightly crazed driver we called Speedy raced me across five hours of Jordan to the Iraqi border. Persuasion got me into sealed no-man's-land camps to interview Indians, Egyptians, Filipinos, and others who fled for their lives from jobs in Kuwait. They were just about the world's only source on the motives and manners of a tyrant who would take us into on-and-off war for the next fifteen years.

Each refugee's words had to be set in a context at which we could only guess from careful questioning and background knowledge. Each story told by excited, scared people had to be checked against others' accounts of the same thing. One tough-looking Indian, a former army sergeant, blustered and bellowed at an American relief worker, himself distraught by his inability to help. I listened for half an hour to await a moment of clarity I suspected would come. Finally, both men broke down in tears and embraced. Each spoke his mind from the heart.

I was able to find reality because AP members had spent millions on my training. That refugee official was an old contact from Africa. I had talked to lots of Indian sergeants over the years. Filipinos opened up because I could reminisce with them about Mindanao and Vigan. Other reporters, friends who were much better at it than I was, shared their own painstakingly gleaned nuggets.

On the way back, Speedy ignored his brake pedal. Morning newspapers were taking shape in America; for the wires, every minute counts. Closing my eyes as we hurtled through the night, with amoebas doing half-gainers in my lower gut, I had one of those epiphanies that foreign correspondents get. No one could pay me enough to do this kind of work. I could not tell my family how close I came, each night, to ending up like former colleagues dead in a ditch. But I loved it, and I was grateful for publishers with a sense of mission who footed my substantial bills.

Anyone with a pencil and a hunger for an excellent adventure can go somewhere and write down quotes. That is not necessarily reporting. And if they get it wrong, the damage to us all is incalculable. Today, in spite of all the cutbacks, plenty of veteran reporters are still out there in the same way I was. But they do not come cheap.

If, from tomorrow morning, we all spent as much on a daily newspaper as we pay for a double cappuccino, we would be halfway toward the light. While free news off the Net is a pretty good deal, we cripple journalism by not paying something toward the price of newsgathering. Of course, there is a free lunch; soup kitchens abound. But when you bum a meal, you take what you get. It does not help to badmouth the menu.

Flawed as they are, we cannot give up on newspapers. Some useful reporting can be found in the lousiest of them. The best give us the heft of thoughtful editors' judgments, with priorities expressed by layout. Yet their economics are skewed. One morning, I saw a *Seattle Times* editorial scolding a man who cut down 120 trees to improve his view of a lake. I agreed, but then I tossed out unread several pounds of classifieds, car ads, and filler copy. How many trees was that? (Over twenty years, WorldWatch estimates, an average reader handles ten thousand pounds of newsprint. That comes to 185 trees; about 35 of them are for classifieds.)

With more circulation, papers would increase display advertising. Paid sales at a fair price would add revenue. Publishers who foreswore obscene profit targets could deliver an honest product in the public interest. We would then have context for TV footage, which, unexplained, so often misleads. Surely, a good newspaper is worth as much as that morning Starbucks.

Some proprietors will simply pocket more profit without improving the product. Revile them noisily and get your friends to join in articulate criticism. If nothing changes, find a better newspaper.

Television is another problem. Viewers have little direct impact on how thoroughly, or effectively, networks cover news. Yet when executives sniff a groundswell of interest, noses twitch. Energetic lobbying can help. Even when it does not, if you understand the players and the issues, disembodied pictures take on more meaning. Once you follow real news, you will know if a flag-waving network is as fair and balanced as it boasts it is.

TV devotes its resources to sizzle, not steak. Until 2006, CBS viewers heard the evening news from Bob Schieffer, who, though weathered from a long life in the real world, is a gifted newsman with gravitas and humor. Then CBS signed a $75 million five-year contract with Katie Couric. That is a lot for someone to read a teleprompter. After Couric's first night, the network president said it all: It was a good "episode."

Couric had excelled on a perky morning program. Under pressure in a new role, she used up much of her twenty-three minutes with offbeat gimmicks to prove she was worth the money. Her mission was impossible. In a news show, what counts is the news, not the show.

Watch *BBC World News* for ten days, with its anchors who are Schieffer-like old men or no-nonsense women reporters in from the cold. Notice how the venerable Beeb focuses on news, with well-edited footage and on-camera interviews that last longer than fourteen seconds. Notice how reporters get across human emotion without transparent gimmickry. Then write to an American network president.

Radio at its best may be the most useful medium of all. Apart from its immediacy, it engages the brain. With evocative words and background actuality, you can visualize what correspondents are talking about. People who matter can express themselves, with their own inflection and emphasis, in long uncut interviews.

With its minimal production costs, radio allows an Amy Goodman to follow her nose, and her conscience, deep into any story she believes is worth the trouble. Radio people like Goodman remember who they spoke to years earlier and what they said back then. And they add context.

If a camera points toward a fragment of reality, you see only that fragment. You might think, for example, that Pakistan is a land of loonies who always wave their fists and denounce something. It is, in fact, a richly textured society with a polo-playing leisure class, fancy women who flirt outrageously, and smart professionals who excel in almost every field. If you can't go places yourself, at least turn off your TV for a while and listen to the radio.

In a book called *Who Stole the News?* I profiled Deborah Amos of National Public Radio, who waxed eloquent about what her medium did that television could not. After corrected proofs went to press, she quit to join ABC-TV. I saw her again in 2006, prepared for some friendly ragging. But she had just quit and returned to radio. Amos found that American TV does not assign reporters to stories as much as it casts them. She could not get to Iraq. ABC wanted dashing male faces on camera. She called Loren Jenkins, foreign editor at NPR, to ask for her old job. Without a word about arrangements or emoluments, he replied, "When can you get there?"

To follow the world, the "mainstream media" should be no more than a starting point. If you navigate wisely and test your sources, broadband gives you access to reality that Edward R. Murrow contemporaries could not even dream about. Such "consolidator" sites as www.mediachannel.org or www.truthout.org get you started. The Reuters Foundation offers www.alertnet.org, a helpful index to hard news, data, and background. Often wise commentary collects on www.commondreams.org. For a lively overall hit, with provocative thought from a main line cast of characters, try Arianna Huffington's monsterblog, www.huffingtonpost.com. Your eleven-year-old nephew can help you with podcasts, RSS, video clips, translated foreign-language media, and the hidden marvels of Google.

When I moved to Provence, my reality links were an iffy phone line and a mailman who avoided my bumpy road. Now a small satellite dish brings the BBC, CNN, Al Jazeera, and all the rest. Online, I watch Jon Stewart, *Frontline* documentaries, and stuff sent by friends across the world. Someone, somewhere, thoughtfully translates media from a hundred languages. I get virulent propaganda and also the wisdom of such journalists as Adam Michnik in Poland, who reminds us: "If you're powerful, you are much more likely to be blind and deaf to signals from the outside."

People such as Michnik, like Václav Havel, kept their spirits alive during ugly times. They know the nature of man's worst side but also how to overcome it. Among my favorite Michnik lines is this: "Americans could never understand the difference between the right and the left in Germany, but they knew that Hitler should be defeated!"

When you find people you admire, check out their backgrounds. Compare what they write today with what they wrote six months earlier. When they refer knowledgeably to distant places, find out if they have actually been there. Read those you disagree with yet still respect as honest.

Such sampling leads to magazines and books. The possibilities are endless. We all believe we are too busy to read, but compare the number of video-rental outlets to bookstores and libraries. Let us get a grip.

Even a fearless daily press that does its job well ought to be seen in context. *Foreign Affairs* is not exactly strong on cover art. Though well edited, its turgid prose can sometimes push insomniacs to deep slumber. But suppose you had thumbed through the last issue of 1998. Two European thinkers explained why Americans' smug assumptions of superiority cost them allies they would badly need. A piece on our vulnerability to terrorism noted: "The World Trade Center bombing [in 1993] scarcely hints at the enormity of the danger." And, in an article entitled "License to Kill," Bernard Lewis focused on a little-noticed declaration of global jihad by Usama bin Ladin. Two vowel changes and a different world later, we can see why we should have paid attention.

The root of bin Laden's wrath was American military presence in Saudi Arabia, Islamic holy ground. Washington laughed that off, opting for the tactical convenience of bases closer to Iraq. We might have tactfully shifted elsewhere without acknowledging bin Laden. One cannot cede to terrorist threats, but one must analyze them carefully. Had we paid attention, perhaps our intelligence agencies would have jointly pursued their essential mission rather than personal and interagency turf wars.

Lewis said most of Islam saw a call for the mass murder of innocents as a travesty. Nonetheless, he concluded, "some Muslims are ready to approve, and a few of them to apply, the declaration's extreme interpretation of their religion. Terrorism requires only a few. Obviously, the West must defend itself by whatever means will be effective. But in devising strategies to fight the terrorists, it would surely be useful to understand the forces that drive them."

If America missed its chance to intercept Al Qaeda's homemade Pearl Harbor, the challenge is just beginning. We cannot eliminate terrorism any more than we can tidal waves. But, as with natural phenomena, we can at least understand its causes. Then we can do things differently to lessen its frequency and intensity.

Some murderous acts are irrational, committed by twisted zealots. Any culture as dominant and profligate as ours will incite some who hate us, no matter what. Yet with generosity of spirit and an even-handed foreign policy that leaves fewer desperate people in dire straits, we can restore the respect. Doing the right thing is a far better defense than deploying muscle-bound armed forces.

However we inform ourselves, what counts most is to evaluate sources. When anyone states a "fact," ask the question Sherman Miller drummed into his journalism students: Who he? Opinions are opinions. Evaluate firsthand reporting by triangulation; when three reasonable witnesses agree on basic facts and a conclusion, you are probably on solid ground.

It is important to step back from the immediacy mania that engulfs the news business. Much of it is marketing hype. For the wires, urgent flashes are vital; they alert editors and reporters to breaking news the way bells wake up firefighters. When big money is at stake, it helps to be warned on events that move markets. But for most of us, how much does it really matter for some Dick Tracy device to buzz on our belt with a snippet of news that will be overtaken many times over before it has meaning?

Consider this: While I was in Miami late in 2006, national news channels went live for hours to follow drama at the *Miami Herald*. MSNBC, CNN, and others said a fired cartoonist charged past lobby security guards with a laser-scope rifle. For one young woman anchor, this became "a laser gun." Others called it a "machine gun" without explaining how a lone man could muscle it up the stairs. Early on, the *Herald* managing editor, one floor below, told an interviewer by phone that the guy had only a toy gun and seemed to be no threat to anyone. But there was no drama in that. Reporters doing stand-ups, in authoritative tones, gave details of the automatic, or semiautomatic, weapon, and each mused on its deadly potential.

Then I left town, driving past the *Herald* and seeing none of the commotion reporters described. Days later, I logged on to the *Herald* Web site and typed "disgruntled" in the search window; that is a reporter's favorite word in these circumstances. Sure enough, it was a toy gun. The guy gave the security guard a Cohiba cigar and waltzed right in. Later, he gave up without fuss. My guess is that more TV time was devoted to the great *Herald* siege in one day than to South Asia or North Korea for the year.

Keep your BlackBerry, but recognize it for what it is not. When the Iraq War turned ugly, I dug into dusty files to find a two-part *New Yorker* piece Milton Viorst had written in 1987. His leisurely account of Shiite life in Karbala and Najaf, with deep-rooted obsessions over the stabbing of Ali in 661, made clear that "freedom" and "democracy" delivered by infidel crusaders would need more than tank fire to implant themselves in that holy ground.

Just before, I found an essay in *Granta* on jihadis by the Indian novelist and journalist Pankaj Mishra. Written early in 2002, the piece recalled Mishra's earlier visits to Pakistan to pin down how the Inter-Services Intelligence Agency used William Casey's discarded Afghani zealots to forge an Islamist sphere across much of Central Asia. Amid his revealing if arcane detail, he offered this small flash of wisdom that framed a larger picture:

"The India I had grown up in had also been radically and often traumatically reshaped by the great imperial power of the West, so I had some understanding of how people in demoralized societies could grow inflexible while trying to protect their older way of living."

Thanks to the Internet, our background news briefings can go back to Sun Tzu, who laid out the first rule of war in the sixth century B.C.: Know thine enemy. And there is Socrates' advice on keeping the peace, a few centuries later: Know thyself. Either way, the operative word is "know." The media alone, whatever its strengths or weaknesses, can only brush the surface.

A ll of this, so far, is preparatory work, guidelines for seeing the world as it is. Confronting the crises we face takes hard choices. We come up against that question, the grandmother of all obstacles: Who gives up what? However we slice things, we all must make short-term sacrifices, which may turn out to be long-term blessings. If we do it right, only the unreasonable will suffer for it. The point to remember is we really have no choice.

If we maintain the status quo, the likely outcome is clear enough. Haves will isolate themselves even further and corner the market on essentials. Have-nots will suffer to their limit and then react in ways we dare not predict. And when nature eventually reaches its tipping points, no one will escape the calamity. Is this too dire? Perhaps. But do we want to risk it? Do our grandchildren agree?

Some challenges are less formidable than they appear. Societies can adapt. Remember litter? When we old guys were kids, we pitched garbage out the car window without a thought. Now, beyond the risk of a fine, littering is a heinous antisocial sin. It only took a different mindset.

Animal lovers cut severely into the use of fur coats by scowling, if not tossing paint, at women who wore pelts of minks and sables raised on farms, just as chickens are raised for the dinner tables. What about Hummers?

Still, token changes at the edges will not do it. If a housewife puts carefully sorted garbage into her Chevrolet Godzilla and drives several miles to a recycling center, is there a net gain? It helps to turn off the tap when brushing your teeth, but what about those gazillion water-guzzling golf courses in southwestern deserts?

With our way of thinking, a Smart Car is pretty dumb. An ecology-minded mother must endanger her child because other mothers protect theirs by spewing CO_2 into the air from hogwagons that, in a collision, crush small vehicles.

We need alternatives; that much is obvious. Someday, we will also have to consider limits on how much is enough for people who believe conspicuous consumption is how we keep score. Free enterprise is fundamental to who we are. Yet that cannot translate into survival of the most piggish.

This is heretical ground in a nation that sanctifies the right to squander heedlessly. Nonetheless, let us think about it. Suppose some New Yorker with a voracious appetite, a low threshold for stepping on others, and bad hair decides to build a pharaonic private estate in Florida that he visits a few days a year. So far so good; that's the American way. But, in an area under stress, can he use unlimited water for splashing fountains and vast gardens?

A sensible society must consider these points. When appeals to human decency fail, do we shrug and let it go? Or do we decide that some things are the finite resources of a planet that we all must share with ever growing numbers? When you are dealing out dwindling supplies in a lifeboat, some things should not be for sale at any price.

Perhaps our greatest challenge is to teach our kids how to think critically. This will take years of committed attention. Even at its best, journalism amounts to no more than a briefing. For a clear sense of what events and trends mean to our reality, we each need to fit news into a broad context. And this has to start in primary school.

In earlier days, most American schooling stopped at eighth grade. But a friend sent me a final exam used in 1895 in Salina, Kansas. The test took five hours. Here are a few questions from the hour-long geography part: How do you account for the extremes of climate in Kansas? Name and describe the following: Monrovia, Odessa, Denver, Manitoba, Hecla, Yukon, St. Helena, Juan Fernandez, Aspinwall, and Orinoco. Name and locate the principal trade centers of the United States. Name all the republics of Europe and give the capital of each. Why is the Atlantic Coast colder than the Pacific in the same latitude? Describe the movements of the Earth. Give the inclination of the Earth.

How about a few grammar points? Define the following, and give examples of each: trigraph, subvocals, diphthong, cognate letters, linguals. Use the following in sentences: cite, site, sight, fane, fain, feign, vane, vain, vein, raze, raise, rays.

Just for fun, answer those questions. Then, to bolster your shattered self-esteem, try them on a Princeton student; she may well do no better.

We must help children to see the larger picture—and to challenge what they hear—from the time they fling their first spoonful of applesauce across the kitchen. Many will never leave their cave. But it takes fewer enlightened young citizens than most of us think to inspire a society.

Better schools with freer curricula are the obvious underpinning. Yet parents, aunts and uncles, and real or symbolic big brothers and sisters all have a role to play. Just about every educator, psychiatrist, and smart mother agrees on the main point: This should start by nursery school and keep on until a kid chooses a path and sets off.

A *New York Times* op-ed piece made this point, under the headline "Young, Gullible and Taught to Hate."[1] It was not about *madrassas* in Pakistan or Parisian *banlieues*. In fact, it was written in August 1993 by Morris Dees, chairman of the Southern Poverty Law Center and founder of Klanwatch.

He described a well-populated underclass: "Vulnerable but streetwise young-sters, who are looking for an excuse to fight, they are easy prey for older white supremacist leaders, who cynically offer a sense of family and purpose—along with a hate-filled ideology."

Change a few nouns, and it sounds familiar today. Dees focused on a particular twenty-year-old who masterminded a plot to ignite a race war that was foiled in July 1993. It was to murder Rodney King, kill worship-pers in a black church, and bomb Jewish leaders and synagogues. It also tar-geted black entertainers and sports figures.

Photos splashed across the front pages back then showed not a shaved-head hooligan in a bomber jacket and tattoos but rather what one newspa-per called "the epitome of an all-American boy." Dees wrote in the *Times*. "The old-guard, armchair extremists have no intention of being anywhere near the front lines if a 'racial holy war' ever occurs."

Barry Austin Goodfield, an American psychotherapist and conflict ne-gotiator who works across the world, sees little difference between today's disaffected young men who join Islamic terrorist ranks and the teenaged brownshirts of the Hitler Youth. It is as Morris Dees said. If you channel all that aggression and energy behind a simplified message, you can shape "ide-ology" in any direction.

People in other cultures will not restore their respect for us until we show signs that we care about them, or at least know who they are. We must get beyond the smug belief in our superiority. If we decide we are better than anyone else, we must at least base that on observation rather than ignorant dogma.

"The media" carries some blame, obviously enough, but it goes deeper than that. In representative democracies, people get the governments they deserve. That applies also to their news organizations. If enough of us de-manded better, we would get it.

The fundamental problem is education, at the hands of both teachers and parents. Children must grow up with intellectual curiosity. At an early age, kids should learn to question, to compare, to take nothing on its face. Any decent editor knows this is far and away the most valuable attribute of a reporter. Writing is only packaging. Substance requires curiosity. Without it, any picture presented will almost certainly be skewed.

Curiosity means more than using a few available facts to catapult toward a conclusion. It is a thought-intensive process of assembling bits of puzzle pieces and fitting them into a logical frame. Questions always remain, and a good reporter, or a good citizen, never stops asking them.

No subject I broached brought more heated response than America's failure to prepare a new generation to understand the world as it is. Curricula are designed to help kids pass tests so no child is left behind.

Among ranking educators, this is a running theme and a constant frustration.

"Our kids don't learn enough early enough," Joel Klein told me in New York. He is chancellor of the city's schools, which are better than most. He sees a tight vicious circle in which neither resources nor faculty are up to the job. Teachers who must act as cops lose their edge, then their enthusiasm. Smart young brains are squandered.

"You have to start young," Klein said, echoing the near unanimous judgment of psychologists, educators, and parents who pay attention to their own kids. "To teach something that makes an impact, give me a three-year-old over a thirty-year-old any day of the week."

But in America today, with religious and nationalistic dogmatists answering questions before they can be asked, the picture is bleak.

In 2006, Jay Bennish, a twenty-eight-year-old social studies teacher in Denver, found this out the hard way. He asked his tenth-grade class to de-construct George W. Bush's State of the Union message. Some of it, he said, "sounds a lot like the things that Adolf Hitler used to say. We're the only ones who are right, everyone else is backwards and our job is to conquer the world and make sure that they all live just like we want them to." He said he was not equating Bush to Hitler but noted "eerie similarities to the tones they use." At the end, he stressed, "You have to figure this stuff out for yourselves. . . . I'm not in any way implying that you should agree with me. . . . What I'm trying to do is think about these issues more in depth and not just take things from the surface."

Bennish was right, of course, as anyone can check by reviewing Hitler's campaign speeches when Germans elected him in free democratic elections. But some weenie in the class taped twenty minutes of the lecture on his MP3 player and gave it to a conservative radio commentator.

The storm echoed far beyond Denver. People called from across the country with Nazi-type threats to "string him up" or kill him slowly along with his family. Colorado governor Bill Owens weighed in, praising the student who ratted out his teacher. "I'll bet that you don't have Mr. Bennish balancing later in the day, talking about the good things that the

United States is doing in Iraq, discussing why George Bush is not similar to Hitler," he said.

But the ending was encouraging. Bush himself defended Bennish's right to free speech in answer to a reporter's question in Washington. About 150 students at Overland High School marched in support, chanting, "Freedom of speech, let him teach." After administrative leave, Bennish went back to the classroom.

There was much to learn from Bennish's challenge to his class. When we hear "Hitler," we think Holocaust. Yet he rose to power legally, in plain view. At first, Nazis preached only that Germans were better than everyone else and that government powers were essential to security. Then they shaped public opinion and retooled the schools. By the time he named himself Führer, and well-meaning Germans saw what they had wrought, what exactly were they to do? Learning about authoritarian rule does not mean glorifying it. It helps us to recognize early warning signs.

When the story broke, however, it was clear that firm lines were already drawn. The headline in the *Denver Post* encapsulated the discourse over Bennish's thoughtful class exercise simply enough: "Teacher caught in Bush 'rant.'"

The standard answer is that we are too busy for complex curiosity—but it does not take long to stop and think. We schedule regular sessions to exercise our heart and lungs. Why not add in brain function? If we are that busy, what explains all those computer games that sell so briskly?

This curiosity business hit home after a midnight landing in Los Angeles. I had spent a month in Afghanistan, just after 9/11. Beat, I looked forward to dozing all the way to Studio City. My driver, it turned out, was an out-of-work actor with time on his hands who seemed intensely interested in the struggle with Al Qaeda.

Tired as I was, I decided to bite the bullet. After all, my spiel runs heavily toward the responsibility of those who happen upon real experience to share it with others. I told the guy where I had just been.

"Oh yeah?" he replied. "Well, let me tell you what's going on there." He did, and I took my snooze. According to my wife, who listened for the next hour, he never asked a single question. He had his own explanation. The trouble, he said, was those A-rabs from I-ran.

During 2006, freed of a day job, I did some teaching of my own. More than anything, I was curious to reconnect with my roots, such as they were, after so many years of looking at other people's societies.

Sometimes, I was pessimistic enough to blow my brains out. More often, I listened, amazed at how much good sense open young minds can produce. In the end, I saw to what extent critics of America confuse stupidity with ignorance. Extremely smart people can be ignorant about important things. That only takes will, and effort, to overcome.

In Tucson, I taught a course on international reporting at my old school, the University of Arizona. Sherman Miller was long gone, but he had left his mark on Jacqueline Sharkey. As department head, she champions the sort of critical thought that eludes so many students coming up through the system. She knows that anyone can learn to craft sentences. Those who hope to be reporters, or simply intelligent citizens, must be able to find the holes in every piece of information they come across.

"If I were empress of the universe," Sharkey told me, "I would triple the salary of every teacher from kindergarten through high school." Much wisdom followed, but the gist is easily summarized: If kids do not learn to think early, are not inspired to be curious, they will as adults be lost to an intelligent society, vulnerable to anyone's flimflam.

Sharkey knows the obstacles inherent to school-board politics. Money is tight; ideology is rampant; power struggles are fierce. But, she believes, none of that is an excuse. People who pay taxes should decide. A career in teaching should not require a vow of poverty. If more qualified teachers are attracted to the job, they can be trusted with some sensible latitude in curriculum.

And Sharkey had another thought, one that I heard from smart Americans across the country: Young people should travel, the earlier the better. Sure, there is a plenty to see in our own vast land, but staying home does not reveal the shape of the world or other people's realities.

Among my seventeen students, I saw what she meant. One young woman, for instance, was a skilled writer who worked on the campus daily. She showed up on time and suffered through my stories. Then a friend came to lecture, and he posed a question I never thought to ask: "What's the population of the United States?" Some came close. One said 450 million. But my promising student ventured: "Six million."

By the end, however, she earned an A. In my optimistic moments, I like to think she has bought a world atlas and, perhaps, a plane ticket might follow.

My brief adventure in academia helped me see why Americans miss so much reality, at home as well as abroad. Obviously, we need better education. Authors and reformers devote lives to making this point. But this cannot happen without national focus and local support. We need school boards and legislators who face the challenge. When strategies are worked out, we must find the money. A trillion dollars squandered in Iraq could have done it.

In Arizona, I reconnected with two friends. Michael Ruby and Merrill McLoughlin had worked together at *Newsweek* and *U.S. News & World Report*. Then they settled in a desert home in Cave Creek, north of Scottsdale. They landscaped in cactus, lived at a human pace, and followed the world via old pals and new technology. It was fun catching up, but our conversation soon plummeted into that familiar zone of despair. Hard-bitten pros tend to dismiss ideas that start with "Change human nature" or "Alter the corporate conscience."

We were eloquent in defining the problem; we just could not solve it. The news business has passed the point where editors can simply decide to do better. If short-sighted managers have not killed their golden goose, they are plucking her to within an inch of her life.

The solution, we decided, lay in people who think for themselves, act on their own, and use today's new tools to energize others. This deep-seated American spirit bubbles up across the country. Dots connect quickly in an Internet age. The trick is to find inspiring examples.

Mike suddenly brightened. In another place and time, he might have shouted, "Eureka!" "Hey," he said, poking a fork toward Mimi, "let's put him in touch with Nick."

The Rubys had met Nicholas Kreider on a Wyoming dude ranch when he worked as a wrangler to pay for his M.B.A. studies at Bond University in Australia. Soon after graduation, that killer tsunami struck South Asia, from Sri Lanka to Indonesia. "I couldn't be so close to all that suffering without doing something," he told me when I finally tracked him down in Los Angeles. With a wispy black beard and dark, piercing eyes, he was having some luck at acting. "A rich friend said he would lend me enough money for a ticket to Sri Lanka, so I went."

Nick made contact with a local relief agency and found a small village to help. The tidal wave had scoured it clean, washing away homes, crops, animals, and no small number of people. He joined in to clean up the mess. Short of money and reluctant to tap the village's meager food supply, he did not eat. People noticed him getting steadily more emaciated. "After that, I was never allowed to miss a meal," he said. "They made a schedule for me. Every day they told me in whose house I would be having lunch and dinner. And they made sure I showed up."

Soon Nick learned Sinhalese, an intricate language of tricky tones along with the usual grammar and vocabulary. Then he set up a factory to process the only thing poor families had at hand: coconut fiber.

"I was able to scrape together a little money for start-up costs, and pretty soon we had jobs for most of the village," he said. "Workers made a small wage and could put their lives back together." When he left after three months, the factory was thriving, feeding the village.

Before Nick moved on to Kenya to do something similar, the village threw him a daylong party. They draped him in flowers and paraded him through the streets atop a painted elephant. The people he helped still regularly scrounge together a week's income to call him up, just to see how he is doing. *They* don't hate Nick Kreider.

G uys like Nick, happily enough, are not especially rare. They combine good works with a good time, and everyone comes away richer for it. But no one who knew Marla Ruzicka had ever met anyone like her. And all of us in that very large group saw in vibrant living color what one committed young American is capable of doing.

Marla laughed when I called her a ditzy blonde; she knew the irony I meant. She was at first glance a storybook surfer chick, quick to giggle or shriek, a star at parties, whose favored term of endearment was "dude." But a micro millimeter beneath the surface, she was as wise, solidly rooted, and sober minded as a person can get.

Born in Lakeport, California, she grew up getting involved. Marla was suspended from high school at fifteen for leading a protest against the first Gulf War. At Long Island University, as a volunteer for the San Francisco–based Global Exchange, she visited Cuba, Guatemala, southern Africa, and the West Bank. Cops carried her off in Texas when she ripped off a sarong to reveal a protest message at a speech by the governor, George W. Bush.

I met Marla in Afghanistan, where she had gone to lobby for compensation for civilian victims. Her one-woman voluntary agency won backing from George Soros and respect from Democratic senator Patrick Leahy of Vermont. Soon she pried $2.5 million from the U.S. government, which grew to $7 million. By the time I found her again in Iraq, she had an admiring retinue of journalists, diplomats, Iraqis of all sorts, and military officers who saw past the surface.

By then, she had already founded Campaign for Innocent Victims in

Conflict. After a look at CIVIC's first briefing, Leahy sponsored legislation that provided $10 million for Iraqi victims. He told colleagues, "Marla Ruzicka is out there saying, 'Wait, everybody. Here is what is really happening. You'd better know about this.' We have whistle-blowers in industry. Maybe sometimes we need whistle-blowers in foreign policy."

More than the money, Marla's impact was personal. She handled babies in hospitals as though they were her own. She engaged senior military officers in conversations that left them convinced. People who called her an idealist did not know her well. Marla knew exactly how the world is built, and what she was up against, and she kept at it.

On April 16, 2005, Marla was killed by a car bomb in Baghdad. She was out saying last-minute good-byes to people she had cared for before heading back home.

"Ruzicka's short life, so packed with adventure and achievement, is proof that belief and resolve can achieve incredible things," Simon Robinson wrote in *Time*. Of all the tributes, perhaps Christopher Dickey of *Newsweek* caught her spirit best. He wrote:

"As flighty as Marla sometimes seemed, and as complicated as she actually was, she drove home one simple and powerful point she never let any of us forget—a terrible, plain truth that too many politicians, soldiers and journalists tend to ignore when they dare to talk about the dead and wounded in war as statistics for history books. 'Each number,' she'd say, 'is a story of someone who left a family behind.'

"As Marla Ruzicka has done. Marla, who was one of a kind."[2]

Exceptional heroism aside, there is no substitute for seeing the world in person. This applies to school kids and adults alike. Travel abroad ought to be as much a federal requirement as paying income tax. It takes only a passport and a little extra lunch money. How can we assess our own place in the world unless we have an idea of how the other nineteen-twentieths live?

Some time back, writing about America as seen by outsiders, I wandered into a Cajun bar in the swamps beyond Lafayette, Louisiana. What with French as a second language, I expected to find a fairly open world-view. When I explained my purpose to a bulky guy with a beer, he asked: "Why do you want to live over there in Europe? Anything you want you can find right here in the USA." I suggested he write me when he found the Parthenon.

These days, of course, that guy could find just about everything except London Bridge in Las Vegas. And the bridge is not far away in Lake Havasu, Arizona. But, of course, it really isn't.

One can debate whether seeing the acid-gnawed remains of the Parthenon is worth dealing with Athens traffic. However, it is more than that. The point is not monuments but the mentalities behind them. In a place where democracy worked two millennia ago, where savants like Plato challenged conventional wisdom, thinking shifts to a meta level. So they dressed in bedsheets. They loved sports and punished iconoclasts with a lethal infusion. *Plus ça change.*

When you go, escape your group. Talk to people with different frames of reference. The more unfamiliar-seeming the place you go, the better. Language need not be a barrier. If you want to communicate with someone on a human level, you will connect.

If you can't get away, do what you can. Go to lectures and stick around to chat afterward. At your favorite ethnic hangout, talk to the owners about more than *rogan josh.* Corner any of the millions of people who have immigrated via the front door or the back. Many will begin on the land-of-opportunity theme. But keep talking.

The more we travel, the more we understand how unlike us people can be. Even more, we realize that people are more like us than they are different. Whatever their culture, they want to protect their families, follow their faith, and get by without serious want. It is how humans were designed. The notion of nationality came later.

Exposure to others does not guarantee anything in particular. I have a friend who has seen much of the world and travels constantly to Europe. He is a psychologist who specializes in reading people's inner circuitry. Recently in Holland, we happened upon a celebration recalling how American troops in World War II seized the crossing at Arnheim, the Bridge Too Far.

Afterward, in a bar, we talked to one of the marchers, a Dutch saxophonist in his forties who grew up on stories of the 82nd Airborne. He did not hate America. As he talked, however, he told us what he thought of Guantánamo, of "rendition" that implicated Europe in our torture, of flying into America, and of the Iraq War in general.

He wanted very much to see again the America he had grown up to love. As I listened, I nodded. That is an old reporter's device, suggesting empathy whatever the message. But I agreed with the man. My friend, meantime, began to fume. When we turned away, he lit into me with fury. How could I run down my country? Everything I told that foreigner was so negative.

We just had different viewpoints. Although I was just as proud of those GIs as he was, I was seeing evidence of how a noble past can be soured by an ignoble present. He believed in America, right or wrong. And he flew a large flag and extolled George W. Bush to prove it.

I distrust that phrase "right-thinking people," which tends to mean those who reflect their interlocutor's wisdom. Who decides what anyone thinks? But at the very least, we might remember a joking slogan we applied to the Columbia University center for foreign students: Join the International House and base your prejudices on fact.

Many workable solutions to crises we face require corporate decision by executives and boards who are not swayed by appeals to conscience. Some of these are very good people, but businesses are not run by emotion or rational outside argument. This, in fact, is not such a difficult obstacle. All that is needed is for these corporate officers to recognize a clear interest.

The key is to speak their language. My Washington attorney friend Jack Blum sympathizes with much of what "the liberal left" has to say. But he often groans at how it is said. An appeal for an undefined common good without some advantage in the mix only marks the appealer as someone who corporate security goons should scrutinize.

"We have this appalling kind of dialogue," he says, "with people on the left who refuse to address things as they are, and people on the right who refuse to listen. It is flat-out protest without engaging. Executives are not going to engage with people who do stuff that's cuckoo in their terms. Critics of oil companies have never produced a barrel of oil. You need solutions that work. You won't change the global direction, but you can modify behavior and certain parameters so we don't destroy ourselves."

Like others, Blum sees a useful chokepoint in taxes. Overhauling how corporations are taxed would modify behavior while helping to unburden families on wages.

"A very small number of people have figured out how to take over a company and take assets for themselves," he said. "This is a terrible disaster for the society. If money is taken out and not reinvested, it must be taxed up the wazoo." But, he adds, "we have no literacy on the subject. No idea of who is paying and who isn't; where wealth is going and where it isn't. We're dealing with reality, forcing political engagement. And that takes work, and that takes thought, and that takes people who go beyond the norm of critique."

Taxes are part of it. Corporations would be more likely to take action to help society if they were not compensated by the government for avoiding it. This gets back to the main point: We can elect better leaders who are independent from the vested interests of big money.

Elections work. Among the Democrat newcomers swept into Congress in 2006 was Gabrielle Giffords, from my hometown of Tucson. Barely out of college, she managed her father's business, El Campo Tire, where we all got our retreads. Then she was elected to the Arizona state legislature, a voice of reason in what is often a loony bin. At thirty-six, she was in Congress. Gabby Giffords is smart, hardheaded, compassionate, amusing, fluent in Spanish, and beautiful to boot. Her "cactus-roots campaign" was funded by small donations.

Giffords believes global warming is a bigger threat than terrorism. She worries about corruption and cronyism in politics. Health care, including for the mentally ill and the elderly, is her top priority. She wants to smooth immigration problems, with a fair shake for Latinos who are eager to do jobs we need filled. Education is crucial, she thinks, and kids must learn about the world early.

When I asked Giffords if Americans were ready to elect people who had a higher regard for doing good rather than just staying in office, she grimaced. "Doubtful," she replied. "In fact, my concern is that Americans are busier and busier with their lives, politically less engaged than fifty, forty, or thirty years ago. Fewer people are determining the outcome of our elections. It depends on who organizes best. Fewer and fewer people register to vote. They just don't want to play anymore."

What we need, she feels, are people who can inspire Americans to get involved and to get themselves to polling places so that sensible ideas become reality.

"I think it starts at the top," Giffords concluded. "Americans will always look to our leadership, with a two-party system and state governor. We have to make sure we elect people who understand complex problems, who value other cultures, other opinions, who can foster good foreign policies. We have to elect people who are intelligent, hardworking, fair, and just."

That seems like an obvious enough course of action. What is stopping us?

Arizona voters rejected a proposal to give anyone who showed up at the polls a lottery ticket for a million-dollar drawing. Considering how hard some people fight for the right to vote, it seems outrageous for Americans to bribe each other to cast a ballot. Plato wanted to reserve voting for people who might choose wisely. Philosophers, for instance. He figured common boobs might get it wrong. America's low turnout is a national shame. Still, it takes fewer motivated voters to sway an election.

Compared to other democracies, our quadrennial presidential sweeps fall between laughable and shameful. Nearly two years before 2008 elections, as hopefuls began campaigns that would cost up to $500 million, columnist Jim Hightower had a suggestion: Candidates should wear patches, like NASCAR drivers, to identify their sponsors.

Others avoid our pitfalls. Parliamentary systems like Britain's use snap elections or votes of confidence to remove an unpopular leader. France has a president, but campaigns are brief with strict funding limits. Candidates draw lots for TV time slots. In long and tough debates, no one escapes with facile sound bites. In other countries, people who come second are seldom shunted aside as losers.

The 2007 turnout in France was 85 percent, twice the usual rate in America. In critical 2004 U. S. elections, only 43 percent of registered voters cast ballots. Since many eligible Americans don't even bother to register, a small fraction of citizens defines our democracy.

By the time we narrow our main choices down to two, both opponents bleed from wounds inflicted by rivals in their own parties. Slick, at times dishonest, TV spots confuse voters and avoid substance. The race is shaped by ad people who market candidates like dog food. Pressure for daily coverage obscures issues. At the end, the winner is heavily compromised by special interests.

Members of Congress who run for president neglect jobs they were elected to do. They have constituents to represent. Legislators are as essential to dealing with the world as the Chief Executive. Kyoto, like so many other important treaties, was signed by a president but left to languish on Capitol Hill. Congress could have prevented the Iraq war. After Democrats won a majority in 2006, squabbling over military and political issues that few understood further worsened our standing abroad.

Congressional fact-finding trips are vital when the purpose is to find facts. Most are rushed and superficial. Soon after Gabrielle Giffords was named to the Armed Services Committee, she went to Iraq. When I asked what she learned, she was refreshingly candid: "I don't know—we didn't get to Iraq. I was in the Green Zone. I saw an awful lot of American SUVs." Having seen the setting, however, she knew what to ask back home.

Too many congressional delegations, or codels, simply waste money. Sometimes they do worse.

In 1991, from Moscow, I saw the first crack in the Soviet monolith. A corner of Nagorno-Karabakh in Azerbaijan declared itself the independent Republic of Shahumian. Semi-autonomous Armenia was sending troops to defend ethic brethren should things turn ugly. In the heat of this, I noticed a press release that Barbara Boxer, then a Democratic congresswoman from Marin County, would visit the tiny new breakaway state. I called her San Francisco office and arranged to join her in Yerevan.

When Boxer arrived, I remarked on her courage. At that, she and her husband exchanged glances. Was this dangerous? Well, I said, things were a little unsettled. She decided instead to visit victims of an earthquake that shook Armenia three years earlier. Officials scrounged enough fuel in their blockaded republic to send our convoy to Leninakan, sixty miles north. Upon arrival, the surprised mayor learned he had the honor of feeding lunch to a U.S. congressional entourage, perhaps fifty in all.

For Armenians, generous by custom and nature, to do guests proud is a solemn duty, even if they come unannounced and uninvited to a city that can barely scrape together enough to feed itself each day. At lunchtime, our motorcade took on yet more precious fuel and headed into the mountains, where the mayor had found a relative who agreed to open his shut-down guesthouse.

A succulent goat, probably the family's last, roasted over coals. A long table groaned under elaborate trimmings. Soon after our arrival, Boxer remarked to our Canadian-Armenian escort that the bathroom had no running water. Earthquake damage, he replied; no one had running water. But the wells worked, and there was soap. Boxer decided we would eat lunch in Yerevan. When her escort urged her to reconsider, she reached for her purse to pay the host for his trouble. This was a mortal insult.

On the way up, my driver was jovial, thrilled that official America cared about a forgotten Armenia that would break free from Moscow. On the way back, he muttered darkly until he could no longer contain himself. Twisting toward the backseat, he shouted until his face grew red. He spoke in Armenian, but I could guess the meaning.

Such things are not major international incidents. Yet people remember them for decades afterward. It is how much of the real world operates. If we want the respect of other societies, we need to understand how to respect them.

Senator Barbara Boxer did better in 2006 at a televised hearing, smacking down Sen. James Inhofe. The hidebound Oklahoma Republican, who insists that global warming is the greatest hoax ever perpetrated on mankind, tried to disrupt Al Gore's testimony that America had to help protect a threatened planet. Perhaps those Armenians were watching.

Although foreign affairs routinely fall behind domestic issues, we need leaders who are wise enough to see that those two categories are the same thing. Navigating a perilous course among day-to-day crises takes skill. But even more, our next administration will have to lead allies and enemies alike toward far greater global security.

The word "security" has got to be broken down, defined, and put through more declensions than a German noun. At one level, it is no more than a catch-all license for a petty official with power issues to do things no sensible society should allow. On a broader plane, however, it has serious meanings. Leaders who shaped the United Nations in the ruins of World War II named the steering committee wisely: the Security Council.

Whether or not we can fix the United Nations, that amorphous collective we call the "international community" needs teeth. This is delicate ground. There is no place for some supranational military that goes beyond clearly drawn mandates. Yet, in cases, why not have a rapid intervention force, perhaps with standing officers and rotating troops on loan from member states, for separating hostile forces while diplomats dither and stall.

Troops with orders to shoot back could have spared up to a million lives in Rwanda and Congo, while discouraging ethnic supremacists elsewhere. Whether the mission is to thump maniacs like the Sudanese *janjaweed* or just to escort food convoys past freelance bandits, the need is urgent and vital. Few powers have the strength to do it alone. Even if any were willing, that would be a bad idea.

When world war threatens, history shows, sparks must be stamped out quickly. It should not have taken months to separate Hezbollah and the Israelis during 2006. If a government fights a stateless militia, negotiations are especially complex. A state under attack has to strike back energetically. But if it hits too hard, it feeds lasting new hatreds.

Our ad hoc system does not work, as anyone who survived Bosnia can attest. Once, in Sarajevo, I asked a French Foreign Legion officer why U.N. troops had such trouble at Serb checkpoints. "Oh, we could get through without slowing down, all right," he said, with a bitter snort, "but what about the poor bastards behind us?" At the time, Serb soldiers made a game of opening the backs of Ukrainian armed personnel carriers and pissing inside.

With no clear mandate and not enough firepower, it was hit or miss in the Balkans. A Danish tank commander who gave me a lift once got fed up with Serb snipers' potshots on one stretch of road. He flipped off his radio and announced to his crew that since they had no contact with headquarters, they had to act on their own. The Danes opened fire. They had no more problems in the future.

A Security Council must enforce its decisions. Why would Saddam Hussein expect anyone to come after him? A few years earlier, he sent the inspectors home and ignored U.N. resolutions. With the Oil for Food program, he avoided the worst sting of sanctions. As a bonus, he got to see how corruptible U.N. officials can be.

In its largest sense, security is a single word for a sweeping set of measures that human societies have to agree on so they can coexist on a small planet under severe stress. That takes statesmen, and stateswomen, whose good sense is fortified by courage. Most past wars were pushed by some lunatic who could have been sat down at a table—or smacked upside the head. If free societies vote wisely, and do not nitpick about their leaders' inconsequential personal habits, it is possible to keep peace.

It all works downward from the top. Fewer aggrieved people means less terrorism and crime. This is, of course, hardly simple. With multiple billions on the planet, we will always have fresh stocks of bad guys, from petty larcenists to murderous multinational psychopaths. But we can do better. In fact, a lot better.

In these matters, glib pundits are little help. We need the guidance of experienced men and women whose track records prove they understand complexity and refuse to compromise basic principles.

During those ugly days in Argentina, I learned to respect a U.S. political officer from Albuquerque named Dennis Jett. Wry and so calm he can seem somnambulant, he listened, evaluated, and offered wisdom. He served in Israel, Malawi, and Liberia. As U.S. ambassador in Peru, he helped defuse a crisis when leftist guerrillas seized the Japanese embassy. As ambassador to Mozambique, and then as a State Department specialist, Jett was deeply immersed in U.N. peacekeeping operations. He, in fact, literally wrote the book on the subject.

Why Peacekeeping Fails, published in 2000, should have been tattooed on Donald Rumsfeld's forearm. In it, Jett notes that peacekeeping is no longer about separating warring states. Mostly, the challenge is to neutralize ragtag factions within a single state, few of which give a damn about any commonweal. To succeed, outsiders must stop the killing but also rebuild a workable state.

The United Nations, a talking shop, can rarely do this. It can give its blessing to an international force. But that requires the political will of major powers ready to put their own interests behind a common cause. That is why Jett entitled his last chapter " 'Inconclusion'—Why Real Reform Might Not Be Possible."

Our current impasse exists not from any lack of assessment or possible remedies, Jett writes, "but because there is always resistance to change, and 'solutions' to this problem are not easily adopted."

The easy way out is always to convene the Security Council, but Jett quotes Sir Anthony Parsons, Britain's ambassador in 1982, on why this seldom works: "If I have learned anything from my experience, it is that problems can ultimately be resolved peacefully only through direct negotiations between the parties themselves. It is no use expecting outside bodies, including the UN, to draw up detailed blueprints and to impose them on recalcitrant parties to a dispute. It simply does not work."

But military coalitions, if not the United Nations, can in the meantime keep combatants from making lasting peace impossible by blasting hot lead at each other's innocent bystanders. Once that happens, resentments are too fresh and deep for negotiators to smooth over. "Democracy" can only work if all sides are willing. The mere act of voting achieves only a public relations victory for negotiators.

When warring factions threaten life en masse, nations equipped to do something must make hard choices and act together, Jett says. This takes wisdom and courage. "How the international community copes with having to be ready to kill some people in order to save others will defy easy answers regardless of what reform takes place."

In 2000, Jett retired to Gainesville as dean of the University of Florida's International Center, but he served as a voluntary adviser to the Defense Department. He resigned the day we invaded Iraq. His letter to Rumsfeld said that because of "arrogance and incompetence," the Bush administration "is responsible for squandering the lives of men and women in our military."

Over the next three years, Jett contributed eighty opinion pieces to newspapers and journals, each filled with wise advice from someone who has seen reality from the inside. Often he is in the national press, but he likes small papers that stick to their principles, like the *Anniston* (Alabama) *Star.* In each, he stomps on humbugs.

Tragic as it was, Jett wrote on September 12, 2006, the 9/11 toll equals that of boat or firearms accidents since then. It was, he wrote, exploited relentlessly by a president who compares it to World War II, in which 60 million people died. "The nation's survival is not at risk," Jett said, "but the values that made it great are. . . . We should never forget what happened on 9/11 nor stop mourning our loss. But we should also not succumb to politically motivated paranoia and should instead reflect on what 9/11 has been used as a pretext to create: a nation of sheep led by a collection of liars, fools, and cowards."

Others have expressed similar thoughts, but Jett knows the true price we paid across a wide world. With his hard-won ability to see how current events lead to future perceptions, he began early on to pose a vital question: When people talk of the Butcher of Baghdad, will they mean Saddam Hussein or George W. Bush?

On a visit in 2006, I found my old friend hardly changed, a weathered version of the Cool Hand Luke I knew in Buenos Aires. We had each stayed outside the cave for the last three decades and, in different places at different times, we had shaped almost identical worldviews.

Some subjects we covered in a single word. I mentioned torture, and the look on his face said it all. Both of us had seen, way too close, what happens when human animals are let loose with victims behind closed doors. In Argentina, we had both admired the FBI attaché who leaked details of official torture. He used to hear piercing screams from behind police stations. As an American diplomat, all he could say was, "Eh, I have to be going."

Now we have seen a president, a vice president, and an attorney general strain to find legal fig leaves to cover the same actions by Americans. "Water boarding" isn't torture? Try this at home: Get some sick lunatic who hates you to hold your head under water until he is pretty sure you have reached your last few seconds of consciousness. And hope like hell he does not guess wrong.

Other subjects kept us talking for hours. In the end, I left feeling hopeful. Guys like him, fearless when it comes to speaking plainly, still keep at it in the State Department. If their consciences force them to move on, they can teach kids at state-run universities and speak out without the requisite sugarcoating of a government post.

Neither embittered nor unduly rosy, Jett takes things as they come. He sees America as a grand nation faced with tough choices. We can pick a better leader in 2008. But each day before and after, he knows, we can take small actions that matter.

This *cri de coeur* began with a simpler purpose, at a time when a profession—really, a calling—I revered was letting us down badly. Reporters on the ground knew what awaited us in Iraq. If they were wrong, it was because few imagined just how bad things would get, and how much America would lose of its moral heft. Their insight and observations seldom made it into print or onto airwaves.

But bludgeoning a disparate profession with a blunt instrument is pointless and unfair. Old friends of mine died doing a damned good job. For all the silly cheerleading, we were also offered keen insight and occasional genius.

The press is hardly a monolith. Dana Priest of the *Washington Post* and Geraldo Rivera of wherever he works both call themselves reporters. A galaxy separates them. Avarice, self-aggrandizement, and corporate blindness have taken a heavy toll on the mainstream. But none of this is fatal. You just have to know where to look.

The tools of the trade are different now. Any news person who dismisses the Internet is like an old-timer who shunned that first stand-up telephone. But the rule is the same: Whether the tip is from a mayor's aide or some doubtful source slurring his words in a bar, check it out.

To escape Plato's cave, our much-maligned media offers a good start—but only a start. Once we get beyond those distorted images reflected off a wall, we have to evaluate news for ourselves. Then we can help enlighten others.

Current-affairs books appear quickly when big news occurs. Some are biased and off base. But many are rich in firsthand anecdote and broad insight. For those in too much of a hurry, there are the cartoonists. The good ones are rich in easily grasped universal truths.

Amid all the words in 2005, Tom Toles caught the crux in a *Washington Post* cartoon labeled "Another one of those trick questions." It posed a quiz: "The Patriot Act lets the government check all the Web sites you've looked at, even if you're not suspected of anything. Okay?" The choices were "Yes, I don't care about my freedoms" and "No, I must be a terrorist who hates freedom."

Later, Garry Trudeau parodied a college professor posing a case for constitutional law. One president starts an endless, bloody, costly war on false premises; approves covert illegal detentions, kangaroo courts, torture;

authorizes wiretapping without warrants of thousands of Americans. The second lies about messing around with an intern. The question is which should be impeached. One student, scratching his head, muses, "This sounds very familiar." Another answers, "The babe hound, right?"

Our common denominator is not a comforting baseline. Fourteen percent of Americans cannot even read. By one survey, the most popular Internet news item of 2005 was a man having sex with his horse. Nor is our standard for morality and taste. A glimpse of Janet Jackson's tasseled nipple is surely less obscene than the sight of grossly overweight kids stuffing down caramel corn.

In the end, keeping track of reality and doing sensible things in the face of it is the business of everyone who inhabits the planet. Many shirk this responsibility, and many more are too caught up in daily survival to do more than hope for the best in their own micro situations. Some use our confused inaction to amass huge fortunes and what we commonly call power. But then there are the rest of us, and that should be enough.

After I was bounced out of daily journalism at the end of 2004, I decided to step back and listen more closely to people whom earlier circumstances had forced me to interview on the fly. I read deeply; I explored back corners of the Web. I went back to sources I had respected over the decades. Mostly, I looked for examples of people who were trying to do the right thing.

I found some of the other kind. In Tucson, I was taken to dinner with a man who had retired from advertising back east. He marketed cars. From the first bite, he spewed venom at "the media." The hapless *Arizona Daily Star,* so painfully balanced that it labels op-ed pieces with disclaimers, was "the Red Star." When I mentioned the *New York Times,* he fumed over its liberal bias. He thought Americans wasted too much aid on lesser beings. It was a depressing meal, not helped by the setting. The guy lived in a water-splashed development bulldozed out of a lovely piece of Tucson's foothills.

Happily enough, such troglodytes are a minority. A thumping majority, I believe, knows we must do better and is prepared to try. There is, for instance, Gina Bentley, a close friend who volunteered uncounted hours helping me with research. Gina, from a family in Kerala, India, grew up in the northern Malaysia town of Alor Star. She studied in America and settled in Seattle with her husband, Brett, a Microsoft security engineer. She is a Christian who respects other faiths. She also cooks a mean fish cutlet.

"For every evil being done," Gina wrote on her blog, "ten acts of good are countering it. . . . [If] I may not be able to stop a war, I can help feed an orphan of the war so that he or she will taste the goodness of the inhabitants of this world. I may not hold all the answers to the whys and hows, but I can help educate a child. I may not have ignited a war, I can be an instrument of peace. But I only can if I put my resolve into action and not just spew the words from my mouth. For my silence will not help, my action will. Facta, non verba! Indeed, it's time for deeds, not words."

And deeds are everywhere, significant if often small. In a Pagosa Springs, Colorado, subdivision, the homeowners' association threatened to fine a couple twenty-five dollars a day unless they removed a four-foot wreath shaped as a peace symbol in their yard. The board called it "divisive"; one member told the local paper it looked like a sign of the devil.

Twenty people in the town of 1,700 carried peace signs to the soccer field and stomped a giant symbol in the snow, three hundred feet across. Houses across Pagosa Springs displayed the sign. Town Manager Mark Garcia put up one of his own, and then he ordered another for the municipal bell tower.

It's a start.

The good news is that we are hardly starting from scratch. A short metro ride from the circus on Capitol Hill takes you to Save the World Circle. It is Dupont Circle, more properly, but within a few minutes' walk in any direction you will find smart, committed, and badly paid people hard at work to confront crises.

The Carnegie Endowment for International Peace is here. So is the Johns Hopkins School of Advanced International Studies. Lester Brown's redoubtable Worldwatch is on Massachusetts Avenue, and his new Earth Policy Institute is around the corner, not far from the World Resources Institute. Voluntary aid agencies, think tanklets, public pressure groups, and consultants make up a very long list. I dropped in on two of them.

My first Dupont Circle stop was up a battered staircase I have frequented since the 1980s. The nameplate says Monitor Consortium, but I call it You Name It, We Save It. Its driving force is Craig Van Note, a former *Time* writer from Southern California, and his wife, Suzie. At its neatest, Monitor's one-room office looks as if a B-52 had bombed it with the contents of the Library of Congress. Still, Craig can pluck any odd yellowed document from beneath the piles whenever discussion requires it.

Van Note puts people together, stirs things up, and lobbies like hell in Washington and abroad. The world's whales owe him much for a comeback from near extinction. His exposure of drug smuggling in tuna fleets, with a slaughter of dolphins, alerted conservationists and lawmen alike. He has helped to stop giant dams and save tiny bats. His briefings on African poaching and illegal wildlife trade launched me into years of reporting. When De Beers mines in Botswana drew too much water from the Okavango Delta, threatening precious wetlands, he stopped them with a simple slogan: "Diamonds are for Death."

In the old days, the Van Notes worked their Xerox machine until it blazed red hot; then they staggered under mounds of packets toward the post office. Now, with Adobe Acrobat, they reach an ever lengthening list. Smart reporters drop in to chat, leaving with enough books and papers to provoke a hernia. Anyone who walks away without a start on a dozen stories—some solid, some unverifiable conspiracy plots—just was not listening.

On this visit, Craig was up to his ears in lawyers. And he was chuckling. Plunderers and polluters have long resorted to a simple tactic against world-savers: They sue on the slimmest of pretexts to bury critics in legal costs and paperwork. But activists are seeing that this works both ways. As more people pay attention to environmental travesty, such lawsuits merely focus more harsh light on the plaintiffs' depredations.

Van Note has been at it for twenty-five years, and I asked him how he kept up his unflagging enthusiasm for agitation and awareness campaigns. "Because," he replied, "they work. And every year, they work better."

It all works if enough people take action and stay interested. We need, desperately now, to understand this.

The second door I knocked on was all glass and glitz. Conservation International's aerie is full of bustling staff aides at humming printers, but it has a simple mission statement: "To conserve the Earth's living heritage, our global biodiversity, and to demonstrate that human societies are able to live harmoniously with nature." In practice, this translates to an ambitious effort to revolutionize how the world thinks about conservation.

"It's no longer enough just to feed a family here or build a house there," explained Claude Gascon, a Canadian ecologist who directs much of the program. "We need to look at the whole scheme. You and I will be long gone when the final results are in, but we have to start now."

CI has identified thirty-four worldwide regions—biodiversity hotspots—where three-quarters of the planet's most threatened species of mammals, birds, and amphibians hang on in dwindling habitats. They total only 2.3 percent of the Earth's surface. Together, CI says, these amount to environmental emergency rooms. The idea is to save fauna and flora by helping people who live among them. It not only spends upward of $120 million a year from its own resources, it also brings in official aid and other nongovernmental agencies. By showing executives a sensible approach toward sustainable yields of natural raw materials, CI attracts big checks from business.

The six-year goal is to put a billion dollars into a Future for Life fund to help enlightened leaders save their own environments. Madagascar, long an exotic but badly run back corner of former French Africa, is a promising case in point. Marc Ravalomanana took over as president in 2002 and got to work. A World Bank report convinced him that saving the island's rare tropical forests was vital to protect the rice paddies and farmland that fed his people. He tripled the national network of protected areas. With income from ecotourism, he energized local economies. A new code attracted investors. In two years, Ravalomanana built 3,600 miles of roads. Now CI is putting together a $50 million fund to leverage for conservation.

"That's a hell of a lot of money for paying direct benefits in a place like Madagascar," Gascon said. Even more, he added, "it is switching around how people relate to natural resources."

You can spend a month walking through doors off Save the World Circle. If snail darters are not your thing, you can find former top-level spooks lifting the corners of rugs or ex–cabinet secretaries tracking secret work to perfect our own chemical weapons, just in case, or freelance activists charting flows of dirty money and modern-day slaves all over the map.

It is not only Washington. In every part of the country, people like Rick Brusca push back despair to make a difference. As an environmental scientist, Brusca sees stupid greed killing sea floors and ancient aquifers. As a father, he watches schools deteriorate. But at the Arizona–Sonora Desert Museum, Brusca shows forty thousand kids a year a world they cannot find online.

The museum near Tucson thrilled us kids when it was a cluster of crude enclosures with a mangy cougar named George L. Mountainlion. Now a vast park of natural enclosures, man-made otter caves, walk-in aviaries, and glass-fronted snake pits, it is a window on vanishing wilds a new generation must protect. My grandnephew Louie Kay, a lover of endangered predator birds, watched one morning as two giant hawks and a rare owl swooped overhead between their handlers. The three raptors cost $100,000 to train, Brusca said, but that is nothing compared to what flies from nearby Davis-Monthan Air Base.

"It is all about understanding the importance of protecting the environment," Brusca said. "We do the research, educate the public, and hope they make the right decisions." His focus begins on eight-year-olds, he said, and the prospects are encouraging. "These kids really get engaged." Then, he adds, they are likely to grow up ready to do some serious good.

In the end, all of these diverse themes are linked, and nearly everyone who confronts world crises we face agrees on a single truth: We may not bother to look out of our cave, but everyone one else is peering at us.

Into 2007, the jury is out. We elected a Democratic Congress, showing a desire for change. But how many of us took the trouble to vote? On election night, victors rejected out of hand the impeachment of a president who repeatedly broke the most basic laws of our land. That was politically expedient, perhaps. But what does it say about our national character and the institutions we boast about?

And our world lacked a wise guiding hand. After his decade at the United Nations, we edged Kofi Annan out the door. He had made mistakes, but he tried hard at an impossible job. For the site of his parting words, he chose the library in Independence, Missouri, that honored Harry S Truman, the sort of American others remember as emblematic of what we proclaim to be.

Annan was blunt: "As President Truman said, 'The responsibility of the great states is to serve and not dominate the peoples of the world.' . . . He believed strongly that henceforth security must be collective and indivisible." Truman, he recalled, brought the Korean conflict to the U.N. "No nation can make itself secure by seeking supremacy over all others."[4]

Respect for human rights and the rule of law must underpin all societies, Annan concluded. America has a primordial role in the world, he said, but when "it appears to abandon its own ideals and objectives, its friends abroad are naturally troubled and confused."

It is not about whether "they" might hate us. What counts is whether others respect us as leaders in what, all hyperbole aside, is a struggle for planetary survival.

Here is a final exercise: Reflect a moment on where America and the world seem to be headed. Do this alone so you are not tempted to defend old positions you may want to change. Forget labels. In the real world, such undefined categories as "liberal" or "conservative" are ludicrous.

Use all the reliable sources you can muster to test your own assumptions and those you have dismissed as incompatible with what you believe. You are by yourself here. Look at things squarely in the face and be honest.

Match any fresh perceptions with your deeply held values, and design a program to inform yourself. If you veer off in any one direction, include enough mainstream to stay aware of the center. Force yourself to see things from a different viewpoint. You may feel your analysis and your facts are 100 percent correct. But when another view is held as firmly as yours, the result is frustrated tension. You don't have to agree; simply listen.

To test your open mind, argue Israel v. Palestine with someone. There has been no clear right or wrong since Moses left Sinai. Any of the groups that believe God gave them a title may well be correct. But we have no way to rule on such jurisdictions. Various sides can continue to duke it out, edging closer toward tactical nuclear mayhem. Or they can find common ground in good faith.

The Holy Land is such a challenge because fanatics on one side or another can be counted on to sabotage peace. The time it came the closest, Yitzhak Rabin was about to commit his wisdom to paper. He was assassinated by a crazed zealot, a Jew. Far more often, such deal-breaking acts come from factions of the other side.

Take your arguments to the logical end. Should Jews own Israel because they were there first? On that principle, are you ready to give your Carolina bottomland back to the Cherokees? Should Israel belong to "the Arabs"? Which of the Arabic factions now killing one another do you have in mind? Okay, so maybe try something easier, like how to reverse global warming.

We must come to grips with what we all face. Whatever we do, or do not do, a lot of pain lies ahead. It would be great if we could all join arms and sing "Kumbaya." Still, we had better not wait for that. Human nature has been what it is since cavemen first scratched stuff on walls. But we have come some ways since then, and it is time to add intelligence to basic instincts.

Rhetoric aside, reality is killing us. The rich and comfortable among us may hold on a while longer, although, most likely, not nearly as long as we think. To act sensibly, we need to know what is going wrong and why.

"The media," our new "press," is no more than a start. Its essence has not changed since that neighborhood kid tossed the *Daily Doormat* into your flower bed and pedaled off to school. You had to go outside and find it, absorb it, and, if you were a responsible citizen, do something about what you learned.

At best, journalists can only sound an alarm that alerts us to action. If they don't, we will eventually smell the smoke. The real point is: Do we react?

In my first week as a foreign correspondent, in 1967, an impossibly tall man, impossibly jet black, strode up to me at the fancy palace in Kinshasa where Africa's leaders had gathered for a summit meeting. A Dinka tribesman, he had walked for weeks to tell the world that Arab Muslims were slaughtering animist Africans in southern Sudan.

Had I the experience back then, I would have known my only real option as a reporter: to walk back with him to see the story for myself. Forty years later, plenty of reporters have since trekked to Juba. The story is the same. Those Arab Muslims' grandkids are slaughtering grandkids of those animist Africans. That Dinka's war is nearing its second half century, after at least one holocaust. And now it is only a Sudanese sideshow.

The El Geneina I saw dying in 1985 was fighting no more than drought and starvation. Now, left to its own devices, Darfur has found worse ways to suffer. Vicious bandits, backed by soldiers, are systematically wiping out a population to steal what remains of fast-vanishing pasture land. The dunes grow bigger, and the last topsoil blows north. Even if there was rain, or seed, who could plant in those conditions?

With a World Darfur Day and full-page newspaper ads, more people can find Sudan on the map. But not nearly enough. In early 2007, I asked one of my students, a 21-year-old journalism senior, to tell me who was fighting. "Us against them?" she answered. I asked her where Darfur was. She replied, "In Europe?"

Darfur caught our attention fast when crisis erupted in 2003. Secretary of State Colin Powell hurried to Sudan. In 2004, Congress condemned "genocide." Yet it rages on. Perhaps 200,000 more people have since been slaughtered; terror spreads into Chad and the Central African Republic. Aid workers are raped and hunted down, but many stay put. President Omar al-Bashir, likely the world's worst despot, was nearly elected by other chiefs of state to head the African Union.

Nick Kristof bangs the alarms in America's leading newspaper. He goes back, again and again. Since leaving the news columns, he writes for the op-ed page so he can say it straight. And people peck at the messenger.

A *Columbia Journalism Review* piece in 2006—"Kristof Becomes Own Worst Enemy"[5]—scored the columnist for shaming a Marguerite H. who had told him by e-mail to stop writing so much about Darfur and focus on problems at home. Her trigger was an appeal for a young woman named Halima.

In reply, under a photo of the woman, Kristof wrote: "So, Marguerite, look Halima in the eye and decide if you're willing to turn away as she is slaughtered, or how many more times you're willing to allow her to be raped."

This is not about the limit to Kristof's patience, or a half-named reader, or a writer who works in a cave at Columbia rather than in Sudan. It is about Halima. In real time, we do not choose our priorities; they choose us.

Is Kristof too much? Try Samantha Power in the *New Yorker,* who, letting simple facts replace any need for a writer's passion, described back in 2004 how *janjaweed* raiders lopped off the head of a woman's baby as she watched them wipe out her family and the rest of her world.

How long, in fact, can we ignore Halima? Every correspondent has seen too many like her. For me, she is a man named Abdul Rahman Diku whom I found by the road in Mopti, Mali, in 1984. He had walked two hundred miles across blistering desert to save the last of his eight kids. Each dawn, he crawled in the dirt to sift dried grains of rice left from the last year's harvest. As he stroked his son's head, I asked what he would do. He looked at me as if I were nuts. "What," he replied, "can I do?" That six-year-old boy may have grown up to hate us. Then again, maybe he got to America, and his own son will find a cure for AIDS.

Africans, no more than Asians or Arkansans, are not distant abstractions. If you take a National Geographic DNA test, you will likely trace your roots to Tanzania, however pale your white ass may be. Yo, we all are brothers. And the Ark we share is leaking fast.

Despite it all, there is plenty of reason for optimism. I love, for instance, this Bill Moyers passage about the Presidio in San Francisco:

> That former military enclave beneath the Golden Gate Bridge is now a marvelous and beautiful center of vital commerce and civic purpose—saved from exploitation and despoliation by citizens who rose up on its behalf. On the wall of one of the main buildings I came upon a painting of an enormous deep blue wave with white caps against an equally blue sky. The artist's inscription beneath the painting reads: "This human wave expresses the concept of people at the bottom rungs of society waking up to using their united strength to claim their universal rights to economic, social, and environmental justice." Put that in your core curriculum. It's America 101.

Even more, I love Moyers's nine-word call to action in a speech he gave at Occidental College in Los Angeles on February 7, 2007. So no one missed the point, he spoke them three times: "The only answer to organized money is organized people."

That is the key. For organized money, read any narrowly focused interests that endanger a wider world. If enough of us take the trouble to see what is going wrong, we can act together. In a democracy that is wired to its farthest reaches, we have all the tools we need.

The last book still on my desk is a fortieth anniversary edition of Rachel Carson's *Silent Spring*. It is dedicated: "To Albert Schweitzer who said 'Man has lost the capacity to foresee and to forestall. He will end by destroying our earth.'" In an epigraph, Carson quotes E. B. White: "We would stand a better chance of survival if we accommodated ourselves to this planet and viewed it appreciatively instead of skeptically and dictatorially."

Silent Spring began as essays in William Shawn's *The New Yorker*. Not much of "the media" competed for attention then, and Carson's eloquent alarm sunk in. She inspired an environmental movement that grows stronger by the year.

Focusing on insecticides, Carson showed how small parts of our biosphere are tied inseparably to everything else within it. Decades later, we ourselves are the imperiled species. Yet with our new ability for each of us to be heard, a Rachel Carson today risks being drowned out in the din. We need, in the end, a collective ability to hear those voices that matter.

Are we to listening to, say, Jim Hansen, the NASA climatologist who refused to censor reality? However we run our world, we need a place to live. He says we have maybe ten years before we cannot save the only one we have.

Such voices can be heard in every field, from statesmen who know why civilizations clash, to economists who factor in humanity, to oceanographers who see our world wither, one coral polyp at a time. The media often fails us. Editors talk about "kicking butt"—that prize-worthy splash—when we need a light held steadily on what happens day-by-day beyond our sight.

In the end, it is up to each of us to see reality and to act. If twenty-three centuries after Plato we stay in our cave, blind to reality, we may well perish inside. Perhaps I am wrong, part of an off-key Greek chorus that wandered into the wrong play. I sure hope so. But let's not bet our children's lives on it.

EPILOGUE

Louis Kay
Baltimore, Maryland

Dear Louie,

Since you used to start your day, at age 6, by perusing the police blotter in the Baltimore Sun, *I'm addressing this to you. It is a note from a loving uncle to you and your pals and other grade-school kids who'll be taking over from us old guys.*

Your parents are as solid as decent people come, and you have the basic stuff down, like that great "neither a borrower nor a lender be" speech from Shakespeare. But this is a practical plan for today based on stuff I've learned the hard way on the road.

First, learn to master the media. You're lucky because for a model you have your own grandmother, Jane Kay, who (I hardly need remind you) is the environmental reporter for the San Francisco Chronicle. *She is so highly regarded by colleagues and sources because she cares passionately about human beings in the context of an evolving reality. Her principles mean more to her than her job. A lot of people use the phrase "without fear or favor," but mostly that is slogan. Janie lives it. Like most journalists (as opposed to "media figures"), she is paid modestly and is widely known in the Bay Area mostly by intelligent people who care about their surroundings.*

So, step one: Look for people like Jane. Beware of the clowns. One especially obnoxious Fox guy just said on TV, "You have to understand the game. It is about getting attention." But it is no game, Louie. Your generation's well-being depends on how well my generation, and your parents', can get things right today.

Don't accept blanket condemnation of any collective. For instance, if someone says, "The media sucks," he is probably pretty dumb. Jim Risen of the New York Times doesn't suck. Neither does Dana Priest of the Washington Post, nor Jon Lee Anderson of the New Yorker, nor Jane Kay, nor thousands of others who work hard to get things right.

Learn something you can call suspended belief. If you read or hear something, wait until you can check it out with other sources you trust. Be critical of those sources. Who are they? What's their authority? Are their facts firsthand? What's their purpose?

Start the day with the New York Times—the real paper so you can hold it in your hands and read it later when you're taking a walk away from your keyboard. It is not "All the News That's Fit to Print." But it is a start. Learn about the writers, especially the columnists. When they say something, go back and compare it to what they said six months, or a year, earlier. That may amuse you. In Baltimore, you'll also want to read what remains of the Sun. Everyone needs to keep up with local news.

Radio is really important. NPR and people like Amy Goodman will widen your scope and get you thinking. Good radio people let other people talk, people from vastly different cultures than ours. Try to imagine their realities and their way of thinking. It doesn't matter whether you agree—or how crazy they may sound. Their take on things, not yours, is what defines their actions.

TV can give you visual background. Your parents are wisely cool toward television, but there is, for instance, the BBC. Some PBS documentaries and special network reports can be terrific. Be wary of glitzy packaging that hides the message. Be grateful for anchors with wrinkles or bad hair. That usually just means they are real journalists.

Don't miss Jon Stewart, not only because laughing helps but also because satirists like him see through what is phony and misleading.

As for the Net, you can waste a whole life straying off into odd directions. Set yourself limits and work from a structure. Sites like www.mediachannel.org give a good overview. I like www.truthout.org, which gathers good material from a lot of places. Whatever you consult, keep your antennae tuned. The fact that anyone can be a "citizen journalist" or post an opinion does not confer credibility. No one can reliably interpret North Korea from a bedroom in North Dakota.

Go deeply into subjects that interest you, whether it is light rail or endangered eagles or kid soldiers in Africa. As you develop expertise, your voice will help others understand complex issues.

Once you are up to speed on informing yourself, do something. All of us can vote, and that is an important start. How do all these crooks and loonies get into office? I just saw a poll that says only 25 percent of Americans respect their congressmen. I mean, Duh. Who hired them, and who reelects them?

Get your friends involved; then widen the circle. Discussion groups are great for brainstorming ideas. Beyond local issues, don't be afraid of agitating for national and global policy. True, not many Americans take the trouble. But that means fewer intelligent, persistent voices can make a difference.

Discussion groups can also help hold big corporations to account. These are far more vulnerable than executives want us to know. After all, each is run by people who will lose their good jobs if their stock prices take a jolt. Make noise. In a country with a lot of consumer choices, the customers rule.

My last chapter has a lot of specifics about the bigger issues. They all come down to a simple fact. "American democracy" is a favorite term for politicians; usually the more they use it, the more trouble they are in. In fact, there are a lot of democracies in the world. The definition is simple: Citizens are free to select their leaders, to advise them on policy, and to replace them if they do a lousy job. We can fix it all, from global warming to the United Nations to stopping people from stealing saguaros in the desert, if enough of us decide these things are important.

And here is a final thing. That Fox clown, selling yet another book, just dumped on a class of Americans he called "secular progressives" (never mind what that is supposed to mean), which he estimated at 20 percent of our population. He said they hate everything about America because they are always criticizing it. His larger group, the "traditionalists," is noble.

Being noble means acting nobly: defining high values and living by them. When someone distorts those values in our name, it is noble to react firmly to protect true integrity. Words do not define who is a patriot. Flying a big flag proves nothing; these days, it is even suspect. Anyone who insists on "my country, right or wrong" is a danger to your future. Many people scorn us precisely because so many Americans believe that, and say that.

Our country can be defined by that badly overworked word which once carried great meaning. It is Awesome. Our founders forged a nation of people who wanted better than Europe could offer. They threw open the doors to people like your great-grandparents who came from all over. Today, when we stand for what they stood for, we inspire plenty of awe without needing the shock.

We all have reason to love America deeply for what it is supposed to be, for what it can be without reserve, and for what it still very often is. It is not up to some moron of any extreme to put us in categories. But we should realize a few things about the bigger world.

Other people also love their countries. Some of them are richer than we are, and others are poor as dirt. But there is no sliding scale. We have no moral superiority. Having more military power gives us no special standing.

These other people judge us by what they see, not by what we insist on telling them with growing stridency. They judge us by today, not by our past actions. Sure, we waded in during World War II, and we tipped the balance. But the enemy then was a Germany that is now our friend, sort of. Times constantly change, and they bring new values, new leaders, and new policies.

It's okay to hate spinach. But love your world. Whatever supreme force that is out there looking after it needs all the help we can give.

Love,
Uncle Mort

ACKNOWLEDGMENTS

Far too many people helped me write this book than I can list here, but many performed duty far beyond any call. Jeannette, Gina, and Peace for reasons mentioned. Geri Thoma, friend and agent, made it happen. Among others are Willis Barnstone, Tad Bartimus, Margaret Binnendyk, Phil Cousineau, Jerome Delay, Christopher Dickey, Jeffrey Fagan, Gene Finley, Pat Finley, Hadley Fitzgerald, Barbara and Larry Gerber, Barry Goodfield, Gretchen Hoff, Robert Hopkins, Nancy Harmon Jenkins, Gary Knight, Terry Maguire, Mary Scarvalone, Peace Sullivan, Paul Theroux, Richard Weening, Craig Van Note.

My focus these days is on young people who care about a world they will have to manage and a noble old profession they want to pursue. In this regard, I am particularly grateful to a pair of committed world-savers, Jacqueline Sharkey at the University of Arizona and Sherman Teichman of Tufts University's Institute for Global Leadership.

NOTES

1. THE CAVE WALL

1. Bill Moyers, *Washington Post*, June 21, 2005.
2. Molly Ivins, Creators' Syndicate, March 23, 2006.
3. Dana Priest, "CIA Holds Terror Suspects in Secret Prisons," *Washington Post*, Nov. 2, 2005.
4. Arundhati Roy, *Nation*, Feb. 18, 2002.

2. THAT FIVE-LETTER WORD

1. Associated Press, July 25, 2006.
2. Sherry Ricchiardi, "The Forgotten War," *American Journalism Review*, August/September 2006.
3. E. B. White in *Harper's*, 1938.
4. Fred Friendly, *Due to Circumstances Beyond Our Control* (New York: Vintage Books, 1967), vi.
5. Viron Vaky: Robert Parry, consortiumnews.com, Nov. 13, 2003.
6. Katharine Q. Seelye, "What-Ifs of a Media Eclipse," *New York Times*, Aug. 27, 2005.
7. Ibid.
8. Ibid.
9. CJRdaily.org, Sept. 1, 2006.

3. WHY *Do* "THEY" HATE US?

1. Associated Press, Jakarta, Oct. 21, 2005; also www.prwatch.org (Center for Media and Democracy).
2. Sidney Blumenthal, *Guardian,* Sept. 30, 2005.
3. Fred Kaplan, Slate.com, Sept. 29, 2005.
4. Jeff Gerth, "Military's Information War Is Vast and Often Secretive." *New York Times,* Dec 11, 2005.
5. www.nobelprize.org, speech delivered Dec. 7, 2005.
6. James Vicini, "US Has the Most Prisoners in the World," Reuters, Dec. 9, 2006.
7. Reporters Without Borders annual Press Freedom Survey 2006, www.rsf.org.
8. Carol Williams, "Covering Gitmo," *Los Angeles Times,* June 18, 2006.
9. Tim Golden, "Voices Baffled, Brash and Irate in Guantanamo," *New York Times,* March 6, 2006.
10. *Washington Post,* Oct. 27, 2006
11. Jane Mayer, "The Memo," *New Yorker,* Feb. 27, 2006.
12. Jane Mayer, "Outsourcing Torture," *New Yorker,* Feb. 14, 2005.
13. Paul von Zierbauer, "Marines Charge 4 with Murder of Iraq Civilians," *New York Times,* Dec. 22, 2006.

4. TERRACIDE

1. James Hansen, "The Threat to the Planet," *New York Review of Books,* July 13, 2006.
2. James Hansen testimony: www.oversight.house.gov/Documents/20070319105800-43018.pdf
3. Cooney: Andrew C. Revkin, "Bush Aide Edited Climate Reports," New York Times, June 8, 2005.
4. "The Heat Over Global Warming," www.pewresearch.org, July 12, 2006.
5. Associated Press, May 13, 2001.
6. "Quenching Las Vegas's Thirst." ABC News, April 5, 2007.
7. James Elsner, *American Geophysical Union News,* Aug. 15, 2006.

5. PLAGUES UPON US ALL

1. Lawrence K. Altman, "Global Program Aims to Combat AIDS 'Disaster'," *New York Times,* Nov. 21, 1986.
2. Zimbabwe. Daniel Howden, *Independent,* Nov. 17, 2006.
3. UNAIDS Annual Report 2006.
4. "Dam-Affected People," www.irn.org.

6. THE GENEROSITY SHAM

1. O.E.C.D. Development Assistance Committee, www.oecd.org/doc
2. Celia W. Dugger, "Poverty Memo: African Food for Africa's Starving is Roadblocked in Congress," *New York Times,* Oct. 12, 2005.
3. Ibid.
4. *Sunday Times,* June 5, 2005.

5. *New York Times*, Dec. 19, 2005.
6. *New York Times*, July 15, 2005
7. "Optimism and Africa," *New York Times*, Oct. 3, 2006.
8. Statistical abstracts, International Office of Migration, www.iom.int.

7. SHOCK AND "AW, SHIT"

1. Iraq poll, University of Maryland School of Public Policy, Nov. 30, 2006.
2. *New York Times*, Sept. 24, 2006.
3. *Wall Street Journal*, Aug. 15, 2002.
4. For the following "media chorus": Norman Solomon, "War-Loving Pundits," www.fair
.org, March 16, 2006.
5. *Lancet* 364 (2004).
6. Peter Johnson. *USA Today*. Sept. 14, 2003.
7. Roy Velez: Associated Press, July 26, 2006.

8. CORPORATE COLONIALISM—AND WORSE

1. *Guardian*, Dec. 2, 2006.
2. Leslie Wayne, "ITT Guilty of Revealing Classified Military Data," *New York Times*, March 28, 2007.
3. David Cay Johnston, "Income Gap Widening, Data Shows," *New York Times*, March 29, 2007.
4. Andrew Ross Sorkin, "Private Firms Lure C.E.O.'s with Top Pay," *New York Times*, January 8, 2007.
5. Democracynow.org, July 28, 2006.

9. THE WORLD, IN FACT, IS ROUND

1. Alison Smale, "Letter from Russia," *International Herald Tribune*, Aug. 25, 2006.
2. "The Practice of Earth Democracy," www.navadanya.org.
3. Tina Rosenberg, How to Fight Poverty, *New York Times*, Talking Points, Nov. 16, 2006.

10. ESCAPING THE CAVE

1. Morris Dees, *New York Times*, Aug. 25, 1993.
2. Simon Robinson, "An Appreciation: Marla Ruzicka," *Time,* April 18, 2005.
3. Christopher Dickey, "Shadowland," *Newsweek.com* April 19, 2005.
4. Warren Hoge, "Annan Urges U.S. to Reject Unilateralism in Diplomacy," *New York Times*, Dec. 12, 2006.
?. CJRDaily.org, Nov. 20, 2006.
?. TomPaine.com, Nov. 1, 2006.
5. "A Time for Anger, A Call to Action," Feb. 7, 2007 www.commondreams.org.

BIBLIOGRAPHY

Abbas, Ferhat. *Autopsie d'une Guerre.* Paris: Editions Garnier Frères, 1980.

Abrahamson, Jennifer. *Sweet Relief*, New York: Simon Spotlight Entertainment, 2006.

Adler, Jeremy. *Franz Kafka.* Woodstock, N.Y.: Overlook Press, 2001.

Anderson, Jon Lee. *The Fall of Baghdad.* New York: Little, Brown, 2005.

Atkinson, Rick. *In the Company of Soldiers.* New York: Owl Books, 2005.

Barmash, Isadore. *The World Is Full of It.* New York: Delacorte Press, 1974.

Becker, Jasper. *Hungry Ghosts: China's Secret Famine.* London: John Murray, 1996.

Black, Edwin. *Internal Combustion.* New York: St. Martin's Press, 2006.

Bogdanos, Matthew, with William Patrick. *Thieves of Baghdad.* New York: Bloomsbury, 2006.

Borges, Jorge Luis. *Obras Completas.* Buenos Aires: Emece Editores, 1974.

Bouyer, Christian. *Au Temps des Isles.* Paris: Tallandier, 2005.

Brock, David. *The Republican Noise Machine.* New York: Three Rivers Press, 2004.

Brown, Lester R. *Outgrowing the Earth.* New York: W. W. Norton, 2004.

———. *Plan B: Rescuing a Planet Under Stress and a Civilization in Trouble.* New York: W. W. Norton, 2003.

————. *Plan B 2.0.* New York: W. W. Norton, 2006.

————. *Who Will Feed China?* New York: W. W. Norton, 1995.

Byrd, Robert C. *Losing America.* New York: W. W. Norton, 2005.

Carrington, Selwyn H. H. *The Sugar Industry and the Abolition of the Slave Trade, 1775–1810.* Gainesville: University Press of Florida, 2002.

Carter, Jimmy. *Our Endangered Values.* New York: Simon & Schuster Paperbacks, 2006.

Carville, James. *Had Enough? A Handbook for Fighting Back.* New York: Simon & Schuster, 2003.

Chandrasekaran, Rajiv. *Imperial Life in the Emerald City.* New York: Alfred A. Knopf, 2006.

Chesnot, Christian and Georges Malbrunot. *Memoires d'Otages.* Paris: Calmann-Lévy, 2005.

Choueiri, Youssef M. *Islamic Fundamentalism.* Boston: Twayne, 1990.

Christianson, Gale E. *Greenhouse: The 200-Year Story of Global Warming.* New York: Penguin Books, 1999.

Clarke, Richard A. *Against All Enemies: Inside America's War on Terror.* New York: Free Press, 2004.

————. *The Scorpion's Gate.* New York: G. P. Putnam's Sons, 2005.

Cockburn, Leslie. *Out of Control.* New York: Atlantic Monthly Press, 1987.

Conason, Joe. *Big Lies.* New York: Thomas Dunne Books, St. Martin's Press, 2003.

Corn, Charles. *The Scents of Eden: A History of the Spice Trade.* New York: Kodansha International, 1999.

Council on Foreign Relations. *Chinese Military Power.* New York: Council on Foreign Relations, 2003.

————. *Foreign Affairs, Winter 1991/2.* New York: Council on Foreign Relations, 1991.

————. *Foreign Affairs, November/December 1993.* New York: Council on Foreign Relations, 1993.

————. *Foreign Affairs, September/October 1995.* New York: Council on Foreign Relations, 1995.

————. *Foreign Affairs, March/April 1996.* New York: Council on Foreign Relations, 1996.

————. *Foreign Affairs, May/June 1997.* New York: Council on Foreign Relations, 1997.

————. *Foreign Affairs, September/October 1999.* New York: Council on Foreign Relations, 1999.

————. *Foreign Affairs, September/October 2002.* New York: Council on Foreign Relations, 2002.

————. *Foreign Affairs, March/April 2004.* New York: Council on Foreign Relations, 2004.

————. *Foreign Affairs, September/October 2004.* New York: Council on Foreign Relations, 2004.

————. *Foreign Affairs, November/December 2004.* New York: Council on Foreign Relations, 2004.

———. *Foreign Affairs, May/June 2005.* New York: Council on Foreign Relations, 2005.

———. *Foreign Affairs, November/December 2006.* New York: Council on Foreign Relations, 2006.

———. *In the Wake of War: Improving U.S. Post-Conflict Capabilities.* New York: Council on Foreign Relations, 2005.

———. *Iraq: The Day After.* New York: Council on Foreign Relations, 2003.

———. *More than Humanitarianism: A Strategic U.S. Approach Toward Africa.* New York: Council on Foreign Relations, 2006.

———. *Russia's Wrong Direction: What the United States Can and Should Do.* New York: Council on Foreign Relations, 2006.

Diamond, Jared. *Collapse.* New York: Viking, 2005.

———. *Guns, Germs, and Steel.* New York: W. W. Norton, 1999.

Diamond, Larry. *Squandered Victory.* New York: Times Books, 2005.

Dunn, Seth. *Micropower: The Next Electrical Era.* Washington, D.C.: Worldwatch Institute, 2000.

———. *Reading the Weathervane.* Washington, D.C.: Worldwatch Institute, 2002.

Easterly, William. *The White Man's Burden: Why the West's Efforts to Aid the Rest Have Done So Much Ill and So Little Good.* New York: Penguin Press, 2006.

Fallows, James. *Blind into Baghdad: America's War in Iraq.* York: Vintage Books, 2006.

Flannery, Tim. *The Weather Makers.* New York: Atlantic Monthly Press, 2005.

Favrot, Lionel. *Tariq Ramadan Dévoilé.* Lyon: Lyon Mag, 2004.

Fishman, Ted C. *China, Inc.* New York: Scribner, 2005.

Flavin, Christopher, and Nicholas Lenssen. *Power Surge.* New York: W. W. Norton, 1994.

Fogarassy, Helen. *Mission Improbable.* Lanham: Lexington Books, 1999.

Forster, Elborg, and Robert Forster, eds. *Sugar and Slavery, Family and Race: The Letters and Diary of Pierre Dessalles, Planter in Martinique, 1808–1856.* Baltimore: Johns Hopkins University Press, 1996.

Fourest, Caroline. *Frère Tariq.* Paris: Grasset, 2004.

Frank, Thomas. *What's the Matter with Kansas? How Conservatives Won the Heart of America.* New York: Metropolitan Books, 2004.

Franken, Al. *Lies and the Lying Liars Who Tell Them: A Fair and Balanced Look at the Right.* New York: Dutton, 2003.

Freeman, Steven F., and Joel Bleifuss. *Was the 2004 Presidential Election Stolen?* New York: Seven Stories Press, 2006.

French, Hilary. *Vanishing Borders.* New York: W. W. Norton, 2000.

Friedman, Alan. *Spider's Web: The Secret History of How the White House Illegally Armed Iraq.* New York: Bantam Books, 1993.

Friedman, Thomas L. *The World Is Flat: A Brief History of the Twenty-first Century.* New York: Farrar, Straus & Giroux, 2005.

Friendly, Fred. *Due to Circumstances Beyond Our Control. . . .* New York: Vintage Books, 1967.

Gannett Center for Media Studies. *Gannett Center Journal, Spring 1989.* New York: Gannett Foundation Program at Columbia University.

———. *Gannett Center Journal, Summer 1993.* New York: Gannett Foundation Program at Columbia University.

Gans, Herbert J. *Deciding What's News.* New York: Pantheon Books, 1979.

Gladwell, Malcolm. *The Tipping Point.* New York: Little, Brown, 2000.

Glaser, Antoine, and Stephen Smith. *Comment la France a Perdu l'Afrique.* Paris: Calmann-Lévy, 2005.

Goodman, Amy, with David Goodman. *The Exception to the Rulers: Exposing Oily Politicians, War Profiteers, and the Media That Love Them.* New York: Hyperion, 2004.

Gordon, Michael R., and Gen. Bernard E. Trainor. *Cobra II: The Inside Story of the Invasion and Occupation of Iraq.* New York: Pantheon Books, 2006.

Gore, Al. *An Inconvenient Truth.* New York: Bloomsbury, 2006.

Granta. *The Last Place on Earth.* London: Granta, 1993.

———. *This Overheating World: Autumn 2003.* London: Granta, 2003.

Grey, Stephen. *Ghost Plane.* New York: St. Martin's Press, 2006.

Gubert, Romain, and Emmanuel Saint-Martin. *L'Arrogance Française.* Paris: Balland, 2003.

Harris, J. D. *War Reporter.* New York: Manor Books, 1979.

Harrison, Neil E., and Gary C. Bryner, eds. *Science and Politics in the International Environment.* Lanham, Md.: Rowman & Littlefield, 2004.

Heisbourg, François. *La Fin de l'Occident.* Paris: Odile Jacob, 2005.

Henry, James S. *The Blood Bankers.* New York: Four Walls Eight Windows, 2003.

Herr, Michael. *Dispatches.* New York: Alfred A. Knopf, 1977.

Hersh, Seymour M. *Chain of Command.* New York: HarperCollins, 2004.

Hess, Stephen. *International News & Foreign Correspondents.* Washington, D.C.: Brookings Institution, 1996.

Hoover, John. *Bullwinkle on Business.* New York: St. Martin's Press, 2007.

Human Rights Watch. *World Report: 2002, Events of 2001.* New York: Human Rights Watch, 2002.

———. *World Report: 2005, Events of 2004.* New York: Human Rights Watch, 2005.

Huntington, Samuel P. *Who Are We?* London: Free Press, 2004.

Ignatieff, Michael. *Virtual War.* New York: Henry Holt, 2000.

Ivins, Molly, and Lou Dubose. *Bushwhacked.* New York: Random House, 2003.

Jett, Dennis C. *Why Peacekeeping Fails.* New York: Palgrave, 1999.

Jian, Ma. *Red Dust.* New York: Vintage, 2002.

Johnson, Chalmers. *Blowback.* New York: Metropolitan Books, 2000.

Judah, Tim. *Kosovo: War and Revenge.* New Haven: Yale University Press, 2000.

Katovsky, Bill, and Timothy Carlson. *Embedded.* Guilford, Conn.: Lyons Press, 2003.

Kennedy, Edward M. *America Back on Track.* New York: Viking, 2006.

Kennedy Robert F., Jr. *Crimes Against Nature.* New York: HarperCollins, 2004.

Kepel, Gilles. *Fitna: Guerre au Coeur de l'Islam.* France: Editions Gallimard, 2004.

Kerry, John. *The New War.* New York: Simon & Schuster, 1997.

Krugman, Paul. *The Great Unraveling.* New York: W. W. Norton, 2003.

Kurlansky, Mark. *Cod: A Biography of the Fish That Changed the World.* New York: Penguin Books, 1997.

Levitt, Steven D., and Stephen J. Dubner. *Freakonomics.* London: Penguin Books, 2005.

Love, Rosaleen. *Reefscape.* Washington, D.C.: Joseph Henry Press, 2001.

MacPherson, Myra. *All Governments Lie! The Life and Times of Rebel Journalist I. F. Stone.* New York: Scribner, 2006.

Malcolm, Noel. *Kosovo: A Short History.* London: Pan, 1999.

Manning, Richard. *Against the Grain.* New York: Farrar, Straus & Giroux, 2000.

Marr, Andrew. *My Trade.* London: Pan Books, 2004.

McNamee, Gregory. *Blue Mountains Far Away.* New York: Lyons Press, 2000.

McPhee, John. *The Control of Nature.* New York: Farrar, Straus & Giroux, 1989.

Miles, Hugh. *Al-Jazeera.* London: Abacus, 2005.

Milton, Giles. *Nathaniel's Nutmeg.* London: Sceptre, 1999.

Mintz, Sidney W. *Sweetness and Power. The Place of Sugar in Modern History.* New York: Viking, 1985.

Moaveni, Azadeh. *Lipstick Jihad: A Memoir of Growing Up Iranian in America and American in Iran.* New York: PublicAffairs, 2005.

Mooney, Brian, and Barry Simpson. *Breaking News.* Chichester: Capstone, 2003.

Moore, Michael. *Dude, Where's My Country?* New York: Warner Books, 2003.

Morgan, Piers. *The Insider: The Private Diaries of a Scandalous Decade.* London: Ebury Press, 2005.

Murphy, Caryle. *Passion for Islam.* New York: Scribner, 2002.

Nabhan, Gary Paul. *The Desert Smells Like Rain: A Naturalist in O'odham Country.* Tucson. University of Arizona Press, 2002.

Naím, Moisés. *Illicit: How Smugglers, Traffickers, and Copycats Are Hijacking the Global Economy.* New York: Doubleday, 2005.

Nicholson, William. *The Society of Others*. New York: Nan A. Talese/Doubleday, 2005.

Obama, Barack. *Dreams from My Father*. New York: Three Rivers Press, 1995.

Packer, George. *The Assassins' Gate*. New York: Farrar, Straus & Giroux, 2005.

Pauly, Daniel, and Jay Maclean. *In a Perfect Ocean*. Washington, D.C.: Island Press, 2003.

Palast, Greg. *The Best Democracy Money Can Buy*. London and Sterling, Va.: Pluto Press, 2002.

Peterson, Scott. *Me Against My Brother: At War in Somalia, Sudan, and Rwanda*. New York: Routledge, 2000.

Pfaff, William. *The Wrath of Nations*. New York: Simon & Schuster, 1993.

Phillips, Kevin. *American Dynasty: Aristocracy, Fortune, and the Politics of Deceit in the House of Bush*. New York: Viking, 2004.

———. *American Theocracy. The Peril and Politics of Radical Religion, Oil, and Borrowed Money in the 21st Century*. New York: Viking, 2006.

Plato. *The Republic*. London: Penguin Books, 1955.

———. *Timaeus and Critias*. London: Penguin Books, 1965.

Pollan, Michael. *The Botany of Desire*. New York: Random House, 2001.

Quandt, William B. *Saudi Arabia in the 1980s*. Washington, D.C.: Brookings Institution, 1981.

Randal, Jonathan. *Osama*. New York: Alfred A. Knopf, 2004.

Reed, Terry, and John Cummings. *Compromised: Clinton, Bush, and the CIA*. New York: SPI Books, 1994.

Reid, T. R. *The United States of Europe. The New Superpower and the End of American Supremacy*. New York: Penguin Press, 2004.

Rich, Frank. *The Greatest Story Ever Sold: The Decline and Fall of Truth from 9/11 to Katrina*. New York: Penguin Press, 2006.

Ricks, Thomas E. *Fiasco: The American Military Adventure in Iraq*. New York: Penguin Press, 2006.

Rifkin, Jeremy. *The European Dream*. New York: Jeremy P. Tarcher/Penguin, 2004.

Roberts, Paul. *The End of Oil*. Boston: Houghton Mifflin, 2004.

Rosenblum, Mort. *Coups and Earthquakes*. New York: Harper & Row, 1979.

———. *Mission to Civilize*. San Diego: Harcourt Brace Jovanovich, 1986.

———. *Who Stole the News?* New York: John Wiley, 1993.

Rosenblum, Mort, and Doug Williamson. *Squandering Eden*. San Diego: Harcourt Brace Jovanovich, 1987.

Rowland, Wade. *Greed, Inc*. New York: Arcade, 2006.

Roy, Arundhati. *War Talk*. Cambridge: South End Press, 2003.

Sachs, Jeffrey D. *The End of Poverty: Economic Possibilities for Our Time*. New York: Penguin Press, 2005.

Sardar, Ziauddin, and Merryl Wyn Davies. *Why Do People Hate America?* New York: Disinformation, 2002.

Schwartz-Nobel, Loretta. *Poisoned for Profit: The Human Equivalent of Global Warming.* New York: St. Martin's Press, 2006.

Sen, Amartya. *Development as Freedom.* New York: Anchor Books, 1999.

Shadid, Anthony. *Night Draws Near.* New York: Henry Holt, 2005.

Smith, Jordan Fisher. *Nature Noir.* Boston: Houghton Mifflin, 2005.

Solomon, Norman. *War Made Easy: How Presidents and Pundits Keep Spinning Us to Death.* New York: John Wiley, 2005.

Sorman, Guy. *Made in USA.* France: Fayard, 2004.

Soros, George. *The Bubble of American Supremacy.* New York: Public Affairs, 2004.

Soto, Hernando de. *The Mystery of Capital: Why Capitalism Triumphs in the West and Fails Everywhere Else.* New York: Basic Books, 2005.

Stewart, Jon, Ben Karlink, and David Javerbaum. *America (the Book).* New York: Warner Books, 2004.

Stiglitz, Joseph E. *Globalization and its Discontents.* New York: Penguin Books, 2002.

————. *Making Globalization Work.* New York: W. W. Norton, 2006.

Stone, I. F. *The Best of I. F. Stone.* New York: Public Affairs, 2006.

————. *The Trial of Socrates.* Boston: Little, Brown, 1988.

Tertrais, Bruno. *War Without End.* New York: New Press, 2005.

Earth Works Group. *50 Simple Things You Can Do to Save the Earth.* Berkeley: Earthworks Press, 1989.

Timerman, Jacob. *The Longest War.* New York: Alfred A. Knopf, 1982.

Tirman, John. *100 Ways America Is Screwing Up the World.* New York: Harper Perennial, 2006.

Tolstoy, Leo. *War and Peace.* Oxford: Oxford University Press, 1991.

Turner, Jack. *Spice: The History of a Temptation.* New York: Alfred A. Knopf, 2004.

Uchitelle, Louis. *The Disposable American.* New York: Alfred A. Knopf, 2006.

Villepin, Dominique de. *Le Requin et la Mouette.* France: Plon/Albin Michel, 2004.

Wallach, Lori and Michelle Sforza. *Whose Trade Organization? Corporate Globalization and the Erosion of Democracy.* Washington, D.C.: Public Citizen, 1999.

Waugh, Evelyn. *Scoop.* Boston: Little, Brown, 1938.

Whybrow, Peter C. *American Mania.* New York: W. W. Norton, 2005.

Woods, Donald. *Biko.* New York: Paddington Press, 1978.

Woodward, Bob. *State of Denial.* New York: Simon & Schuster, 2006.

World Resources Institute. *Pilot Analysis of Global Ecosystems: Freshwater Systems.* Washington, D.C.: World Resources Institute, 2000.

Worldwatch Institute. *State of the World, 2005*. New York: W. W. Norton, 2005.

————. *State of the World, 2006*. New York: W. W. Norton, 2006.

————. *Vital Signs, 1992*. New York: W. W. Norton, 1992.

————. *Vital Signs, 2002*. New York: W. W. Norton, 2002.

————. *Vital Signs, 2003*. New York: W. W. Norton, 2003.

————. *Vital Signs, 2006–2007*. New York: W. W. Norton, 2006.

Worldwatch Institute with World Resources Institute. *Watersheds of the World*. Washington, D.C.: Worldwatch Institute, 1998.

Wright, Lawrence. *The Looming Tower*. New York: Alfred A. Knopf, 2006.

Zakaria, Fareed. *The Future of Freedom*. New York: W. W. Norton, 2004.